The Wagner Complex:
Genesis and Meaning of
The Ring

Tom Artin

For Cynthia

visionary

CONTENTS

ACKNOWLEDGMENTS

I am indebted especially to Sally Henry for her meticulous reading of the manuscript, and for her generous and acute critiques of both substance and style, from which I learned more about good writing than from all my teachers in school.

Warmest thanks are due Gerald Dugan, an early reader of the manuscript, for his enthusiastic support and encouragement, as well as his penetrating responses to its argument in lengthy and detailed correspondence, grounded in a deep knowledge of Wagner's operas.

D. W. Robertson, Jr. taught me the nature of allegory. Thanks also to Gordon Harper for reading and commenting on the manuscript.

Though he died unexpectedly before I was clever enough to have posed the myriad questions I now wish I had asked, I am grateful to Mark Brunswick for sowing the seeds of a passion for Wagner's music and an abiding admiration for the person and accomplishments of Sigmund Freud, whom Mark had been privileged to know intimately.

Chapter 1

Introduction: the Unconscious

To begin with a commonplace: *The Ring* is a circle. Wagner's title, that is, implies a structure as much as it indicates a plot; the ring is not only the glittering circle forged for Alberich, around which the dramatic action swirls from theft of gold to fall of gods; it is also the operatic tetralogy itself. As the Hall of the Gibichungs tumbles into incendiary ruins, igniting Walhall, spelling the doom of the gods, the banks of the Rhine overflow and flood the stage, returning us to the primeval under-water of *Rheingold* where the Rhine maidens frolic in celebration of their fiery gold restored.

The drama thus ends where it has begun. But such a structure has implications of its own. For instance, if *The Ring* is a circle, then it ought to have, strictly, neither beginning nor end; perhaps Wagner's prologue, *Rheingold*, is the "beginning" only by virtue of the exigencies of fiction. Fiction, namely, has to be acted out in time, which is not circular, but linear. Accordingly, time is seen to be as fictional an element as character or setting. The history of the drama's composition hints at this view.

Wagner had originally conceived a single opera called *The Death of Siegfried*, corresponding closely to what ultimately became *Götterdämerung*. This opera, however, already contained in exposition the story of *The Ring*, only wrenched from the axis of time and interpolated into the action of a few days. As a result, in this original version, Alberich's theft of the gold from the depths of the Rhine both was the beginning, and wasn't. The audience was to understand the theft as initiating a sequence of events culminating in Siegfried's death, but because it had occurred long in the past, and was recounted in retrospect, not depicted, it was not the beginning of the opera. To appreciate the logic of events onstage, the audience was to sort out the sequence of past events. And yet the very structure of the opera, which broke up and scattered the past in dialogue, undermined the sense of that sequence by telescoping it. The present, then, contained the past, and set it forth more or less simultaneously and as a unity. *Siegfried's Death* achieved through its telescoped plot the same timeless unity, or simultaneity, as that given *The Ring* by its ultimately circular structure. In *The Ring* this effect is heightened by the interpolation throughout of numerous lengthy recapitulations of past events in the form of exposition which, from the perspective of plot alone, seem superfluous.

The circular structure (implicitly a *cyclical* structure) is a transmutation into narrative (and thus into time) of a complex of ideas defying simple logic. Take the Old Testament history of Israel, telling and retelling essentially the same plot: a people is divinely chosen, transgresses God's law, is punished with affliction and exile, is eventually led to redemption, only to transgress God's law once again: an eternal round of blessing and chastening. The pattern is repeated until time itself ceases, until as it were the fiction of time is transcended and the veil of complexity falls away.

In the meantime, however, the allegoric veil remains, obscuring vision, necessitating that ever-recurring plotline to express the Judaic conception of the human. To be human means election, blessing, sinning, damnation, forgiveness and redemption, not so much in that order as paradoxically all at once. The effect of reading the history of the Old Testament, with its ever-recurring pattern is finally to see beyond the order of events fixed along the linear axis of time, and to apprehend the whole circle at once, without beginning or end, a single fact: a ring.

The circling back at the end of *Götterdämmerung* to the primal waters of the Rhine indicates that though the gods are destroyed, it is not the end of everything; in fact it is as much the beginning of something. This indication of cyclical time conforms with Wagner's sources in Nordic mythology, in which the cosmic cataclysm of Ragnarok is not an ultimate annihilation, for the gods are to be reborn through a resurrected Balder, the beautiful and beloved son of Odin. Like any mythology, that of the Teutons functioned (like the cyclical history of the Jews) as an elaborate metaphor for existence, a projection outwards into concrete images and historical events of a culture's inward experience, its sense of self — too complex and contradictory to express overtly.[1]

---

[1] More precisely [following Owen Barfield, *Poetic Diction* (London, 1964), pp. 60-92], mythology represents the perception of inner and outer experience as identical. Here, for clarity's sake, the focus is on the metaphorical side of the transaction, however, since only modern, self-

Now unless we are to ascribe Wagner's interest in these mythological sources (and that of his audience) exclusively to antiquarian curiosity or to the vogue in the 19th Century generally of things medieval, we are confronted by a considerable problem of meaning—an exegetical problem. For this cycle of operas composed in the modern, mechanistic era, is based on the mythology of a culture that flourished in the particular historical and geographical context of Northern Europe more than a thousand years earlier. Whatever those tales of gods and men once vividly expressed about the worldview of resourceful, often berserk warriors of pre-Christian Europe, they bear little relation to the life of a bourgeois conductor and composer of operas at the first turbulent cresting of the Industrial Revolution. The problem of meaning is thrown into bolder relief in light of the artist's dedication of twenty-five years to *The Ring*'s composition, and his grandiose aspiration not only to revolutionize operatic production, but to regenerate the fragmented and decadent culture of the German people. What, then, were Wagner's purposes in adopting for his operas a mythology, albeit Germanic, so far removed and so alien in spirit to his own time? To pose the question more pointedly, how exactly do the stories of the gods and giants and dwarves of Nordic mythology serve to express also the inner world of Richard Wagner and his contemporary audiences?

G. B. Shaw, in his characteristically brilliant and entertaining guide to *The Ring*, *The Perfect Wagnerite* (a title, incidentally, that suggests we are to learn as much about Shaw as about

---

conscious recreation of myth is under discussion, not primitive consciousness.

Wagner), argues that Wagner adapted the old mythology to an allegory of modern life conceived along socialist lines, depicting the rise and corruption of state power (Wotan's violation of his own laws in dealing with the giants), the oppression of the working class by bourgeois capital (the enslavement of the Nibelungs by Alberich, wielding the "Plutonic" power of the ring), and the redemption of society by the fearless, joyful, innocent revolutionary (Siegfried's penetration of the illusory fire surrounding Brünnhilde). Undeniably, the text of *The Ring* was composed during the period of Wagner's most intense commitment to revolutionary politics. The first prose sketch, "The Nibelungen Myth as Scheme for Drama," was written during October, 1848; the completed *Ring* poem was published privately early in 1853 in Switzerland where Wagner was living in exile for the role he had played in the Dresden uprising of May, 1849. So Shaw's reading of the text as allegory of Wagner's revolutionary worldview seems plausible.

Yet Wagner was skeptical of his own conscious intentions. He confesses in a letter of August 23, 1856 to August Röckel, one of his co-instigators of the Dresden uprising, that he has come to recognize a split within himself between the conscious and the unconscious. And the unconscious seems to him his more authentic self. "Now, the strange thing is," he writes, "that in all my intellectual ideas on life, and in all the conceptions at which I had arrived in the course of my struggles to understand the world with my conscious reason, I was working in direct opposition to the intuitive ideas expressed in these works. While, as an artist, I *felt* with such convincing certainty that all my creations took their coloring from my feelings, as a philosopher I sought to discover a totally opposed interpretation of the world; and this interpretation once discovered, I obstinately held to it, though to my own surprise, I found that it had invariably to go to the wall when confronted by my spontaneous and purely objective artistic intuitions." Thus, Shaw may be correct in arguing that Wagner intended a socialist allegory. Wagner himself, though, affirms that these conscious intentions are offset by fundamentally opposite unconscious intentions, and that ultimately the unconscious intentions have prevailed.

Shaw was of course aware of this letter to Röckel, but he dismisses it as an attempt long after the fact to justify the inconsistency of *The Ring* with the Master's latest enthusiasm—the pessimism of Schopenhauer. "Wagner's determination to prove that he had been a Schopenhauerite all along without knowing it only shows how completely the fascination of the great treatise on The Will had run away with his memory."[2] Shaw attempts to demonstrate that the tendency in *The Ring* that Wagner wished to believe intuitively Schopenhauerean was in fact optimistic, not pessimistic. "Now Wagner was, when he wrote The Ring, a most sanguine revolutionary Meliorist, contemptuous of the reasoning faculty, which he typified in the shifty, unreal, delusive Loki, and full of faith in the life-giving Will, which he typified in the glorious Siegfried. Not until he read Schopenhauer did he become bent on proving that he had always been a Pessimist at heart, and that Loki was the most sensible and worthy adviser of Wotan in The Rhine Gold."[3] So he concludes, "that Wagner's explanation of his works for

[2] George Bernard Shaw, *The Perfect Wagnerite,* in *Selected Prose* (New York, 1952), p. 296.
[3] *Ibid.,* p. 297.

the most part explain nothing but the mood in which he happened to be on the day he advanced them, or the train of thought suggested to his very susceptible imagination and active mind by the points raised by his questioner. Especially in his private letters, where his outpourings are modified by his dramatic consciousness of the personality of his correspondent, do we find him taking all manner of positions, and putting forward all sorts of cases which must be taken as clever and suggestive special pleadings, and not as serious and permanent expositions of his works."[4]

Shaw is correct: the tenor of Siegfried's story is optimistic up until that climactic moment when the hero, having redeemed Brünnhilde from both the prison of fire and the shackles of sleep, cajoles the drowsy virgin into letting the chips fall where they may. The remainder he dismisses as a degeneracy into mere "grand opera," although even this portion is not pessimistic, for it proposes a solution. "At the point where The Ring changes from music drama into opera," Shaw explains, "it also ceases to be philosophic, and becomes didactic. The philosophic part is a dramatic symbol of the world as Wagner observed it. In the didactic part the philosophy degenerates into the prescription of a romantic nostrum for all human ills. Wagner, only mortal after all, succumbed to the panacea mania when his philosophy was exhausted, like any of the rest of us."[5]

"I made my most remarkable discovery in this respect," continues Wagner in the letter to Röckel concerning unconscious intention, "with my Nibelung drama. It had

---

[4] *Ibid.*, p. 300.
[5] *Ibid.*, p. 266.

taken form at a time when, with my ideas, I had built up an optimistic world, on Hellenic principles; believing that in order to realize such a world, it was only necessary for men to wish it. I ingeniously set aside the problem, why they did not wish it. I remember that it was with this definite creative purpose that I conceived the personality of Siegfried, with the intention of representing an existence free from pain. But I meant in the presentment of the whole Nibelung myth to express my meaning even more clearly, by showing how from the first wrongdoing a whole world of evil arose, and consequently fell to pieces in order to teach us the lesson that we must recognize evil and tear it up by the roots, and raise in its stead a righteous world." Here is the optimism, the "meliorism," that Shaw insists remains the informing attitude of *The Ring*, regardless of what Wagner said in retrospect. "If The Ring says one thing, and a letter written afterwards says that it said something else, The Ring must be taken to confute the letter just as conclusively as if the two had been written by different hands," maintains Shaw.[6] As his authority he quotes Wagner from the same letter to Röckel: "How can an artist expect that what he has felt intuitively should be perfectly realized by others, seeing that he himself feels in the presence of his work, if it is true Art, that he is confronted by a riddle, about which he, too, might have illusions, just as another might?"

Shaw disputes the Master's *ex post facto* exegesis; whatever intuitive tendency was operating below the rational surface in the composition of *The Ring*, it wasn't Schopenhauerean pessimism. Yet Shaw misses what is crucial in Wagner's

---

[6] *Ibid.*, p. 300.

explanation. Its critical distinction, namely, is not between philosophical optimism and pessimism, but between *conscious* and *unconscious* intention. Optimism and pessimism appear as purely rational, not affective concepts. If Wagner truly was guided in composition by the unconscious—as he says he finally *allowed* himself to be—then the tendency of that guidance must have remained unconscious, even after he had come to sense there was more at play than he could rationally account for.

That Wagner is able—whether before or after the fact—to formulate Schopenhauerean pessimism as the unconscious tendency in his work makes that interpretation itself suspect. The unconscious is, after all, *unconscious*. Wagner himself admits he stands before his work as before a *riddle*, a riddle, moreover, of cosmic proportions. "I was scarcely aware," he goes on, "that in the working out, nay, in the first elaboration of my scheme, I was being unconsciously guided by a wholly different, infinitely more profound intuition, and that instead of conceiving a phase in the development of the world, I had grasped the very essence and meaning of the world itself in all its possible phases."

Theodor Adorno describes this ambitious scheme: "This basic idea is that of totality: the Ring attempts, without much ado, nothing less than the encapsulation of the world process as a whole."[7] Wagner concludes that this essence of the world is its "nothingness," in the Schopenhauerean sense. Let us adopt

---

[7] Theodor Adorno, *In Search of Wagner*, trans. Rodney Livingstone (NLB, 1981), p. 101.

Shaw's skepticism regarding this conclusion, at least, in order to explore the thematic implications of the unconscious, cosmic nature of Wagner's intuition.

"The very essence and meaning of the world itself" — the grandiosity of the phrase seems to raise *The Ring* from the level of mere opera to that of mythology. That of course was Wagner's intention: a mythology conveyed through the agency of the *Gesamtkunstwerk* (after the model of ancient Greek dramatic festivals) around which the splintered soul of the German Folk might be unified. True mythologies, however, expressive of a culture's essence, are intrinsically collective, rather than individual creations. Moreover, if the core experience of mid-century German culture — politically disunited and in the throes of the Industrial Revolution, with its class divisions and warfare — was alienation, then a unifying mythology seems in principle an impossible aspiration. Perhaps at best, in the modern age, each man in the isolation of sleep dreams a private, idiosyncratic, and entirely separate mythology.

We return circuitously to the question how ancient Nordic mythology could have served the purposes of Wagner's self-expression. "Dream is the personalized myth, myth the depersonalized dream," writes Joseph Campbell; "both myth and dream are symbolic in the same general way of the dynamics of the psyche. But in the dream the forms are quirked by the peculiar troubles of the dreamer, whereas in myth the problems and solutions shown are directly valid for all mankind."[8]

---

[8] Joseph Campbell, *The Hero with a Thousand Faces* (Cleveland, 1956), p. 19.

Campbell's formulation is equally useful in relating myth to dream and in distinguishing them. In its light, moreover, one can explore the implication inherent in the fact that Wagner's *Ring* is both myth *and* dream: myth insofar as it is built from the narrative elements of the ancient Teutons; dream insofar as those narrative structures have been reshaped to express the modern consciousness of the artist (not to say "quirked by the peculiar troubles of the dreamer"); and myth once more to the extent that the private dream of the artist invites and evokes a public response.

Wagner's acquisition of plot from pre-existing sources does not constitute a relinquishing of control over meaning. In many instances, of course we see Wagner altering and conflating elements of the ancient stories to suit his conscious purposes. But quite apart from these alterations, his intention obviously informs the narrative structure. Whatever the stories may originally have meant, their outlines adumbrated in Wagner's perception of them new and entirely personal meanings that he in turn embedded in the narratives in reworking them.

These were not neutral narratives in their historical context; surely they evoked a complex of affective and cognitive responses (or meanings) in the skalds who authored and the Teutonic audiences who heard them, responses that were culturally, not personally determined. Resurrected by the antiquarian interest of the 19th Century and viewed as artifacts of the past, however, the same stories were no longer invested with the capacity to trigger analogous responses. Received by Wagner as essentially neutralized narrative material, they evoked different, wholly personal responses, both conscious and unconscious, and suggested underlying content (i.e., meaning) arising out of 19th Century, not pre-Christian Germanic consciousness.

Wagner's stories are old bottles filled with new wine. Their content reveals itself less in the bare details of the narrative than in verbal formulations and the feeling tone of language, in the texture of the verse, in the transformation of people and things into symbols, in the peculiar characterization of mythological stereotypes, in the emergence of pervasive thematic issues, in the underscoring and highlighting accomplished by the music, and so on. Wagner is not simply retelling old tales; he has appropriated them. We are justified in regarding the operas he constructed from these narrative materials as personal fantasies, "quirked" by his own particular anxieties, wishes, and compulsions. In much the same way, dreams are constituted out of bits and pieces of "objective," waking reality, distorted and reorganized according to a different, though parallel logic.

Mythology was characterized above as "a projection outwards into concrete images and historical events of a culture's inward experience." Ultimately, individual experience is always unique, so that on the level of the concrete, the actual, communal life may appear chaotic. Mythology gathers up and expresses fictionally what is common (or wished to be common) to the life experience of the group; it lends coherence to the otherwise disparate lives of individuals. Culture is impossible without this cohesiveness, so that in some measure mythology *is* culture. In quasi-Platonic terms: the palpable experience of the individual, though it seems real, is but the shadow of the higher reality expressed in a culture's myths.

In the 19th Century, romantic and Victorian alike bemoaned the withering of mythology in the modern age; some tried rehabilitating old mythologies or fashioning new ones, others gave in to despair. Their own time, many regarded as a barren present, stripped of the graceful habiliments of belief. Iron horse, factory, and Eiffel Tower seemed the dreary monuments of the bourgeois world. Characterizing the malaise of the age, Erich Auerbach writes of Flaubert that, "like so many important nineteenth-century artists, he hates his period; he sees its problems and the coming crises with clarity; he sees the inner anarchy, the *manque de base théologique*, . . . but he sees no solution and no issue; his fanatical mysticism of art is almost like a substitute religion, to which he clings convulsively, and his candor very often becomes sullen, petty, choleric, and neurotic."[9]

It was Freud's insight into 19th Century social culture, however, that revealed in what sense it was not after all lacking a mythology of its own, that on the contrary the actual, the concrete, the quotidian, in the service of repression, had itself become a modern mythology. For reality, in Freud's estimation, lay not in the conscious *appearances* of modern life, but in the buried and unconscious emotional life to which the actual referred by a symbolism of displacement and distortion. This is not necessarily to decry Victorian mores as hypocritical. For hypocrisy entails *conscious* dishonesty. Rather, by a process beyond rational control, Victorian culture

---

[9] Erich Auerbach, *Mimesis* (Garden City, NY, 1957), p. 430.

had been erected on the foundation of unconscious denial of instinctual wishes intolerable to contemporary moral consciousness. Men and women for the most part acted out lives distanced from the instinctual by this elaborate symbolism. The Freudian view is thus an essentially Platonic one. The actual is merely a shadow of the real; the world as sense relays it is a matrix of symbols for the psyche's impalpable world of forms. Put another way, what appeared real, the actual lives of 19th Century men and women, was a projected fiction, beneath which lay true reality, the unconscious life of feelings and drives.

Freud's most radical statement of this proposition, asserted in *Civilization and its Discontents*, was that culture itself is the fundamental neurotic symptom. Other contemporaries held similarly Platonic views of the world. The transcendentalists, for example, considered the sensible world a symbol of indwelling divinity. Freud's symbolism, however, was more concrete than the mysticism of Thoreau or Emerson. And his worldview was essentially tragic. A further and critical distinction was that whereas the transcendentalists held the inner reality symbolized by the external world to be *higher*, that is, celestial, Freud perceived it as distinctly *lower*, viz., unconscious and instinctual.

Corollary with this relation between the higher level of manifest life and the lower level of its underlying reality, in Freud's view, was the peculiar character of concealment necessitated by repression. The appearance of everyday life served to deny exactly what psychoanalysis showed it to symbolize. The nature of literary allegory is to conceal meaning, paradoxically, only in order to reveal it; one thing is said while another is meant. Like hide-and-seek, though, the game of allegory is pointless if what is concealed cannot (at least by those with eyes to see, ears to hear) be discovered. So meaning in allegory constructed by the artist is disguised by analogy, not contradiction. 19th Century gentility and earnest striving, however, not only masked but actually symbolized their very opposites: intolerable sexual and aggressive instincts. Genteel bourgeois culture was life turned upside down; real life, as Alice found, had gone underground, to be glimpsed in the looking-glass, reversed.[10]

Classical mythologies are enacted in a separate, empyreal world, while the actual life to which they refer occurs on the sublunary level of the earth below. Modern life viewed as mythology takes place likewise above the level of the real, which we think of as "buried," or "underground," not only because it is unconscious, but because it is centered in the organs of sex and elimination situated in the lower regions of the body, as opposed to the organs of thought and communication, indeed the very consciousness of self, located atop the body in the head.[11] Mythology, which the 19th Century longed so earnestly to resuscitate, was after all never

---

[10] The project of psychoanalysis is to decipher even this apparently padlocked psychic code. As Philip Rieff writes, "Repressions both conceal and betray. The psychoanalytic interpreter looks for tell-tale ways in which repressed material manifests itself: in dreams, by the eruption of symbols, distortions of logic and sentiment; in the pathology of daytime, by an unusual arrangement of the patient's words, a forced expression or gesture, an accidental clumsiness." *Freud: The Mind of the Moralist* (Garden City, NY, 1961), p. 120.

[11] "The polarity in religion between the manifest literal and the latent ethical exactly reverses the Freudian. What is hidden by the religious text is 'high' (or at least 'higher'), while what is hidden by the psychic symptom — even a normal symptom like the dream — is 'low.'" *Ibid.*, p. 121.

far to seek. It was under their noses, masquerading as reality. Not mythology, but real life had gone astray, and the romantics who looked for it in imagination, in mesmeric experiments with the unconscious, and in the ravings of lunatics were nearer the mark than either anachronistic theologians, or rationalistic scholars like the tedious Casaubon in *Middlemarch*, "a little buried in books," compiling his encyclopedic "Key to all Mythologies." The task now was to descend into the unconscious where the stuff of life had crystallized, and bring it to light.[12]

That exploration of the psychic underground climaxes in the work of Freud, but though he was the first psychoanalyst,[13] Freud did not "discover" the unconscious, nor was his theory of psycho-dynamics entirely unanticipated. More than a century of scientific inquiry had gone before and prepared the ground for him.[14] To be sure, it was Freud's genius to consolidate the insights and intuitions of the earlier research and hypothesis into a systematic theory.

Still, others had preceded Freud, not only scientists, philosophers, and physicians, but artists, whose insights Freud acknowledged often to have been more readily in touch with the unconscious than his own laborious researches. E. T. A. Hoffmann and Fuseli, Blake and Coleridge, Poe and Lewis

[12] Adorno, *op. cit.*, p. 117, notes that, "It is as if Wagner had anticipated Freud's discovery that what archaic man expresses in terms of violent action has not survived in civilized man, except in attenuated form, as an internal impulse that comes to the surface with the old explicitness only in dreams and madness."
[13] Erik Erikson, "The First Psychoanalyst," *Insight and Responsibility* (New York, 1964), pp. 17-46.
[14] Lancelot Law Whyte, The Unconscious Before Freud (New York, 1960); Henri F. Ellenberger, *The Discovery of the Unconscious* (New York, 1970).

Carroll, and Arthur Schnitzler come readily to mind. The artist's tactic is fantasy. Fantasy creates a world parallel to the sensible world, referring to the same inner reality, only transparently. The world in which daily life plays out is opaque—normally we do not see that it *has* inner meaning, much less comprehend it. We take life for what it appears on its mundane surface to be.

Fantasy, by contrast, erects a world whose unreality invites interpretation, whose magical or fabulous character says: more is here than meets the eye. We may fail to understand the relation of the fantasy to reality, but we sense at least that it exists. We cannot regard it seriously without conceding the necessity of interpretation. Actual life is an obscure symbol, then, whose meaning lies in the unconscious; the unconscious in turn generates fantasies that render the symbolic nature of actuality transparent.

Beginning with the earliest prose sketch of 1848, *The Ring* was informed with Wagner's passion for revolution, whether he happened to be in his "meliorist" phase in which he longed for the destruction of the ancient order from whose ashes would arise a golden age, or in his pessimistic phase (under the influence of co-conspirator Bakunin, whose politics consisted more or less in advocating the immolation of everything except—he confessed in a weak moment— Beethoven's 9th Symphony).

In April, 1849, one month before the uprising in Dresden, Wagner mythologized his concept of revolution in an article printed anonymously in August Röckel's radical democratic newspaper, *Volksblätter*. Revolution is personified as a mighty woman. Ernest Newman characterizes Wagner's piece as "a paean to the red goddess in her most incarnadine aspect."[15] "The old world is in ruins from which a new world will arise," Wagner proclaims, "for the sublime goddess REVOLUTION comes rushing and roaring on the wings of the storm, her august head rayed round with lightnings, a sword in her right hand, a torch in her left, her eyes so sullen, so punitive, so cold; and yet what warmth of purest love, what fullness of happiness radiate from it towards him who dares to look steadfastly into that sombre eye!"

The telling attribute of Wagner's revolutionary goddess is her maternal function. "Rushing and roaring she comes, the ever-rejuvenating mother of mankind; destroying and blessing she sweeps across the earth; before her pipes the storm; it shakes so violently all man's handiwork that vast clouds of dust darken the air, and where her mighty foot treads, all that has been built for ages past in idle whim crashes in ruins, and the hem of her robe sweeps the last remains of it away." Wagner's allegory is recognizably the two-sided, life-giving and life-destroying mother of mythology and depth psychology. Whence this figure's paradoxical nature? The mother who bestows life, the unconscious assumes, can as easily take it away. *Alma mater's* other face is the face of the "terrible mother." The mother who nourishes also devours. "I am the ever-rejuvenating, ever-creating Life; where I am not is Death. I am the dream, the balm, the hope of all who suffer. I annihilate what exists, and whither I turn there wells forth fresh life from the dead rock. I come to you to break all the

<hr>

[15] Ernest Newman, *The Life of Richard Wagner* (Cambridge, 1976), vol. II, p. 54. The text of Wagner's article is found translated on pp. 54-56.

fetters that oppress you, to redeem you from the embrace of Death and to pour young life into your veins. Whatever is must pass away: such is the everlasting law of Nature, such is the condition of Life; and I, the eternal destroyer, fulfill the law and create eternally youthful life. From its roots upwards I will destroy the order of things under which you live, for it has sprung from sin, its flower is misery and its fruit is crime; but the harvest is ripe and I am the reaper!"

Death, Wagner declares, is "the everlasting law of Nature." It is "the condition of life," and Revolution fulfills this law by eternally destroying and renewing. The statement of this "law" puts forth a cyclical view of history. Revolution (etymologically as well as politically a *turning*) is a circle. But Wagner's formulations suggest also that he is groping for what he described in the letter to Röckel as "the very essence and meaning of the world itself in all its possible phases." On the face of it, this "essence and meaning" is contained in the principle of revolution Wagner is extolling. But as Shaw notes, Wagner's revolutionary zeal gradually waned, eventually to be transformed into its reactionary mirror image. All the while, work on *The Ring* proceeded to its ineluctable completion. *The Ring*, we may accordingly conclude, must be informed by some other fundamental "essence and meaning."

To all appearances, the Master here employs the mother figure as a symbol for revolution: actually, the truth is the other way around. "Revolution" presents itself to Wagner as a guise for the figure of the universal maternal, a particular guise easily discarded for another when expedient. Not revolution, but the maternal principle is Wagner's "very essence and meaning of the world itself in all its possible phases."[16]

The maternal principle transcends the political or philosophical enthusiasm of the moment, be it meliorist revolution, Bakuninist nihilism, or Schopenhauerean pessimism. Yet for Wagner, it symbolically encapsulates — paradoxically to be sure — the affective experience and underlying meaning of all of them. "Mother" is both giver and destroyer of life; from the nothingness of life in her womb we are born, and to it we long to return, as it were, in death. Revolutions, counter-revolutions, fashions in philosophy come and go; the maternal endures. "Two peoples only are there henceforth: the one, that follows me, the other that withstands me. The one I lead to happiness: over the other I tread, crushing it as I go; for I am the REVOLUTION, I am the ever-creating life, I am the one God whom all creation acknowledges, who comprises and animates and fills with happiness all that is."

From this perspective we may resolve the Wagnerite confusion over optimism and pessimism. These are not so much — as they appear — opposing philosophical systems between which we are obliged to choose. Rather, they are complementary attitudes corresponding to the two faces of mother: the good mother, the "terrible mother." The confusion over them lies in the realm of logic, which is consciousness. But we are venturing into the unconscious, where contradiction is not merely tolerated, it is the rule. This is the realm of the "mother with two faces," evoking the

---

[16] Cf., "Alles Vergängliche/Ist nur ein Gleichnis . . .
Das Ewig Weibliche/zieht uns hinan," Goethe, *Faust*, Part II.

linked experiences of desire and terror. Desire and terror co-exist easily there until intuition of them rises into consciousness, and they become transmogrified (and, we might say, disguised) into "philosophies." Then it appears (because consciously we are thralls to logic) that a choice must be made.

But Wagner was unable, finally, to make that choice, although he shifted enthusiasms periodically. Shaw shrugs off Wagner's inconsistencies as part and parcel of his genius. "As in all men of his type," he writes, "our manifold nature was so marked in him that he was like several different men rolled into one . . . Wagner was not a Schopenhauerite every day of the week, nor even a Wagnerite. His mind changes as often as his mood."[17] "Mind," the superstructure of consciousness, is made rigid by logic and brittle by contradiction. But "mood" arises from the unconscious where, because contradiction flourishes, there is no contradiction at all.

It needs to be stressed that what is at issue is not the nature of mother or of the maternal itself so much as the child's ambivalent relation to her—a more intricate matter, since it is a *continuing* relation, characterized by an evolution. This evolutionary relation is recognized as having multiple stages, notable among them what Freud named the Oedipus Complex. In Freud's view, it was the determinative nucleus of personality, and in turn of personal destiny. The Oedipus Complex was in effect Freud's "very essence and meaning of the world itself in all its possible phases," his reduction of life to a single genetic principle. Freud employed the term

---

[17] G. B. Shaw, *Op. cit.*, p. 300.

complex to characterize a complicated affective system; complexes, he explained, are "circles of thoughts and interests of strong affective value."[18]

The Oedipus Complex refers neither to an event in the life of the child, nor simply to its unconscious wish for sexual possession of the opposite sexed parent, but to the complicated psycho-sexual economy that evolves among the child and its parents. Since it is a dynamic economy, it is based on a system of tensions that tend continually toward resolution. But since the possible resolutions to Oedipal conflict are inevitably compromises, the tensions are never finally unstrung, and continue to determine the evolving psychology of the adult. Caught in a double bind, the male child wishes to monopolize his mother, and eliminate the competition of father and siblings. But neither can he accomplish his desire without suffering guilt, nor can he suppress his desire or transfer it to some substitute object without suffering frustration. The Freudian view of the course of psychic life, then, is that the individual periodically accomplishes merely provisional resolutions of Oedipal conflict, only to see each resolution unravel, requiring a new effort at resolution—a continuing rhythm of regression and growth, a spiral, a series of circles.

---

[18] Sigmund Freud, "Sixth Lecture," *A General Introduction to Psychoanalysis*, trans., Joan Riviere (Garden City, NY, 1953), p. 114. All subsequent quotations from Freud's writings will be from *The Standard Edition of the Complete Psychological Works of Sigmund Freud*, ed., James Strachey, 24 vols. (London: Hogarth Press, 1963). Ms. Riviere's translation of this phrase, is closer to Freud's German, "affektmächtige Gedanken-und Intressenkreise," to be found in *Vorlesungen zur Einführung in die Psychoanalyse* (Leipzig and Vienna, 1918), p. 112. The term "complex," adopted by Freud from Jung's usage, had been coined originally by the German psychiatrist, Theodor Ziehen.

On the foundation of the genetic principle of the Oedipus Complex, Freud erected a structural theory of the psyche, a metapsychology. The ramifications of the Oedipus Complex as he saw it playing out in his own life and the lives of his patients suggested the roles of three functional psychical agencies: id, representative of the drives; ego, the mediator with the environment; and superego, repository of moral prohibitions and commands, as well as of ideal aspirations. Freud's theory of personality can be roughly divided, then, into two parts, the dynamic principle of the Oedipus Complex determining the individual's life story, and the metapsychological scheme describing the architecture of the psyche as comprising id, ego, and superego.

In his later work, Freud revised his estimate of how exclusively the Oedipus Complex, as originally formulated, determined character, recognizing that a crucial period of development occurred in the life of the infant before the emergence of the father as a major figure, and that prior to the triadic Oedipal relation, there existed a dyadic relation comprising only (or primarily) mother and infant. As Freud's collaborator Ruth Mack Brunswick puts it, "The relation of the child to the mother is obviously the fundament of its psychic life, the basis and prototype of all later love relationships."[19] Still implicitly retaining the primacy of the Oedipus Complex, however, Freud named this the "pre-oedipal" period.

Later theorists have further de-emphasized the nuclear Oedipus Complex. Fairbairn's assessment that Freud put the cart before the horse is exemplary: "The role of the ultimate

---

[19] Ruth Mack Brunswick, "The Pre-oedipal Phase of the Libido Development,"*Psychoanalytic Quarterly* (1940), p. 304.

cause, which Freud allotted to the Oedipus situation, should properly be allotted to the phenomenon of infantile dependence. In conformity with this standpoint, the Oedipus situation presents itself, not so much in the light of a causal phenomenon as in the light of an end-product. It is not a basic situation, but the derivative of a situation which has priority over it not only in the logical, but also in the temporal sense. This prior situation is one which issues directly out of the physical and emotional dependence of the infant upon his mother, and which declares itself in the relationship of the infant to his mother long before his father becomes a significant object."[20]

What persists, however, despite refinements and revisions of Freudian theory is general agreement that the infant's earliest relations to its mother (whatever the role — if any — played by the father) are determinative of its personality and future relationships. Whether the concept of the Oedipus Complex is broadened to include the pre-oedipal, or the Oedipus "situation" is viewed as an appendage of the primary dyadic relation to mother, what we might loosely term the "mother complex" is for orthodox Freudians and revisionists alike the core of a first principle . . . we might say "the very essence and meaning of the world itself in all its possible phases." It is at once the genetic nucleus of personality, and the foundation on which the Freudian metapsychological structure is built.[21]

---

[20] W. R. D. Fairbairn, *An Object Relations Theory of the Personality* (New York, 1954), p. 120.

[21] Cf., Bryan Magee, *Wagner and Philosophy* (Allen Lane, The Penguin Press, 2000), "[Wagner] sees what is ultimate in character as being something universal. For this reason he chose to base most of his mature works on myths or legends, because they possessed this quality of universality. . .

My aim in this study is not to construct an exhaustive interpretation of *The Ring*. In fact its view is purposely somewhat narrowly focused on the tetralogy's striking semantic and figural parallels to the insights and terminology of psychoanalytic theory. Like all great and complex works of art, *The Ring* lays itself open to multiple interpretations, which though radically different may not be mutually exclusive — in fact taken together begin to mirror the richness of the work itself.[22] The Freudian concept of the Oedipus Complex (including its pre- and post-oedipal ramifications) and the Freudian metapsychological hypotheses offer paradigms that illuminate many of the obscurities of *The Ring*. My point of departure is that Freud's psychoanalytic theory and Wagner's *Ring* are historically parallel manifestations of the same underlying social reality — childhood, family life, and sexual relations in the middle-class German/Austrian household of the 19th Century.[23]

This is one reason why Wagner's works have such deep appeal to many who are oriented towards analytic psychology: they deal successfully in archetypes and other universal attributes of the human psyche, with proto-Freudian and proto-Jungian insight. Before Freud was born, Wagner publicly analysed the Oedipus myth in terms of its psychological significance, insisting that incestuous desires are natural and normal, and perceptively exhibiting the relationship between sexuality and anxiety." pp. 84, 85.

[22] By the same token, the subtitle of the current book, *Genesis and Meaning of The Ring*, pointedly omits the definite article as modifiers of "Genesis" and "Meaning."

[23] To be underscored is the distinction between Freudian intra-psychic theory based on his metapsychology, on the one hand, and the therapeutic practice of psychoanalysis on the other. The efficacy of Freudian therapy has been assiduously questioned in recent decades, not to say disparaged. I take no position in this clinical dispute here, nor is it relevant to the subject at hand.

We tend to think of psychoanalysis as lying on this side of the watershed 1900 publication date of *The Interpretation of Dreams*, and thus to regard Freud as belonging to, even iconically representative of the 20th Century. In fact, Freud's theory was in important ways actually retrospective. It was out of 19th Century bourgeois culture that his theoretical system emerged, and to which it largely referred. Even when psychoanalytic treatment occurred after 1900, the childhoods of the patients on whose clinical histories Freud based his speculations had been lived in the 1800's. Freud was himself born only six years after mid-century, in 1856, the year Wagner completed the score of *Walküre* and began the score of *Siegfried*. He was twenty in 1876, the year *The Ring* premiered at Bayreuth. The basic patterns of Viennese family life in the second half of the 19th Century were not essentially different from those of Wagner's Dresden or Zürich or Munich of the forty-odd years earlier. And of course Freud's most celebrated patient, whose analysis furnished more raw material than any other for the construction of the psychoanalytic edifice, was Freud himself.

Underlying construction of *The Ring*, too, must have been an intuitive process akin to Freud's famous self-analysis. *The Ring* is the precipitate of this process, like the trail of a particle across a vapor chamber. Embedded in the fantasy of *The Ring* are images of events and relations from Wagner's life, as well as representations of his deepest wishes and anxieties. But though it has its genesis in the author's psychic life, *The Ring* is not an encoded psychic autobiography. Just as Freud's self-analysis led to the formulation of a general theory, Wagner's work transcends the personal through inflation to mythology.

We might say it is through intuitive and only partially conscious self-analysis that Wagner arrives at myth.

It is no denigration of Freud's work to regard it also as a mythologizing endeavor. The very naming of the central "complex" after a Greek myth suggests this. Likewise, it is suggested by the personifying and topographical tendency of Freud's metapsychological concepts of *unconscious*, *preconscious*, *id*, *ego*, and *superego*. Like a mythology, psychoanalytic theory attempts to order the chaotic multiplicity of experience through paradigms with which all behavior accords. The paradigms are formulated as generalizations and abstractions rather than as pictorial and narrative representations. Nevertheless, abstraction is akin in the economics of the mind to the process of deification, which elevates aspects of the mundane to the level of the divine. Abstraction elevates the typical or ordinary to the level of destiny, or natural law, or scientific principle. Both intellectual processes achieve order by unifying in the mind what is multifarious in experience.

At the core of 19th Century European consciousness generally was alienation (for which psychoanalysis coined the term *separation anxiety*); myth—formerly the medium of social cohesion—becomes individualized as the dream. Freud's theory is based on his *self*-analysis, and is launched with the publication of *The Interpretation of Dreams*. The fantasy of the lone dreamer, isolated in sleep, is thus publicized as universal myth. There is more than a trace of megalomania in this, but it is a megalomania endemic to the culture. For as classical style entails the submersion of individual identity in the perfection of forms that are, as it were, the artistic commons, romantic style entails the opposite, inflation of the personal, the idiosyncratic into a principle of form itself.

Mime's three questions to the Wanderer in *Siegfried* — "What race dwells under the earth? What race dwells on the earth? What race dwells on the cloudy heights?" — intimate that *The Ring* sets forth not an ordinary fantasy but a cosmography. Yet these images of an external universe are symbols of inner experience. The cosmos is the psyche turned inside out. The myth *is* its creator, as the dreamer is his dream. *The Ring is* Wagner, as psychoanalysis *is* Freud, or as *Madame Bovary is* Flaubert. The personal nevertheless attains universality because alienation — the painful loneliness of individuality — is at the heart of Everyman's story.

The Ring is a circle, or a series of circles, corresponding in its intricacy to that economy of psychic development Freud named the Oedipus Complex. Leaving aside the scientific and clinical validity of the concept, this book argues that *The Ring* refers to the same experiential reality of 19th Century life on which Freud grounded his insights and paradigms, and which became manifest and even reified in the edifice of psychoanalytic theory, and that it emerged from a common *Zeitgeist*.[24]

The Ring's complexity comprises three distinct components: a geography, a hierarchical cast of characters, and a time scheme. In general, its topography symbolizes the body *as represented in the mind*, that is, the psychical image of the body. Through this landscape move figures identifiable with the

---

[24] Lionel Trilling posits just such a *Zeitgeist* in his 1940 essay, "Freud and Literature," in *The Liberal Imagination*, (HBJ, New York, 1979), pp. 33-38.

people crucial to Wagner's life-history — again, as they exist in the mind: to appropriate the terminology of psychoanalysis, as introjected "objects" incorporated into the structure of the psyche. Time, finally, is the dimension of psychic life-history, or evolution; the unidirectional time-vector of the fiction subserves the underlying cyclical pattern of conflict, regression, resolution.

Freud's theoretical edifice and Wagner's operatic drama are viewed here as parallel manifestations of their historical milieu — mental constructions pertaining to a largely common referent. The striking parallels observable between the fiction of *The Ring* and Freud's psychoanalytic theorizing (Wagner will be seen often as presenting almost picture-book illustrations of abstract psychoanalytic principles)[25] is not so much to be understood as an uncanny anticipation of Freud's insights. Rather, the uncanny parallels point to the fact that both arise from a common underlying reality. *The Ring* is only on one of its multiple layers "about" dwarves and giants and gods and dragons, the fabulous images traversing its elaborate surface. On other levels, *The Ring* is about the real life of its time. Its surface narrative is an allegory: it says one thing and means another. What it says is patently fabulous. But this fabulous narrative refers to the realities of 19th Century European life by a systematic symbolism.

Freud's vision of the human psyche can likewise be regarded not so much as the scientific discovery of a system of absolute

---

[25] Cf. B. Magee, *Aspects of Wagner*, rev. ed. (New York: Oxford University Press, 1988), p. 36: "[Wagner's operas often seem] like animated textbooks of psychoanalysis . . . While archetypal psycho-sexual situations are being acted out and discussed at exhaustive length, the orchestra is pouring out a flood of the otherwise inexpressible feelings associated with them."

truths, independent of his historical context, as the systematic expression—as it were the projection—of psychic life in the social matrix of his time. This book does not seek to determine (or even take a position on) the scientific validity of psychoanalytic theory. In the sense I intend it, the Freudian concepts adumbrated in the Wagnerian text need not even be seen as absolutely "explaining" it. Conversely, the Freudian text is itself subject to interpretation.[26] The psychoanalytic concepts do elucidate the text by connecting its fabulous narrative to a concrete social reality. Thus, the present study, beyond its obvious literary purpose, asks to be regarded as an essay in intellectual history.

It is less plausible to propose that Freud's theoretical world-view was a singularity, isolated from the intellectual currents of his time.[27] Parsimony suggests rather that the *Zeitgeist* from which Freudian theory emerged engendered other, more or less parallel manifestations, among which, I contend here, Wagner's *Ring* is to be numbered.[28] Psychoanalytic theory

---

[26] By interpretation, I do not mean works of revision, or even commentaries such as Rieff's *Mind of the Moralist,* or Norman O. Brown's *Life Against Death.* I have in mind studies such as John Murray Cuddihy's *The Ordeal of Civility* (New York, 1974), which interprets Freud's psychoanalytic theory as an allegory of Jewish emancipation and assimilation—the rejected, unruly "yid" regarded as metamorphosed into the theoretical *id* of the genteel personality.

[27] The evolution of the idea of the unconscious, of which Freud's work represents one of numerous summits, is well documented. See especially L. L. Whyte, *The Unconscious Before Freud* (Basic Books, 1960); Henri F. Ellenberger, *The Discovery of the Unconscious* (Basic Books, 1970); Leon Chertok, Raymond de Saussure, *The Therapeutic Revolution : From Mesmer to Freud,* (New York, 1979).

[28] If Wagner can arguably be said to have anticipated Freud in important respects, it is interesting to know what Freud (the younger of the two) knew about Wagner. On this point, see Cora L. Diaz de Chumaceiro,

provides one kind of structure for organizing the apparent chaos of individual wishes, fantasies, and associations. *The Ring* furnishes another. The former is interpretive, diagnostic, and (in aspiration at least) therapeutic; the latter, aesthetic and visionary. This book aims to illuminate Wagner's encyclopedic work by the light of Freud's.

To this end I scrutinize the Wagnerian text. Two questions guide the inquiry: to what Freudian paradigms do the elements of Wagner's text correspond? and to what concrete social reality, or actual experience might each element refer? For example, I frequently identify the figure of Wotan with the superego. I mean by this identification that Wotan's function corresponds to that component of actual psychic life reified by Freud in the concept of the superego. When I draw an analogy between Alberich's relation to the Rhinemaidens and that of Wagner to his sisters, I do not mean that *Das Rheingold* is disguised autobiography, but that Wagner's characterization of the universal experience of infantile helplessness is informed and infused by a particular personal experience: the idiosyncratic, generalized and elevated to the level of myth. The parallels with Wagner's life experience — which we know from his autobiographical writings — illuminate ambiguous situations in the operas. We must always remember we are confronting works of art, not biography.

At times, I have recourse to psychoanalytic writers other than Freud, his contemporaries as well as more recent

Richard Wagner's Life and Music: What Freud Knew, in *Psychoanalytic Explorations in Music*, 2nd Series (Madison, CT, 1993), Feder, Stuart, Karmel, Pollock, eds., pp. 249-278.

theoreticians. This is not to introduce any element of the revisionist debate, or take sides in it. The passages cited are meant to fill explanatory gaps in the Freudian text,[29] and are not, I believe, inconsistent with the general theory.

Nor do I propose to psychoanalyze Wagner. To be sure, analytically informed speculations are made with regard to biographical details that bear on the text of *The Ring*. But this is a literary study, not a diagnostic one. I am not an analyst. Even if I were, it is doubtful that, lacking the "patient's" associations — the crucial material of any analysis — such an endeavor would be particularly enlightening. My interpretations of Wagner's biography, to the extent they bear a psychoanalytic stamp, are aimed at elucidating the text and its genesis. My purpose is to coax out literary, not clinical meaning.

This study is also intentionally not musicological. Occasional observations are made concerning the music, but no effort is made at a systematic harmonic analysis, or analysis of the leitmotifs. Such have been (and continue to be) carried out copiously and admirably elsewhere. Wagner was first and foremost, of course, a musician. But he was also a remarkable poet and dramatist, and it is this side of his genius on which I choose to concentrate here.

There is ample precedent for a purely literary approach to *The Ring*, not least, Shaw's really splendid *Perfect Wagnerite*. But another consideration has dictated my focusing on the poetic text. Psychoanalysis is by its nature a verbal discourse. To be sure, the unconscious processes it refers to are essentially non-

---

[29] I.e., with respect to Wagner.

verbal.   But they become accessible to psychoanalytic interpretation only by conversion into words. It is difficult to imagine what significant psychoanalytic insights are to be gained from an analysis of the musical score, however such a task might be approached. To ascribe specific unconscious meaning to music seems an unusually tenuous enterprise. It is true that music, the continuously fluid medium in which the *Ring* drama plays out, does embody the emotional content of the words of the text.   More particularly, the leitmotifs of Wagner's operas are vehicles of clearly formulated thematic meanings.   But these meanings are *conscious* ones, whereas psychoanalytical exegesis is aimed at the unconscious. Unless some discrepancy exists between a feeling suggested by the music or the association borne by a leitmotif and what — viewed psychoanalytically — is "really" going on in the drama, unless some displacement or distortion determines the music at some point, the commentator can only recapitulate the composer's conscious intentions. In the instances where such discrepancies *have* been apparent to me, I have taken them up. But they seem to me the exception, not the rule.

It should be said that this reading is unstintingly and comprehensively corporeal, referring frankly to bodily parts and functions. *The Ring* is a representation of the human condition, which is, first and last, a bodily one: to it we are born; to it we succumb in death, and between those two terminals of life (to quote W. B. Yeats), "Love has pitched his mansion in the place of excrement." This corporeal dimension has been neglected in interpretive considerations of *The Ring*.

In the chapters that follow, each opera of the tetralogy is taken up in turn. And we begin in the depths of the Rhine.

CHAPTER II

Rheingold: Anxiety

Wagner was a life-long sufferer from gastric disorders, skin eruptions and rheumatism — afflictions Ernest Newman (like the composer's contemporaries) attributes to hypochondria. Wagner himself blamed his perennial ill-health on "nervousness." On Sept. 12, 1852, for example, he writes to Röckel, "My nervous system is in a bad way and is gradually getting worse — the necessary result of my abandoning myself to that passionate and hectic sensitivity in virtue of which I am the artistic being that I am." To Liszt on July 20, 1856, he writes from one of the several "hydropathic" institutions he patronized, "I go thoroughly to work in using this new and careful treatment and feel sure of being completely cured of my ailment, which, after all, was caused by nervousness."

Laymen were not alone in this diagnosis. In 1856 the Swiss hydropathic Dr. Vaillant, whom Wagner praises in *Mein Leben*, warned his patient against hot sulfur bath water and strong mineral waters. "'*Monsieur, vous n'êtes que nerveux*. All this will only excite you more; you merely need calming. If you will entrust yourself to me, I promise that you will have so far recovered by the end of two months as never to have erysipelas again.'"[30] Dr. Vaillant settled the Master's nerves to

---

[30] Richard Wagner, *My Life*, 2 vols. (New York, 1911), p. 645.

the extent that the erysipelas erupted again only after twenty-three years.

Wagner could not fully have appreciated that what he experienced as "bad nerves" had a deep psychological basis. But his association of a nervous condition with the artistic temperament reflects the growing awareness in the nineteenth century that unconscious mental processes have somatic consequences.

Hypochondria, excessive sensitivity that results in the exaggeration of symptoms, is in modern psychological terms a primitive defense mechanism (like projection and denial). It substitutes a bodily anxiety for an emotional one. Thus hypochondria, unlike purely physically based dysfunction or disease, is *significant*, or symbolic, in that sensory or bodily experience stands for inner or emotional experience. Wagner's morbid obsession with his health (Newman characterizes him also as a valetudinarian) indicates that his symptoms constituted not merely a physical condition but that they had — consciously or unconsciously — a meaning.

Accordingly, Wagner devotes himself like a fanatic to the theory and praxis of hydropathy. Obsessed with his symptoms, he is devout in his faith in the healing properties of water, as expounded in a book (Wagner writes in *Mein Leben*), "by a certain Rausse, which pleased me greatly, especially by its radical principles, which had something of Feuerbach about them." It is the rebellious, revolutionary Wagner to whom hydropathy's radicalism appeals: "Its bold repudiation of the entire science of medicine, with all its quackeries, combined with its advocacy of the simplest natural processes by means of a methodical use of strengthening and refreshing water." For Wagner, the principle of revolution is as we have seen the well-spring of creativity, appearing in his imagination in the guise of a powerful woman. In his encomium to hydropathy, we might well see (mother) nature, in the form of the water cure, overthrowing a discredited father science.[31]

As early as 1850, the Master has begun a routine of taking cold baths and drinking quantities of cold water; in 1851 he is conscientiously wearing the "Neptune Girdle," a new-fangled cold compress belt. On Sept. 16, 1851 he submits to the regimen of the hydropathic institution at Albisbrunn under the direction of Dr. Christoph Zacharias Brunner of Winterthur. Wagner describes the daily routine:

1. At half-past five in the morning, wrapping up in a wet sheet until seven; then a cold tub and a walk. Eight o'clock, breakfast—dry bread and milk, or water.
2. Another short walk; then a cold compress.
3. About twelve, a rub-down with damp towels; a short walk; another compress. Then dinner in my room, to avoid unpleasant consequences: An hour's idleness; a stiff walk of two hours, alone.
4. About five, another damp rub-down and a short walk.
5. About six, a hip-bath, lasting a quarter of an hour, followed by a walk to get my circulation up. Another compress. Supper about seven—dry

---

[31] *Ibid.*, p. 569.

bread and water. Then a whist party until nine,
after which another compress and about ten o'clock
to bed.[32]

This regimen was the practical application of Rausse's theory that conventional medicines are effectual only insofar as they are poisonous to the system. Patients constitutionally weakened through absorption of these "medicinal" poisons can be restored only by flushing the poison through the skin with water. When he discovered Rausse's work, Wagner tells us, "I naturally thought of the disagreeable sulfur baths I had taken during the spring, and to which I attributed my chronic and severe state of irritability . . . For a long while after this I did my best to expel this and all other poisons which I might have absorbed in the course of time, and by an exclusive water regimen restore my original healthy condition."[33]

From Albisbrunn (Nov. 20, 1851) he writes Liszt that he is virtually cured, and admonishes his friend to follow him down this unique path to salvation.

> My previous continual anxiety about my health has
> also now been relieved by the conviction I have
> since gained of the all-healing power of water and
> of nature's medicine; I am in the way of becoming
> and, if I choose, of remaining a perfectly healthy
> man. If you wretched people would only get a good
> digestion, you would find that life suddenly assumes
> a very different appearance from what you saw
> through the medium of your digestive troubles. In

---

[32] Letter to Uhlig, quoted in Newman, *The Life of Richard Wagner*, vol. II, p. 247.
[33] *My Life*, pp. 569-570.

fact, all our politics, diplomacy, ambition, impotence,
science, and, what is worse, our whole *modern
art*, in which the palate, at the expense of the
stomach, is alone satisfied, tickled, and flattered,
until at last a corpse is unwittingly galvanized —
all this parasite growth of our actual existence
has no soil to thrive in but a ruined digestion.
I wish that those could and would understand me to
whom I exclaim these almost ridiculously sounding
but terribly true words!

Characteristically, Wagner reduces all existence to single, universal principles. At this moment, it happens to be digestion. Bad digestion, good digestion. And the simple element water is the universal panacea.

Water means cure. It means cure to the chronically afflicted Wagner as it means cure to the hopelessly wounded Amfortas in *Parsifal*. And yet Wagner, for all his hydropathic treatments, like Amfortas with his ineffectual baths in the lake of the Grail Knighthood, is no better, possibly worse off than before. There is this curious twist: water is at once cause *and* cure. The Flying Dutchman's salvation from water is water. Finally and mercifully he drowns in the water he cannot otherwise escape. So it is for Wagner.

For if his artistic temperament is the cause of bad nerves and ill-health, it is nevertheless finally art, for Wagner metaphorically also a kind of water, that redeems him. Once again immersed in composition, he assures Minna in a letter of October, 1854 that he has "plunged" into the "sea" of his music. To Liszt he writes that he will "cast everything aside to dive up to the ears into the fount of music." (April l3th, 1853) Complaining of his wretched existence to Liszt on another occasion: "If I am to dive into the waves of artistic fancy in order to find contentment in a world of imagination, my fancy should at least be buoyed up, my imagination supported. I cannot live like a dog; I cannot sleep on straw and drink bad whiskey." (January 8, 1854) He finds Liszt's own music to be like water. When he reads through one of his friend's scores, Wagner writes, "I feel every time as if I had dived into a deep crystal flood, to be there quite by myself, leaving all the world behind me, and living for an hour my real life. Refreshed and strengthened, I rise again to long for your presence." (July 20, 1855)

Here, Wagner evokes another aspect of his water symbolism. Water cures not only by cleansing, but by inundating, salving the bruised soul with oblivion. The Dutchman escapes his life on the water by drowning in it. "You know, or might imagine," Wagner writes Liszt (May 8, 1859), "that I do not live a life in the proper sense of the word; the only thing that could help me [is] art, art to the verge of drowning and world-forgetfulness." It offers escape from everyday life in the depths of fantasy. Early in 1852 he has written Liszt that he hopes only for a more or less private realization of his Nibelung drama, "in some beautiful solitude, far from the smoke and pestilential business odour of our town civilization . . . If I now turn to my great work, it is done for the purpose of seeking salvation from my misery, forgetfulness of my life. I have no other aim, and shall think myself happy when I am no longer conscious of my existence." (Jan. 30, 1852)[34]

We can now appreciate the significance of Wagner's story of the *Rheingold* prelude's conception and composition. The poem of *The Ring* had been finished for some time. But, unable to begin composition, and depressed in the wake of a visit from Liszt, Wagner went to St. Moritz in the summer of 1853 for yet another cure. The waters only irritated his bowels and nerves the more, however, and he returned to Zürich in August. Two weeks later, he was off for Italy in hopes travel would restore him.

"My only object still," he writes, "was to find a refuge where I might enjoy the congenial peace suited to some new artistic creation. In consequence, however, of thoughtlessly indulging in ices, I soon got an attack of dysentery, which produced the most depressing lassitude after my previous exaltation."[35] To escape the noise of the Genoese harbor, he fled to Spezia. But the voyage was ill-fated, as severe head-winds and heavy seas tossed his steamer mercilessly.

> The dysentery became worse, owing to sea-sickness, and in the most utterly exhausted condition, scarcely able to drag myself another step, I made for the best hotel in Spezia, which to my horror, was situated in a

---

[34] Wagner gives the triple theme of art, water, and oblivion its most celebrated form in the *Liebestod*; Isolde metaphorically transforms the fancied breathing of Tristan's corpse step-wise into music, then breezes, then water, in which she ecstatically drowns.
[35] *My Life*, p. 603.

noisy narrow street. After a night spent in fever and sleeplessness, I forced myself to take a long tramp the next day through the hilly country, which was covered with pine woods. It all looked dreary and desolate, and I could not think what I should do there. Returning in the afternoon, I stretched myself, dead tired, on a hard couch, awaiting the long-desired hour of sleep. It did not come; but I fell into a kind of somnolent state, in which I suddenly felt as though I were sinking in swiftly flowing water. The rushing sound formed itself in my brain into a musical sound, the chord of E flat major, which continually re-echoed in broken forms; these broken chords seemed to be melodic passages of increasing motion, yet the pure triad of E flat major never changed, but seemed by its continuance to impart infinite significance to the element in which I was sinking. I awoke in sudden terror from my doze, feeling as though the waves were rushing high above my head. I at once recognized that the orchestral overture to the *Rheingold*, which must long have lain latent within me, though it had been unable to find definite form, had at last been revealed to me. I then quickly realized my own nature; the stream of life was not to flow to me from without, but from within.[36]

Whether or not this well-known story is fanciful, it reveals, as only fantasies can, what the music's genesis means.

---

[36] *Ibid.*, p. 603.

Commonly, water symbolizes birth, referring to the life of the fetus suspended in amniotic fluid. There is nothing new, or especially "Freudian" about this particular symbolism. It is found universally in myths, and is the conscious symbolism of Christian baptism, in which the font is a "womb" from which the soul is "reborn." Paradoxically, the font is also regarded in Christian exegetical writings as a tomb; to be reborn the soul first must die. The dual significance of this water symbolism is understandable, for the horror of drowning is a counterpoise to the blissful fantasy of life in the deeps. Freud explains the ambivalence as the unconscious assumption that mother's womb, which has power to give life, can also take it away. "Phantasies and unconscious thoughts about life in the womb," he adds in a footnote to *The Interpretation of Dreams*, ". . . contain an explanation of the remarkable dread that many people have of being buried alive; and they also afford the deepest unconscious basis for the belief in survival after death, which merely represents a projection into the future of this uncanny life before birth. *Moreover, the act of birth is the first experience of anxiety, and thus the source and prototype of the affect of anxiety.*"[37]

The symbolic implication of Wagner's underwater fantasy of inspiration is that cure is birth, or rebirth, or regression to the intra-uterine stage. The power of rebirth does not reside, however, in the substance of his water cures; since rebirth is a fantasy, it occurs only in symbolic water — in Wagner's case, the water of *Rheingold*, that is to say, his work. "I realised that the fact which refreshed and invigorated me was not the

---

[37] Sigmund Freud, *The Interpretation of Dreams, Standard Edition*, vol. V, pp. 400-401, n. 1, Freud's emphasis.

renewal of my delight over Italy, but the resolve to take up my work again. And indeed, as soon as I made up my mind to alter this plan, the old condition set in once more, with all the symptoms of dysentery. I thereupon understood myself, and giving up the journey to Nice, I returned direct by the nearest route."[38]

But cure is also cause. The womb is the object of desire as well as the source of anxiety. Wagner's fantasy is curative, but terrifying, like drowning. In Zürich once more, he does not get down to work. He is restless and defers his composition until after meeting with Liszt in Basel and Paris where he is "terribly depressed," and "tortured by continually recurring nervous headaches."[39] Not until the first of November, 1853, two months after his underwater fantasy, can Wagner conquer his ambivalence and begin the music of *Rheingold*.

"The pure triad of E flat major never changed, but seemed by its continuance to impart infinite significance to the element in which I was sinking." "Infinite significance" is a formulation equivalent to "the very essence and meaning of the world itself," a product of Wagner's penchant for grandiose and universal principles, prefiguring the "oceanic feeling" about which Romain Rolland questioned Freud. Rolland thought the "oceanic feeling" was the fundament of all religion. Freud, skeptical of this notion in the opening pages of *Civilization and its Discontents*, regards it rather as the "primitive ego-feeling" preserved from infancy. If the "very essence and meaning of the world" is what we are loosely calling the mother complex, including this "primitive ego-

---

[38] *My Life*, p. 604.
[39] *Ibid.* p. 607.

feeling" of identification with the mother, then the "infinite significance" of water becomes clear. In the prelude to *Rheingold*, desire for mother, re-identification with her, as it were, is transformed into the fantasy of immersion in water, symbolically the womb.

The fantasy's aim is resolution of Oedipal conflict, as hypochondria's is masking it. *The Ring* consists essentially of a sequence of tentative resolutions proposed symbolically through fantasies whose outlines are drawn from Norse mythology and medieval legend. Return to the intra-uterine stage is logically (if not developmentally) the first of these tentative resolutions, solving the conflict between desire and guilt by combining total identification with (or absorption by) the mother and loss of consciousness. Thus the apparent stasis of the *Rheingold* prelude. The triad of E flat major seems *by its continuance* to impart infinite significance to the water. The wish is to return to life in the womb, with this difference — that one would never be born, suspended forever in lubricious passivity.

But this resolution in fantasy lasts no longer than the 136 bars of the prelude. The music itself belies the wish that gives it birth. For although the triad remains, the undulating arpeggios double and redouble their speed, rushing toward the climax marked by Woglinde's babbling. How deceptive, that seemingly static pedal point with which the prelude begins. The climax is birth, the infant's ineluctable separation from mother. Appropriately, what Woglinde first sings are not words at all, but an infant's warbled nonsense. Soon she begs the water (the mother) to rock her as though in a cradle.

A second stumbling block now appears. It is the discovery — in the dark, watery paradise — of Alberich. The water of *Rheingold* is the womb. It is also the unconscious, the depths of the Wagnerian self, from which emerges a fantasy that is essentially self-reflexive. The action of *The Ring* occurs first of all inside the circle of Wagner's head. Womb and unconscious are logically fused in the symbol of water, since intrauterine life represents primal unconsciousness.

The wish is to resolve inner conflict over Oedipal desires by returning to the womb. But bliss is short-lived because the dreamer finds there what he most wishes to avoid. He finds Alberich, a hateful dwarf, made ludicrous by lust. The complexity of the water symbolism suggests that he finds "Alberich" not only in the putative paradise of the womb, however, but also in himself. The figure in the Dreamer's ontogeny who matches that description, who has preceded him into mother's womb, and is simultaneously part of the dreamer himself, is the dreamer's arch-rival, his father.

It is generally accepted that Wagner's biological and his legal father were not the same man. Wagner was certain his actual father was Ludwig Geyer, the man who became his step-father a little over a year after his birth, whose surname he carried till the age of thirteen. While Wagner's mother's husband kept rendezvous with a local actress, Geyer generally "filled his place in the lap of the family," writes Wagner in *Mein Leben*.[40]

---

[40] On page 2 of the English edition of *My Life*, this passage is translated, "the worthy actor generally filled his place in the family circle," a rendering that obscures the *double entendre* noted by Gutman, below.

This figurative "lap of the family" contains in German a double meaning absent from the English: *"im Schosse seiner Familie."* Robert Gutman points out this ambiguity. "Since the word *'Schosse'* must in German do double duty for 'lap' and 'womb,' it is difficult to imagine that the Wagner who was one day to make even his Kundry speak in puns was completely unaware of the implications of the idiom he chose to employ."[41] Whether Geyer was Wagner's biological father in fact—in mother's "womb" in advance of the son—what matters is that Wagner believed him to be.[42] The double meaning of the pun reflects what is expressed symbolically in the figure of Alberich in the waters of the Rhine.

As a portrait of his father, the figure of Alberich has undergone distortion of the sort Freud found to be the normal mechanism of the "dream-work." Wagner loved the physically normal and artistically gifted Geyer, whereas Alberich is a hateful and ridiculous dwarf. This distortion conforms with the diagnosis of Wagner as a hypochondriac.

Hypochondria was characterized (above) as the substitution of somatic complaints for psychic conflict—that is, as a symbolic illness. A modern clinician defines hypochondria more particularly as:

> The transformation of reproach towards others arising
> from bereavement, loneliness, or unacceptable,
> aggressive impulses into, first, self-reproach, and, then,
> complaints of pain, somatic illness, and neurasthenia.

---

[41] Robert Gutman, *Richard Wagner* (Harmondsworth, Middlesex, England: Penguin, 1971), p. 31.
[42] On the question of the Wagner paternity, see Newman, vol. II, Appendix, and Gutman, pp. 24-36.

It includes those aspects of introjections which permit traits of an ambivalently regarded person to be perceived as within oneself and causing plausible disease. Unlike identification, hypochondriacal introjection produces dysphoria and a sense of affliction; hypochondriacal introjects are "ego alien." The mechanism may permit the individual to belabor others with his own pain or discomfort in lieu of making direct demands upon them or in lieu of complaining that others have ignored his wishes (often unexpressed) to be dependent.[43]

The term introjection is most familiar in regard to the development of the superego, the internalized system of parental morality, roughly identifiable with the "conscience." The superego is an image of the parents imbedded in the psyche. There is, moreover, a negative and a positive aspect to the superego, a carrot and a stick. On the one hand it enunciates prohibitions and commands, which delimit behavior, and on the other it represents an ego-ideal in the image of the parents. Parental prohibitions and commands, by their very existence, imply that this child, left to its natural impulses, would behave unacceptably. Conversely, the ego can assure itself of the love and esteem it feeds on by becoming like the parents who dispense them. In the male, introjection of the parents occurs at separate stages.

---

[43] George E. Vaillant, M.D., "Theoretical Hierarchy of Adaptive Ego Mechanisms," *Archives of General Psychiatry*, (Feb., 1971), vol. XXIV, no. 2, p. 117. It is a coincidence without significance that the author of this article shares the surname of Wagner's hydropathic physician.

First mother is introjected to circumvent the catastrophic loss of her love. Introjection of the father is itself a provisional resolution of the Oedipus Complex. Unable to compete with father for mother's love, the child temporarily renounces Oedipal ambitions and identifies with the rival in order to incorporate his power, and to protect himself from castration anxiety.

Since Alberich is a representation of Geyer not in reality, but as introjected father, he is an aspect of Wagner himself. Small and loathsome as he is, his sexual desires make him ridiculous, just as the boy, contrasting his own penis with father's, sees himself as a puny rival whose suit for mother's love is doomed to rejection. Alberich is stubbly and disgusting, as tabooed sexual wishes are experienced as "dirty." The ego's response to this discovery of self as dwarf is the provisional resolution of Oedipal guilt through identification with the idealized father, Wotan. For Wotan, explicitly in Wagner's text of *The Ring*, is the obverse of Alberich. Wotan is "Light-Alberich," as Alberich is "Black-Wotan." Wotan and Alberich are the complementary faces of the introjected father, the Geyer *within* Wagner.

Of course the splitting of the father image into Wotan and the Nibelung (in *Siegfried*, Alberich's brother Mime plays the role) reflects the actual situation of Wagner's childhood. He had in fact two fathers. But it corresponds to the normal complication of infantile development that Freud identified as the positive and the negative Oedipus Complexes. Freud ascribed the cause of this complication "to the bisexuality originally present in children: that is to say, a boy has not merely an ambivalent attitude towards his father and an

48

affectionate object-choice towards his mother, but at the same time he also behaves like a girl and displays an affectionate feminine attitude to his father and a corresponding jealousy and hostility towards his mother." Wotan, whom the son regards affectionately, is the father of this "negative Oedipus Complex." The Nibelung is the father of the "positive Oedipus Complex," hated rival for mother's love.[44]

Wagner's hypochondria may well have been, according to the cited definition, the transformation of reproach towards his parents, "arising from bereavement, loneliness, or unacceptable aggressive impulses into, first, self-reproach, and, then, complaints of pain and somatic illness." Wagner was in fact considerably deprived of the warmth and tenderness of mother love. At seven he was sent to live with a parson in a nearby village closer to his school. When father Geyer died a year later, he was sent to live at Eisleben with Geyer's brother Karl Friedrich Wilhelm. Only the following year, when his uncle's decision to marry made his continued presence in the house inconvenient, did the boy return to his

---

[44] Sigmund Freud, *The Ego and the Id*, *Standard Edition*, vol. XIX, p. 33. A variation of this rationale is offered by Fairbairn, *Object Relations Theory*. In Fairbairn's view, the father becomes (considerably later than the mother, but analogously) a cathected object. The infant cannot long ignore that whereas sometimes father answers its demands for care and affection, at other times he does not. In an effort to subject rejection and deprivation to inner control, the infant splits the image of father into a "good" father, who satisfies its demands, and a "bad" father, who frustrates them. The "bad" father is internalized, where he is once more split. That aspect which the infant longs for, but is denied (Fairbairn calls it the "exciting object") is detached from the aspect that rejects the infant's demands, called the "rejecting object." This latter differentiates itself as the "internal saboteur." According to this scheme, Wotan would represent the father as "exciting object," while Alberich would represent the fusion of "rejecting object" and "internal saboteur." See also Appendix.

mother in Dresden. But at thirteen, the very cutting edge of puberty, his mother and sisters moved to Prague, leaving Richard in Dresden to continue his studies.

In *Mein Leben* Wagner recalls that his mother's "trying position at the head of a numerous family (of which I was the seventh surviving member), the difficulty of obtaining the wherewithal to rear them, and of keeping up appearances on very limited resources, did not conduce to evolve that tender sweetness and solicitude which are usually associated with motherhood. I hardly ever recollect her having fondled me. Indeed, demonstrations of affection were not common in our family, although a certain impetuous, almost passionate and boisterous manner always characterized our dealings."[45] Wagner's defensive justification of his mother's aloofness is somewhat undermined by passages revealing ways he compensated for what she denied him.

Geyer's death left Richard (when he was not boarding elsewhere) surrounded by a household of females — Wagner's mother and four sisters. His brothers Albert and Julius were grown and living on their own. To this feminine atmosphere Wagner attributed "the development of the sensitive side of [his] nature," by which he meant in particular an obsessive fascination with the world of fantasy and the supernatural. Because life at school was exclusively male, Wagner opines, "the opposite characteristics of womanhood, especially such as were connected with the imaginary world of the theatre, created a feeling of such tender longing in me."[46]

---

[45] *My Life*, p. 15.
[46] *Ibid.* p. 15.

The longing was twofold. First, it was the longing for feminine tenderness. What his mother withheld, however, was in part supplied by his sisters, so that, for example, "the more elegant contents of my sisters' wardrobes . . . exercised a subtle charm over my imagination; nay, my heart would beat madly at the very touch of one of their dresses."[47] Second, it was the longing to retreat from tedium and frustration into a realm that promised to restore infantile omnipotence. "What attracted me so strongly to the theatre . . . was . . . the fascinating pleasure of finding myself in an entirely different atmosphere, in a world that was purely fantastic and often gruesomely attractive. Thus to me a scene, even a wing, representing a bush, or some costume or characteristic part of it, seemed to come from another world, to be in some way as attractive as an apparition, and I felt that contact with it might serve as a lever to lift me from the dull reality of daily routine to that delightful region of spirits."[48]

Wagner's immersion in fantasy includes a masochistic attraction to terror. The world he conjures up is not always a rosy bower; rather, it is often a place as bizarre as the settings of the contemporaneous tales of E. T. A. Hoffman. His favorite theatrical piece as a child was Weber's *Freischütz*, "mainly on account of its ghostly theme." He continues that, "The emotions of terror and the dread of ghosts formed quite an important factor in the development of my mind. From my earliest childhood certain mysteries and uncanny things exercised an enormous influence over me. If I were left alone in a room for long, I remember that, when gazing at lifeless

---

[47] *Ibid.*, p. 15.
[48] *Ibid.*, p. 14.

objects such as pieces of furniture, and concentrating my attention upon them, I would suddenly shriek out with fright, because they seemed to me alive. Even during the latest years of my boyhood, not a night passed without my waking out of some ghostly dream and uttering the most frightful shrieks, which subsided only at the sound of some human voice. The most severe rebuke or even chastisement seemed to me at those times no more than a blessed release."[49]

The attractiveness of fantastical terror lay in its function of providing in imagination both the maternal attention he craved (even if in the form of the "terrible" mother), and the punishment the boy unconsciously felt he merited. Thus, a similar memory is of the room in which he slept at his Uncle Adolf Wagner's house in Leipzig. This room was hung with portraits invested by the young boy with a terrifying power, "particularly those of high-born dames in hooped petticoats, with youthful faces and powdered hair. These appeared to me exactly like ghosts, who, when I was alone in the room, seemed to come back to life, and filled me with the most abject fear. To sleep alone in this distant chamber, in that old-fashioned bed of state, beneath those unearthly pictures, was a constant terror to me . . . Never a night passed in which I was not a prey to the most horrible ghostly visions, my dread of which would leave me in a bath of perspiration."[50] These "high-born dames," gazing down on the boy in his bed, suggest a fantasy of the not-so-nurturing mother, looming gigantically (and threateningly) over the infant in its crib.

---

[49] *Ibid.*, p. 14.
[50] *Ibid.*, p. 8. These "ghosts, who . . . seemed to come back to life . . . " may be an early instance of the necrophiliac motif discussed below in Chapters III and IV in relation to Brünnhilde's sleep and awakening.

Music, Wagner's principal escape from the everyday, was from his childhood freighted with these same ghostly associations. "The mysterious joy I felt in hearing an orchestra play quite close to me still remains one of my most pleasant memories. The mere tuning up of the instruments put me in a state of mystic excitement; even the striking of fifths on the violin seemed to me like a greeting from the spirit world." These fifths had, moreover, a quite specific association for Wagner. He had first heard a violin as he was passing a small palace in Dresden, and the sound seemed to his impressionable mind to emanate from the sculptured musicians adorning the walls. Even much later in life he could not pass this palace, he confesses, without a shudder.

As a young man he used to listen to the Zillman Orchestra almost every afternoon. "One may imagine," he writes, "the rapturous thrill with which I drew in all the chaotic variety of sound that I heard as the orchestra tuned up: the long drawn A of the oboe, which seemed like a call from the dead to rouse the other instruments, never failed to raise all my nerves to a feverish pitch of tension, and when the swelling C in the overture to *Freischütz* told me that I had stepped, as it were with both feet, right into the magic realm of awe. Anyone who had been watching me at that moment could hardly have failed to see the state I was in, and this in spite of the fact that I was such a bad performer on the piano."[51] On the whole, Meyerbeer's *Robert le Diable* disappointed him: "The only thing that impressed me," he writes, "was the unearthly keyed trumpet which, in the last act, represented the voice of the mother's ghost." No wonder Wagner, for whom "music was a

---

[51] *Ibid.*, p. 35.

spirit, a noble and mystic monster,"[52] eroticized his own music as no composer ever had.   Sensuousness came to assume the equivalence of maternal affection.

Sisters also served a maternal function. His closest childhood playmate was his younger sister Cäcilie. His much older sister Rosalie he regarded consciously as a surrogate mother. Her age, "her charming gravity and her refined way of speaking place[d] her above the younger children." Richard was as solicitous of her affection and esteem as of his actual mother's. "Of course," he writes penitently, "I had been the one member of the family who had caused the greatest anxieties both to my mother and to my motherly sister, and during my life as a student the strained relations between us had made a terrible impression on me. When therefore they [mother and motherly sister] tried to believe in me again, and once more showed some interest in my work, I was full of gratitude and happiness. The thought of getting this sister to look kindly upon my aspirations, and even to expect great things of me, had become a special stimulus to my ambition. Under these circumstances a tender and almost sentimental relationship grew up between Rosalie and myself, which in its purity and sincerity could vie with the noblest form of friendship between man and woman."[53]

When Wagner's mother and sisters moved from Dresden to Prague, leaving the thirteen year old boy with the Böhme family, he acquired in effect a new set of sisters. Wagner's earliest memories of "boyish love" are flirtations with the Böhme girls and their friends. "On other occasions I recollect

[52] *Ibid.*, p. 37.
[53] *Ibid.*, p. 84.

pretending to be too helplessly sleepy to move, so that I might be carried up to bed by the girls, that being, as they thought, the only remedy for my condition. And I repeated this, because I found, to my surprise, that their attention under these circumstances brought me into closer and more gratifying proximity with them."[54] Wagner's strategy for gaining attention is regression to passive dependence. His surprise at the strategy's success hints at an underlying sense of worthlessness. By putting himself into the position of helpless infant, he maneuvers his adoptive sisters into supplying affection he regarded as unmerited.

Passive dependence became Wagner's alternate strategy for coping with the exigencies of the everyday life he also escaped through art. He was a notorious accumulator of debts. Constantly pleading for money, staving off creditors, he perversely courted ruin by living extravagantly beyond his means. His greatest wish, practically speaking, was to be patronized by some nobleman or wealthy widow — that is, adopted by surrogate parental figures. One may concur with Ernest Newman in retrospect that the world did owe Wagner a living in return for the treasure he gave it with his art and yet nonetheless perceive the strategy of dependence as bespeaking regressive emotional neediness.

Inferiority and helplessness are the keynotes to Wagner's relationship with his first wife, the actress Minna Planer, with whom he had worked as conductor of the Magdeburg theater orchestra. Three or four years his senior, she appeared utterly in control of herself and her future. "The strange power she

---

[54] *Ibid.*, p. 18.

exercised over me from the very first," Wagner writes, "was in no wise due to the fact that I regarded her in any way as the embodiment of my ideal; on the contrary, she attracted me by the soberness and seriousness of her character, which supplemented what I felt to be wanting in my own, and afforded me the support that in my wanderings after the ideal I knew to be necessary for me."[55] In the future, Minna was to provide a secure base of operations for Wagner's perpetually adolescent waywardness. She would play the role of patient mother, waiting anxiously for her prodigal son's return home.

Minna conformed to the Oedipal paradigm of the desirable woman also in that initially, she seemed unavailable. Not only older than Wagner, she was virtually betrothed to one young (though impecunious) nobleman, and was courted by others, who must have seemed far more eligible than the struggling, young conductor. But in the event, Wagner's strategy proved successful. "All his life long," writes Ernest Newman concerning this episode, "women who pitied him felt an impulse to mother the highly-strung, self-torturing little man who was visibly incapable of running his own life with ordinary prudence; and more than once this impulse was the insidious opening chord in the overture to a drama of love. His tactics were half instinctive, half calculated, and they varied slightly according to circumstances; but they were generally successful. Minna's was the first case in which we see them operating with signal success."[56]

The seduction was accomplished on the lines of the ruse he had used with the Böhme girls. He finagled himself into

---

[55] *Ibid.*, p. 160.
[56] Newman, vol. I, p. 189.

Minna's bed by falling "helplessly" asleep in her apartment. Invited to tea with Minna and another woman of the theater company, whom he detested, he had become inebriated killing time over a game of whist to delay his arrival. Finding the obnoxious interloper still ensconced at Minna's apartment, he hastened her departure by his coarse behavior. Minna felt she had no choice but to allow the inebriated *Kapellmeister* to collapse in her bed, in which, come sunup, she had yielded to his "importunities."

But Wagner was not alone in his romantic conquest of Minna; he was given to fits of jealousy over the past and present attentions of other men, and came to feel he never fully possessed his wife. He recounts one such explosion over his discovery of Minna's relationship with a Jewish tradesman named Schwabe. "There was a violent scene between us, which was typical of all our subsequent altercations. I had obviously gone too far in treating a woman who was not passionately in love with me, as if I had a real right over her; for, after all, she had merely yielded to my importunity, and in no way belonged to me."[57] In retrospect, Wagner says Minna never "felt any sort of passion or genuine love for me." Indeed, he did not believe "that she was capable of such a thing, and [he] can therefore only describe her feeling for [him] as one of heartfelt goodwill, and the sincerest desire for [his] success and prosperity inspired as she was with the kindest sympathy, and genuine delight at, and admiration for [his] talents."[58]

---

[57] *My Life*, p. 161.
[58] *Ibid.*, p. 115.

Minna's relation to Richard, then, mirrored his mother's coolness. And since mother knows best, he was forced into pacifying Minna by owning himself wrong in the argument over Schwabe, a capitulation all the more infantilizing in that it climaxed what had apparently been a violent tantrum—a boy's impotent rage over the impossibility of ever truly possessing his mother. "Such was the end of this and all subsequent scenes, outwardly, at least, always to her advantage. But Peace was undermined forever."[59]

Also like his mother, Minna's appreciation for Richard's art was limited by mundane concerns. If she was "inspired" with "sympathy, and genuine delight at, and admiration for" Wagner's talents, she—like Wagner's mother, who had done her best to discourage a career in the musical theater, and had "often even threatened [him] with her curse should [he] ever express a desire to go on the stage"[60]—had a more sincere desire for his material "success and prosperity."

Neither Minna nor his mother sympathized with Wagner's "incomprehensible conception of [his] art and its proportions," so that his authentic vocation was fraught with prohibition and defiance. In the middle of the marriage ceremony, Wagner realized the profound division between his bourgeois life as husband and provider and his career as artist. "I saw, as clearly as in a vision, my whole being divided into two cross-currents that dragged me in different directions: the upper one faced the sun and carried me onward like a dreamer, whilst the lower one held my nature

[59] *Ibid.*, p. 161.
[60] *Ibid.*, p. 12.

captive, a prey to some inexplicable fear."[61] He required the strictures of marriage, the dullness of domesticity, to experience the exhilaration of escape, however. That is why none of his escapes — his plan to run off to Greece with Jessie Laussot, his dream of continuing indefinitely an idealized liaison with Mathilde Wesendonck — could ever be fully realized. He dared not consummate them, prey as he was to that "inexplicable fear." The bad boy, the enfant terrible, the "Cossack," as Geyer had nicknamed him, was after all more firmly tied to the strings of his mother's apron than his more outwardly obedient siblings.

This paradox is illuminated by one of the conspicuously few reminiscences in *Mein Leben* in which Wagner writes about his mother directly. As a student in Leipzig Wagner had developed a passion, among other dissipations, for gambling. "In vain," he writes, "did my poor mother try everything in her power to induce me not to come home so late at night, although she had no idea of the real nature of my debauches." But Wagner, neglecting his studies, avoiding his companions, sank deeper into the habit, which he characterizes as a mania:

> I now lost myself in the smaller gambling dens of
> Leipzig, where only the very scum of the students
> congregated. Insensible to any feeling of self-
> respect, I bore even the contempt of my sister
> Rosalie; both she and my mother hardly ever
> deigning to cast a glance at the young libertine whom
> they only saw at rare intervals, looking deadly
> pale and worn out: my ever-growing despair

---

[61] *Ibid.*, p. 165.

made me at last resort to foolhardiness as the
only means of forcing hostile fate to my side. It
suddenly struck me that only by dint of big stakes
could I make big profits. To this end I decided
to make use of my mother's pension, of which I was
trustee of a fairly large sum. That night I lost
everything I had with me except one thaler: the
excitement with which I staked that last coin on
a card was an experience hitherto quite strange
to my young life."[62]

The intoxicated young gambler won on that play, and went on
winning until he had regained his mother's pension, and
enough extra to pay off his sizable debts. His grandiose
excitement was heightened by the conviction that he would
never gamble again. "My sensations during the whole of this
process were of the most sacred nature: I felt as if God and
His angels were standing by my side and were whispering
words of warning and of consolation into my ears." Once
more he stole home at dawn, climbed over the gate and up to
bed, only "this time to sleep peacefully and soundly and to
awake very late, strengthened and as though born again."

As early as 1897 Freud hypothesized that the seemingly
inexplicable compulsion to gamble, like other "bad habits,"
was traceable to guilt over masturbation. "It has dawned on
me that masturbation is the one major habit, the 'primal
addiction' and that it is only as a substitute and replacement
for it that the other addictions — for alcohol, morphine,

---

[62] *Ibid.*, p. 61.

tobacco, etc. — come into existence."[63] In a 1928 paper, Freud interpreted Dostoevsky's gambling mania. In particular, the aspect of play in gambling suggests masturbation, commonly euphemized as "playing with oneself." In Wagner's case the pun on playing extends to his twin careers in the theater, where roles are *played* in *plays*, and in the concert-hall, where music is *played* on instruments manipulated with the hands. In dreams, writes Freud elsewhere, "Gratification derived from a person's own genitals is indicated by any kind of play, including playing the piano."[64]

Like Wagner, Dostoevsky was a habitual debtor. "As often happens with neurotics," Freud remarks, "Dostoevsky's burden of guilt had taken a tangible shape as a burden of debt." He gambled under the pretext of repaying his creditors. "But this was no more than a pretext . . . " Freud continues. "All the details of his impulsively irrational conduct show this and something more besides. He never rested until he had lost everything. For him gambling was another method of self-punishment." Thus, the gambling ritual included passionate self-castigation and perennial promises to his young wife never to gamble again. But breaking the promises was also part of the ritual. "When his losses had reduced himself and her to the direst need, he derived a second pathological satisfaction from that. He could then scold and humiliate himself before her, invite her to despise him and to feel sorry that she had married such an old

---

[63] Sigmund Freud, letter to Fliess, Dec. 22, 1897.
[64] Sigmund Freud, *Lecture X, Introductory Lectures on Psycho-Analysis, Standard Edition*, vol. XV, p. 156.

sinner; and when he had thus unburdened his conscience, the whole business would begin again next day."[65]

Self-denunciation is likewise crucial to Wagner's gambling tale. He "lost" himself in places where "only the very scum" congregated. He had abandoned his self-respect, and deserved the scorn of mother and motherly sister. The next morning, however, as though his grand adventure would win mother's approval, he was eager to confess. "No sense of shame deterred me from telling my mother, to whom I presented her money, the whole truth about this decisive night. I voluntarily confessed my sin in having utilised her pension, sparing no detail."

Wagner feels compelled to gamble by a "hostile fate," which Freud in the Dostoevsky paper interprets as a projection of the introjected father, the superego bent on punishing Oedipal wishes. Similarly Sophocles has disguised the meaning of Oedipus' crime "by projecting the hero's unconscious motive into reality in the form of a compulsion by a destiny which is alien to him." So a hostile fate, that same alien though introjected father visible in the figure of Alberich, exacts Wagner's degradation to atone for Oedipal wishes. But he is suddenly inspired by the intuition that "foolhardiness," wagering his mother's pension (in effect, his deceased father's money), can coerce "hostile fate" over to his side.

English usage of "spend" to mean both the paying of money and the ejaculation of semen[66] parallels the symbolic

---

[65] Sigmund Freud, "Dostoevsky and Parricide," *Standard Edition*, vol. XXI, pp. 190-191.

association of the gambling mania with the habit of masturbation, whose guilt derives from Oedipal fantasies accompanying the act in puberty. What follows masturbation, in Freud's view, is the conscious or unconscious fear of castration by an avenging father. If the exhilaration of gambling replaces the pleasure of masturbation, the abasement of gambling substitutes for guilt and castration. But Wagner arrives at a provisional resolution of the Oedipal conflict giving rise to gambling mania: he identifies with father, appropriating his penis as it were, spending his semen, with the double effect of first destroying father's power over mother (squandering the money), and then displacing him as provider (winning it back). Symbolically, gambling represents the fulfillment of desire for mother; thus, the excitement: "an experience hitherto quite strange to my young life."

Yet, the episode really does achieve a resolution of sorts, for he is cured of this particular mania. "I felt as if God and His angels were standing by my side and were whispering words of warning and of consolation into my ears . . . And, truth to tell, gambling had lost all fascination for me from that moment." He has disrupted this vicious cycle by modifying his relation to the introjected father from passive receiver of punishment to "identification with the aggressor," in order to share the spoils.

---

[66] See, for instance, *A New Pronouncing Dictionary of Medicine*, John M. Keating, M.D., LL.D., Henry Hamilton, 2nd ed., (Philadelphia, 1893), p. 646.

Hypochondria was described as symptomatic of the mostly unconscious sense that unacceptable traits of some introjected person, traits alien to the self's ego are within the body, causing disease. Geyer, the "ambivalently regarded person"[67] in Wagner's case, indeed, the only father Wagner had any opportunity to introject (his legal father died when he was half a year old), was "alien" in the same sense that all fathers are intruders into the infant's monopoly relationship with mother.

He was "alien" also in being legally regarded as a step- rather than a true father. Finally, evidence suggests Wagner harbored the suspicion Geyer was Jewish. Thus Jewish blood (he perhaps feared) flowed in his own veins. Geyer, German for vulture, is (like Adler, "eagle") a common German-Jewish name. Although modern research has failed to discover any actually Jewish branch on the Geyer family tree, Wagner seems to have been plagued by doubts. Throughout his life it circulated as an open secret among his enemies that this virulent anti-Semite was himself at least partially Jewish.[68]

Robert Gutman hypothesizes that Wagner must have been taunted from early childhood by accusations of being Jewish. "Not only had the Norns of destiny in a malevolent hour given the boy a Jewish name; they had also placed his birth on the Brühl, the centre of the Leipzig Jewish quarter, and had, to

---

[67] See footnote 43, p. 47, above.
[68] Bryan Magee, *The Tristan Chord*, (New York, 2000), p. 358, writes: "Geyer was not Jewish . . . He came from a long line of church musicians; for generations his forbears had been Lutheran cantors and organists." Magee's seemingly cogent dismissal, however, leaves out of account what may be conjectured about Wagner's irrational and unconscious fears.

crown their mischief, given his features a hawk-like cast with prominent nose, pointed jaw, and high, intellectual brow; his oversized head was perched upon a stunted but energetic body at an angle suggesting . . . a close escape from deformity; in short, the boy had physical characteristics which ignorance and prejudice associate exclusively with the Jews." A lifelong, obsessive anti-Semitism, that formed, as Gutman puts it, "one of the cornerstones of Wagnerian thought in art and politics," disguised the secret fear that he himself was a Jew.[69]

Wagner's most notorious anti-Semitic outpouring was the essay "Judaism in Music," published in 1850, but sketched in Dresden, before 1849. The formulation of these ideas coincides with the composition of *The Ring* poem. His thesis is simple. The sources of true art lie always in the artist's connection with the instinctive life of "the folk." The Jew, an alien in whatever land he happens to inhabit, is segregated from the mainstream of life of "the folk" by the "natural repulsion" he inspires in the non-Jewish native. His own traditions, moreover, are irretrievably corrupt. Therefore Jews are incapable of creating true art, Mendelssohn, Meyerbeer, and Heine (in Wagner's assessment) by no means to the contrary. Jews are capable only of pandering to the Philistine tastes of the public by fashioning a simulacrum of art, and transforming the creative process into a sordid business transaction.

While at the outset, Wagner pretends to cast a cool, objective eye on things just as they are, he lapses almost immediately into venomous racism that betrays deep emotional

---

[69] Robert Gutman, *Richard Wagner*, p. 29.

entanglement with his subject. "I consider it important to bring some clarity to the subject," he writes dispassionately in his opening paragraph, ". . . a subject which critics either shy away from or become overexcited about. I shall not attempt to say anything new but shall explain people's instinctive dislike of Jewishness. What I refer to is simply what exists: I have no interest in imaginative theorizing. Criticism destroys itself if, whether on the attack or the defensive, it attempts to do more."[70]

Wagner's supposedly rational enquiry begins with the irrational nature of prejudice. "We shall attempt to understand the involuntary repulsion aroused in us by the personality and customs of the Jews." This pose of objectivity is a pretense, however, for at no point does he examine the Gentile mind that experiences this "instinctive dislike," this "natural revulsion aroused by Jewishness." Instead, "in order to justify this instinctive feeling which is obviously stronger and more overpowering than our desire to be free of it," (25) he deals exclusively with the objective situation of the Jews that makes genuine artistic creation — in his view — impossible.

There are two distinct aspects to the essay: first is Wagner's need to express his own instinctive hatred for Jewishness, which seems, as the essay progresses, ever more like a compulsion to spit, or vomit; second is his need to rationalize that irrational revulsion through a purportedly dispassionate

---

[70] Richard Wagner, "Judaism in Music," reprinted in *Stories and Essays*, ed., Charles Osborne (New York, 1973), p. 24. Page references in parentheses following quotations in my text refer to this edition.
For an exhaustive analysis of the term and category "Judaism" in European thought and culture, see David Nirenberg's brilliant *Anti-Judaism: The Western Tradition*, (W.W.Norton, 2013).

analysis of the consequences of genetics and the diaspora. Wagner concedes that the sources of his prejudice are deep-seated and unconscious, yet he can only displace the burden of this affect onto its object.

Wagner's image of the alien Jew appears readily as a projection of his internalized father. Accordingly, he attributes to Jews the omnipotence an infant typically attributes to its parents. Decrying the recent emancipation of the Jews, he argues it is on the contrary non-Jews "who require emancipation from the Jews. As the world is constituted today, the Jew is more than emancipated, he is the ruler. And he will continue to rule as long as money remains the power to which all our activities are subjugated." Particularly the realm of art concerns Wagner: "the artistic taste of our time. [has been given] into the custody of busy Jewish hands . . . What the great artists have toiled to bring into being for two thousand years, the Jew today turns into art business." (25)

Wagner's attack on Jewish art parallels his father's many-faceted life in art. Forced by the economic consequences of his own father's untimely death to abandon studies in law and painting, Ludwig Geyer had pursued a motley career as hack portrait painter, actor, singer, and playwright, an artistic jack-of-all-trades. Ernest Newman surmises that, because he abandoned study of serious painting prematurely, Geyer remained all his life "something of a brilliant amateur."[71] He disliked the theater, whose inner workings and politics he knew all too well to have romantic illusions, and he tried to

---

[71] Newman, vol. I, p. 16.

keep Richard Wagner out of it. Geyer was the model (somewhat less than successful) of the *Gesamtkünstler* Richard was to become. But where Geyer had remained a "brilliant amateur," Wagner became the totally committed, passionate professional. Where Geyer was deflected from his own inner purpose by economic necessity, Wagner uncompromisingly rejected financial security to keep his passion and art pure. Geyer was the model who taught by the cautionary tale of his own failure.

The Jew has "taken over" modern art, and the "Aryan" must be emancipated from his dominance. Likewise, Wagner's father, *Gesamtkünstler* Geyer, is a master of art, though mercenary only, and the unconscious Oedipal project becomes to dethrone and replace him. "Art," that crystal spring, that billowing ocean into which Wagner habitually dived "up to the ears," is not only healing for the hypochondriac, but is imbued with the essence of the maternal.

"But if emancipation from Judaism seems to us a prime necessity, we must test our strength for this war of liberation. We shall not gain this strength merely by an abstract definition of the situation, but by an intimate knowledge of the nature of our deep-seated, involuntary feeling of repugnance for Jewish nature. By this unconquerable feeling, what we hate in the Jewish character must be revealed to us, and when we know it we can take measures against it. By revealing him clearly, we may hope to wipe the demon from the field, where he has been able to thrive only under the protective cover of darkness, a darkness that we good-natured Humanists ourselves have offered him to make his appearance less disgusting." The protective darkness concealing the Jew also pervades the underwater of *Rheingold* — the maternal womb, where the ego was surprised and dismayed to find Alberich lurking.

Like Alberich, the Jew "strikes us first by his outward appearance which, whatever European nationality we belong to, has something unpleasantly foreign to that nationality." (26) The Jew is an "unpleasant freak of nature," whose "exterior could never be acceptable as a subject for a painting." Wagner's own somewhat dwarf-like appearance caused Nietzsche's sister to write, "at first, I was somewhat confused at finding Wagner such a pigmy compared to Frau Cosima,"[72] and Gutman to characterize his head as hawk-like and oversized. Precisely his own features arouse instinctive repulsion in Wagner, but he projects them onto "the other" so that, "We instinctively feel we have nothing in common with a man who looks like that."(26) Projection transforms the glass of nature into a magic-lantern.[73] The assertion that "we have nothing in common with a man who looks like that" is echoed in Siegfried's emphatic denial, when he sees his own image reflected in the stream, that Mime could ever be his father. Yet that denial is curiously offset by the admitted identity of Wotan and Alberich: Light-Alberich/Black-Wotan. As in the gambling episode, the superego wrings a confession from Wagner, though disguised behind the mask of a symbol.[74]

---

[72] *The Nietzsche-Wagner Correspondence*, ed., Elizabeth Foerster-Nietzsche (New York, 1921), p. 59.

[73] See also footnote 78, p. 73, below.

[74] Cf. Theodor Adorno, *In Search of Wagner*, pp. 24, 25. Adorno sees in the grotesque characterization of Mime and the other Nibelung dwarves a projected self-image: "However, this idiosyncratic hatred is of the type that [Walter] Benjamin had in mind when he defined disgust as the fear of

If Alberich and Mime are thinly disguised Jews in *The Ring* fantasy, so is the whole race of Nibelungs, wretched dwarfs who dwell in the bowels of the earth, hoarding and working their gold. Gutman claims that Wagner has made the Nibelungs speak a kind of Jewish-German (not quite Yiddish), as well as gesticulate in a manner he conceived of as typically Semitic.[75] Certainly the characteristics of Jewish speech described by Wagner in "Judaism in Music" are reminiscent of the Nibelungs' chatter. "We are repelled in particular by the purely aural aspect of Jewish speech," he writes. "The shrill, sibilant buzzing of his voice falls strangely and unpleasantly on our ears. His misuse of words whose exact shade of meaning escapes him, and his mistakenly placed phrases combine to turn his utterance into an unbearably muddled nonsense. Consequently, when we listen to Jewish speech we are involuntarily struck by its offensive manner and so diverted from understanding its matter." One thinks of

---

being thought to be the same as that which is found disgusting. Newman places particular emphasis on the description of Mime in the original version . . . Wagner's fear of caricature which, after all, in theatrical terms, would not have provided an inappropriate contrast with the serious underworld deity, Alberich, suggests . . . that Wagner recoiled with shock from the similarity between Mime and himself. His own physical appearance, disproportionately small, with over-large head and protruding chin, bordered on the abnormal and only fame preserved him from ridicule . . . He pursues his victims down to the level of their biological nature because he saw himself as having only barely escaped being a dwarf. However, the fact that all the rumours concerning Wagner's own Jewish ancestry can be traced back, according to Newman's investigations, to . . . Nietzsche, who had opposed Wagner's anti-Semitism, is a phenomenon that has its own logic. Nietzsche knew the secret of Wagner's idiosyncrasies and broke their spell by naming them."
[75] Robert Gutman, *Richard Wagner*, p. 235.

Mime's conversation with Siegfried after the slaying of Fafner, when, because he has tasted the dragon's magical blood, the hero understands the evil import of the dwarf's hypocritical words. "When we listen to a Jew talking we are unconsciously upset by the complete lack of purely human expression in his speech. The cold indifference of its peculiar 'blabber' can never rise to the excitement of real passion. And if we, in conversation with a Jew, should find our own words becoming heated, he will always be evasive, because he is incapable of really deep feeling."(28)

Since opera comprises both speech and song — Wagner argues — if Jewish speech is offensive, the spectacle of a Jew singing is doubly so. Song, Wagner says, is speech heightened by passion, of which music is the language. "If the Jew's already ridiculously vehement manner of speech is to be heightened, we shall be further alienated from him. If we were repelled by his appearance and his speech, his song will engage our attention only to the extent that we exclaim at so absurd a phenomenon. It is understandably in song, as the most indisputably vivid expression of personal feeling, that the offensive peculiarity of the Jewish nature reaches its peak." (29)

Rheingold's curtain opens to reveal shimmering, undulating mermaids, swimming as though weightless, warbling blithe nonsense, absorbed in the childish delight of play. The contrast presented by Alberich's entrance on this scene shifts from the pathetic to the ludicrous at the moment he opens his mouth to woo the Rhinemaidens in song. Though his hopeless longing is pitiable, the sympathy of the audience is solidly with the taunting Rhinemaidens, for Alberich's lustful suit is patently inappropriate and clumsy, and his song absurd. Jewish song has for native inspiration only the music of Jewish worship, which (Wagner contends), though once animated by genuine feeling, is now a lifeless shadow. "Who has not had feelings of repulsion, horror and amusement on hearing that nonsensical gurgling, yodeling and cackling which no attempt at caricature can render more absurd than it is?" (32)

The interior of the earth is symbolic of the maternal interior just as the world under the water is. While the intruder Alberich is discovered in the paradise of the Rhine, Nibelungs swarm in the bowels of the earth. A Jew has gotten there first, and bred a nestful of Jews who are—the logic of the symbolism says—siblings in competition for mother's body. This accords with Freud's clinical observation that brothers and sisters are often symbolized in dreams as *little animals* or *vermin*.[76]

The specific targets of Wagner's essay are the popular and successful Jewish musicians Mendelssohn and Meyerbeer. Why do Jews dominate 19th Century music? Because after Beethoven, music died. "The Jews could never have taken over this art until they had proved, as they have, the insufficiency of its inner life. As long as the separate art of music possessed a really organic need for life, up until the time of Mozart and Beethoven, there were no Jewish composers to be found: it was impossible for an element completely foreign to this living organism to take any part in its growth. Only when a body's inner death is evident can

---

[76] See Sigmund Freud, "Lecture X," *Introductory Lectures*, p. 153; *Interpretation of Dreams, Standard Edition*, vol. V, p. 357.

outside elements gain entry, and then only to destroy it. Then the flesh of that body is transformed into a swarming colony of worms. But who, looking at it, could imagine such a body to be alive? The spirit, that is, the life fled from this body back to its essence, and this is just life itself. Only in true life can we too rediscover the soul of art: not in its worm-devoured corpse." (38,39. Last two sentences, my trans.)

Wagner employs the identical image to describe the Nibelungs in his 1848 essay "The Nibelung Myth as sketch for a Drama." "From the womb of night and death was spawned a race that dwells in Nibelheim (Nebelheim), that is, in gloomy subterranean clefts and caverns: Nibelungen are they called; with restless nimbleness they burrow through the bowels of the earth, like worms in a dead body."[77] Jewry is a swarm of maggots in the corpse of music, as the Nibelungs fester inside the symbolic maternal body. Years later, the image still bedevils him; Cosima Wagner's entry in her diary for July 20, 1881 reads, "R. had a somewhat restless night, he dreamed first of all that I did not love him, then that he was surrounded by Jews who turned into worms." Maggots are carrion feeders, like vultures. Recalling that the German word for vulture is *Geyer*, Wagner's father's name—we see this is a displacement requiring but a short leap.[78]

---

[77] Trans. in *Wagner on Music and Drama*, eds., Albert Goldman and Evert Sprinchorn (New York, 1964), p. 281.

[78] Denial at once conceals and reveals the truth. A comparable ambivalence is apparent in Wagner's scrupulousness over the vulture crest he deputized Nietzsche in 1870 to have embossed on the cover of *Mein Leben*. "The crest turned out very well and we have every reason to be grateful to you for the careful attention you gave the matter," he wrote his young disciple on January 16, 1870. "However, I still have the same misgivings in regard to the *vulture*, which unquestionably will be taken for

As a kind of postscript to "Judaism in Music" Wagner takes up the case of two Jewish writers, Heine and Börne. To Heine he concedes considerable talent, not, indeed, as a true poet, but a prophet (able to emerge only because German poetry, like music, has died), whose mission was to reveal, "in a most fascinating manner, the endless acidity and Jesuitical hypocrisy of our versifying which still thought of itself as poetry." (39) Wagner admires him particularly for scorning the artistic pretensions of even his Jewish contemporaries. Geyer's compromised career served Wagner as a negative model, and he regarded Heine similarly.

We can see the association between Wagner's feeling for his father and for Jews. "Nothing deceived him," he writes of Heine. "By the remorseless demon of denial of all that seemed fit to be denied, he was driven on without respite, through all the illusion of our modern self-deception, to the point where he deluded himself into poetry." Denial—which is to say, negation—is glorified and personified in demonic form, and culminates in self-annihilation. Thus, the denial Wagner sees

an eagle at the first glance . . . It is of the greatest importance, on account of the association, that the 'vulture' be instantly recognizable, and for this reason we beg that you secure the best available picture of such a beast and instruct the engraver to hang the characteristic ruff of the vulture around the neck of our bird." The vulture crest serves as an explicit symbolic statement of the Geyer paternity. Jewishness may, for Wagner, also have been embedded in the emblem. As a vulture is distinguished from an eagle by "the characteristic ruff . . . around the neck," Gentile is distinguished from Jew by the foreskin around the head of the penis. Whether this symbolism constitutes denial (the vulture is not a Jew, for it has its ruff intact around its neck), or distortion by inversion (the badge of the Jew becomes that which the Jew does not have), Wagner's focus on this iconographic detail points to the same underlying meaning.

as the essential element in Heine is akin to the nihilism that had so drawn him to Bakunin and Schopenhauer. Wagner finally ascribes to Heine in particular and to Jewry in general the function of a kind of perverse public superego. "He was the conscience of Judaism, just as Judaism is the bad conscience of our modern civilization."(39) The Jew, inextricably woven into our culture, is an implacable mirror, showing us our worst, our "Judaic" aspect, that perhaps we might reform and find redemption.

In the unconscious, contradiction rules alongside logic. Thus, the curious love-hate that Gutman observes in Wagner's relation with Jews: "He often delighted in them in particular but always loathed them in general. His friendships with Jews extended from his childhood sweetheart, Leah David, and his school chum, Lippert né Levy, to those close and emotional but ambiguous relationships of his final years with Joseph Rubinstein, Hermann Levi, and Angelo Neumann."[79]

The (putative) Jew Geyer is envied for having achieved the wished-for return to the womb. But identification with and emulation of the Jew to share that blissful state is encumbered with punishment: Jewishness. To be Jewish is to be a dwarf, a helpless infant. By way of object lesson, the superego assumes the guise of dwarf (in place of imposing, punitive father-figure), revealing in its own deformity the reality of the castration threat. Even Wotan, the idealized father, is almost entirely under the thumb of his manipulative and shrewish spouse, Fricka, and is treated with contempt by his heroic son Siegfried.

---

[79] Robert Gutman, *Richard Wagner*, p. 29.

Freud hypothesized that aversion to the Jews is grounded in the fear of circumcision, consciously or unconsciously imagined as castration, a fear that may have figured in Wagner's phobia. The Jew, serving the project of the superego, chastens by bearing abhorrent witness in its own circumcision to the threat of castration. That the Jew simultaneously has sexual possession of the mother is a paradox, the sort of contradiction that flourishes in the unconscious. For the very circumcision feared as a type of castration is popularly imagined to bestow a magical sensitivity, an extraordinary sensuality on the Jew. Terror and desire are thus merged in the Judaic rite.

A parallel thematic thread appears in *Parsifal*, where the diabolical magician Klingsor, unable to control his lust, has resorted to self-castration in vain hopes of acceptance into the Brotherhood of the Grail. "On himself he laid his sinful hands," the libretto has it, a circumlocution denoting castration, but suggestive sub rosa of circumcision and masturbation — that "primal addiction" whose most calamitous punishment is imagined to be castration. Jewishness is disguised here as exclusion from the Grail Brotherhood. It is also encoded in Klingsor's castration, as it were an extreme, catastrophic form of circumcision.

Wagner might be describing Klingsor's situation when he generalizes about the "cultured Jew who has gone to great trouble to rid himself of the obvious distinguishing features of his fellow-believers: in many cases he has even had himself baptised as a Christian. But this seal has not brought the cultured Jew the rewards he has hoped for. It has served merely to isolate him and to render him the most heartless of all men, thus losing him the sympathy we once felt for the tragic history of his race . . . The cultured Jew stands alien and alienated in the midst of a society he does not understand, with whose tastes and aspirations he is not in sympathy, and to whose history and evolution he is indifferent." (30)

Wagner unconsciously displaces the cutting away of circumcision and castration onto the Jew's cultural isolation. "Completely cut off from this community by the nature of his situation, equally completely torn [*gänzlich herausgerissen*] from all connection with his own race, the more distinguished Jew can only consider his acquired culture as a luxury which he does not know how to put to practical use."(30) Thus, Klingsor acquires power, but only to pervert the purposes of the Grail, not to save himself. If the cultured Jew enjoys any contact with society it is only with "that outgrowth which is cut off [*gänzlich losgelösten Auswuchse*] from the main, healthy stem [*Stamm*]."(31) This transparent phallic analogy suggests that only the "foreskin" of Gentile society consorts with Jews.

Wagner's final paragraph is devoted to the Jewish writer Börne, who, "From his Jewish isolation . . . came to us seeking redemption," by renouncing his Judaism—in other words through cultural self-annihilation. Börne, Wagner writes, "teaches us that this redemption cannot be achieved easily or in comfortable complacency, but only by sweat, want, anguish and the depths of sorrow and suffering." Jewishness, Wagnerian psychic code for Oedipal longings and punishment, is a curse from which the only redemption is oblivion. "Join dispassionately in this redemptive work of rebirth through self-annihilation, then will we be united and undifferentiated [*ununterschieden*]," urges Wagner. (*My trans.,*

1869 version. In the 1850 text the last word is "untrennbar," "inseparable.")

"But remember," Wagner concludes his essay, "that your redemption from the curse laid on you can be achieved by only one thing, and that is the redemption of Ahasuerus — going under [*Untergang*]!" Ahasuerus, the Wandering Jew, whose curse is life, is redeemed at the Second Coming, when he finds the oblivion of death. This despised and accursed Wandering Jew appears disguised as the hero of Wagner's *Flying Dutchman*, with whom he strongly identified, again revealing the double nature of the Master's self-image: self-annihilation is at once imbued with shame and heroism.

Rheingold opens with a tableau emblematic of infantile impotence. The disposition of the characters on the stage bespeaks this theme.[80] The Rhinemaidens hover, while Alberich is stuck down below. "You up there," shouts Alberich. "What do you want down there?" the water-sprites reply. This distinction of place becomes the basis of the Rhinemaidens' taunt. The miserable dwarf begs them to descend to his level; they tempt him to rise to theirs. The Rhinemaidens tease by swimming down towards him, but always slip up out of his reach. Their power over Alberich is

---

[80] This opening scene is adumbrated in an image from "Judaism in Music" of the "cultured Jew," to whom the "lovelessness [of his relation to gentile society] must be ever more obvious when, seeking nourishment for his artistic creation he descends to the ground [*Boden*] of this society: not only is everything here stranger and more incomprehensible, but the instinctive revulsion of the folk towards him confronts him in its most devastating nakedness . . ." [*my trans.*]

On the use of relative height of position as a symbolic element on the operatic stage, see Patrick J. Smith, *The Tenth Muse: A Historical Study of the Opera Libretto* (New York, 1975), pp. 22, 23.

their superior position. The figure of the dwarf, gazing helplessly up at the Rhinemaidens, represents the child's relation to adults. The world and its furnishings dwarf the child, to whom adults seem giants. The Rhinemaidens have been set by Father to guard the gold, to keep watch over "the slumberer's bed." When Flosshilde sees Alberich approach, she thinks she recognizes his intentions, for "Father warned us against such a foe."

But Alberich is not after the gold. Indeed, he has no idea of its existence. The dwarvish libido is focused on the Rhinemaidens themselves, who, though superior, are not parents, but as the text indicates, sisters. This displacement of the Oedipal wish onto sisters represents a provisional resolution of the Oedipus Complex, especially since Wagner's sisters were indeed more affectionate than his emotionally distant mother. "How lucky that you three are not one!" Alberich declares. "Among many surely I'll appeal to one: where there is only one, none would choose me!" *The one* is the unique mother; *the many*, the sisters with whom Wagner had more luck. Uniqueness is a recurrent theme in *The Ring*, always with the same Oedipal implications.

The infant gazes up at his sisters. He longs to join them in play, but he is too small. "Just dive down deeper if you would reach me," begs Alberich. "Am I near enough now?" Wellgunde teases—the sister, as though bending over baby brother on the floor. "Not quite enough," the frustrated dwarf cries.

The diminutive infant merits the erotic attention of neither mother nor sisters. But Alberich is not only small. "Are you moon-struck, and longing for love? Let's see, my beauty, what you're like to look at," Wellgunde replies. Seeing, she exclaims, "Pfue, you hunchbacked, horrible gawk! Swarthy, scurvy, sulfurous dwarf!" Sulfurous alludes to the odor of feces, a euphemism encountered later in *Rheingold*, when Wotan and Loge descend into Nibelheim. Alberich's grotesqueness, like his stature, has distinct unconscious meaning. Beneath the exterior of the infant writhes a bundle of instincts (Freud's *id*) which the world views as obscene. The infant experiences instinctual life as authentic, but learns to disguise that self behind a mask of innocence. Alberich's character and situation are analogous to Freud's controversial hypothesis about childhood sexuality.

Freud gave the name "cloacal theory" to the often encountered idea that babies are born through the anus; "in the unconscious [babies and feces] are often treated as if they were equivalent and could replace one another freely."[81] Thus the child normally identifies its own body with feces, although once defecation becomes stigmatized by shame and disgust, this identification submits to repression.

In short, Alberich embodies the image of the self as unlovable. His rejection by the Rhinemaidens is inevitable. The Rhinemaidens are only sisters, but their rejection recapitulates mother's rejection of the infant's suit, an experience Fairbairn characterizes in uncompromising terms as, "singularly devastating. In the older child this experience is one of intense humiliation over the depreciation of his love . . . At a somewhat deeper level (or at an earlier stage) the experience is

---

[81] Sigmund Freud, "On Transformations of Instinct as Exemplified in Anal Erotism," *Standard Edition*, vol. XVII, p. 128.

one of shame over the display of needs which are disregarded or belittled. In virtue of these experiences of humiliation and shame he feels reduced to a state of worthlessness, destitution or beggardom." In Alberich's particular case, as in Wagner's, the self feels "belittled" to the state of a dwarf. Fairbairn explains further that, "His sense of his own value is threatened, and he feels bad in the sense of 'inferior.' The intensity of these experiences is, of course, proportionate to the intensity of his need; and the intensity of need itself increases his sense of badness by contributing to it the quality of 'demanding too much.' At the same time his sense of badness is further complicated by the sense of utter impotence which he also experiences. At a still deeper level (or at a still earlier stage) the child's experience is one of, so to speak, exploding ineffectively and being completely emptied of libido. It is thus an experience of disintegration and of imminent psychical death."[82]

This sense of exploding, of being drained of life-sustaining substance ties the rejection of Alberich's love to the extortion of his gold in a way that will appear shortly. Alberich is driven by the same impulse that will appear heroic in Siegfried, who demands of Brünnhilde no less than the dwarf asks of the Rhinemaidens. "Madness and love, wild and powerful, stir up my desire," he cries. "Laugh and lie as you will , but lustfully I long for you, and one of you must yield to me." Of course his threat is empty. As he clambers over the rocks, the Rhinemaidens slip easily away; in utter frustration he clenches a fist and gestures. "If this fist could but catch one. . ." His empty fist in lieu of intercourse — expressive of

---

[82] W. R. D. Fairbairn, *Object Relations Theory*, p. 113.

both desire and impotent rage—hints at the dwarf's remaining recourse, masturbation.

For masturbation is another provisional resolution of Oedipal conflict. The new-born infant moves ineluctably from the experience of omnipotence to the realization that its power to manipulate external reality is severely limited. Though the world will not gratify its erotic needs, the infant can withdraw into fantasy and autoerotism to regain the omnipotence of that period when every cry for attention was answered with warmth and feeding. Autoerotism, which begins with thumb-sucking, manifests itself in anal erotism before it settles into genital masturbation. Powerless over the real world, the solitary autoerotic controls at least the world he creates in his fantasies.

Fairbairn describes the process in compelling, albeit technical, terms. "The greatest need of a child is to obtain conclusive assurance (a) that he is genuinely loved as a person by his parents, and (b) that his parents genuinely accept his love . . . In the absence of such assurance his relationship to his objects is fraught with too much anxiety over separation to enable him to renounce the attitude of infantile dependence; for such a renunciation would be equivalent in his eyes to forfeiting all hope of ever obtaining the satisfaction of his unsatisfied emotional needs. Frustration of his desire to be loved as a person and to have his love accepted is the greatest trauma that a child can experience; and it is this trauma above all that creates fixations in the various forms of infantile sexuality to which a child is driven to resort in an attempt to compensate by substitutive satisfactions for the failure of his emotional relationships with his outer objects. Fundamentally these substitutive satisfactions (e.g., masturbation and anal erotism) all represent *relationships with internalized objects, to which the individual is compelled to turn in default of a satisfactory relationship with objects in the outer world.*"[83]

The compensatory essence of autoerotic satisfactions leads logically to the next of *Rheingold*'s themes. Not until his nose has been rubbed in his failure to seduce the Rhinemaidens does Alberich become aware of a substitute enticement, the gold. Water and gold are the primal elements of the drama. Water represents the maternal. Gold is power. Omnipotence is the psychic issue. In the fictional realm of the opera, it becomes world domination. In the words of the text, "inheritance of the world," ("*der Welt Erbe*"). Inheritance is what father passes on to son; receiving his inheritance, the son assumes father's role. This inheritance is the world itself, the earth, mother's body. Such, at least, is the fantasy. "Inheritance of the world he would win for himself whoever could forge from the gold of the Rhine the ring that bestows on him measureless power," Wellgunde tells Alberich.

This magical gold has power to resolve the conflicts of the Oedipus Complex by offering the son his father's role. But this omnipotence is yielded only when the gold is forged into a ring. The standard psychoanalytic interpretation of gold is familiar. In the semantics of dream and fantasy, money and gold are equivalent to feces; as Freud explains of money, "in the course of life this precious material attracts on to itself the psychical interest which was originally proper to faeces, the product of the anal zone." This identification is of course

---

[83] *Ibid.*, pp. 39, 40 (emphasis, Fairbairn's).

accomplished in retrospect, for the infant knows nothing of money or gold. To the infant, feces seem part of its own body, "precious material," not offal, because defecation is accompanied by erotic pleasure.[84]

This identity of feces and self may inform Alberich's horrified response when Wotan finally demands the ring. "The ring?" he gasps, "Take my life, but not the ring! . . . Redeeming my body and my life, I must redeem the ring too; hand and head, eye and ear are no more mine than this red ring!"

Gold, then, is associated with omnipotence for a reason beyond its exchange value. The infant, who has suffered already the blow of its impotence, is confronted with the demand that it control the excretory functions it once exercised indiscriminately, and even derived erotic gratification from. The feces, which it views as contents of its own body, are now made to seem shameful. Obedience and regularity are the demands of toilet training. Love is withheld as punishment for defying the demand for control, and

---

[84] Sigmund Freud, "Anal Erotism and the Castration Complex," *Standard Edition*, vol. XVII, p. 72. For a survey of the psychoanalytic interpretation of this symbolism, see Ernest Borneman, *The Psychoanalysis of Money* (New York: Urizen Books, 1976). Discussing the gambling episode recounted above, money was equated with semen. If this be inconsistency, it is such as inheres in unconscious processes. Symbols are as fluid as the dreams and fantasies that contain them. Cf. Chapter V, n.176, p.218, below. More to the point, however, the unconscious tends to equate all forms of *excreta*, as it equates vital fluids and bodily contents. Thus, it is less inconsistent than at first appears that equivalent symbols (money and gold) should mean semen in one instance and feces in another, particularly in light of the anal-erotic themes apparent in *The Ring*. In *Parsifal*, similarly, blood drips from the tip of the "holy" (*viz.*, patently phallic) spear, implying the equivalence of semen and blood. Cf., Chapter V, pp. 230-31, below.

dispensed as the reward for compliance. Control over the infant's own body determines mother's love, the primary object of the infant's desire, so that self-control comes to seem tantamount to omnipotence. Thus, Wellgunde's characterization of Alberich as "sulfurous" is quite pointed. Like the infant who has not learned to control its excretory functions, the dwarf smells of feces. The Rhinemaiden likens his passion to a sulfurous fire, sizzling in the waves.

Furthermore, the agent of control over feces (the "gold hoard") is the anal sphincter, that circular muscle analogous to the golden ring at the heart of the tetralogy. That elsewhere in the tetralogy the ring symbolizes the vagina (as, for instance, when Brünnhilde gives it as love token to Siegfried) does not contradict its anal character; the association of anus and vagina is well attested in psychoanalytic literature. The childhood fantasy of anal birth is one instance of the confusion. More particularly, the anus in the present context becomes a substitute vagina, for through sphincter control the infant secures the maternal love whose ultimate form is reoccupying the womb. The first scene of *Rheingold* closes as the solitary dwarf retreats with the token of his autonomy into the bowels of the earth.

That chronic bowel problems — flatulence, diarrhea, and occasional constipation — were life-long, not merely infantile, issues for Wagner is attested by Chris Walton, who writes, "Wagner's bowels and his muse seem to have existed in a strangely symbiotic relationship; indeed it seems almost as if his creativity was in some measure dependent upon his 'control over [his] orifices' [Wagner to Ignaz Heim, July 13, 1856] (or lack of it). . . There is little doubt that Wagner was in regular physical pain that had real physical causes, and of a kind that must have brought considerable social embarrassment with it. Indeed, one cannot but marvel at his productivity as writer, composer, conductor and organizer when one considers the chronic conditions from which he suffered. One can even sympathize with the immensity of his ego when one contemplates the degree of willpower and self-confidence that he must have developed in order to feel able to show himself in public, when his face was blotched with red and the air around him pungent with the flatulent odors of his discomfort."[85]

For Alberich, control will mean constipation, hoarding. Ironically, during his visit to Nibelheim Wotan asks Alberich just what Alberich earlier asked the Rhinemaidens: what use is the hoard? The Rhinemaidens, like infants in the anal period, play with it, in pure, immediate pleasure. Alberich, the miser, merely hoards it, defering to some ever-receding future any actual use of it; for him, the gold is useless.

If Alberich has resembled an infant smelling of feces he has no control over, he will counteract the Rhinemaidens' repugnance through mastery. The anus is a substitute vagina. Alberich renounces love but not (the text suggests) erotic pleasure. "Though I cannot wrest love, cunningly perhaps I may wrest pleasure," he reasons. ("*Erzwäng' ich nicht Liebe, doch listig erzwäng' ich mir Lust?*")

Alberich's renunciation is conventionally regarded as exchanging love for power — the dwarf's own formulation of it

[85] Chris Walton, *Richard Wagner's Zurich: The Muse of Place* (Boydell & Brewer, 2007), pp. 98-99.

notwithstanding — because after the opening scene of *Rheingold*, he no longer appears lecherous. Power, however, has been eroticized as the miser replaces erotic pleasure with the hoarding of money. "We are accustomed," writes Freud, "to trace back interest in money, insofar as it is of a libidinal and not of a rational character, to excretory pleasure, and we expect normal people to keep their relations to money entirely free from libidinal influences and regulate them according to the demands of reality."[86] But Alberich is hardly a paragon of normality.

In the second scene, *Rheingold*'s action ascends from lower depths to lofty heights. But since Wotan and Alberich are aspects of a single psychic entity,[87] this scene parallels Alberich's humiliation, and suggests a major theme of *Rheingold*: the male's infantilization at the hands of women. As the scene opens, Wotan and Fricka (whose union resembles Wagner's loveless marriage with Minna) are asleep. It is the joyless, punitive Fricka who wakes first, and attempts to rouse her husband. But Wotan goes on dreaming of his "holy hall of delight," towering gloriously into the clouds. That Wotan, chief among Gods, sleeps through the building of Walhall is a puzzle so conspicuous as to invite interpretation. His passivity mirrors Wagner's strategy for seduction: counterfeit sleep.

---

[86] Sigmund Freud, *op. cit.*, p. 72.

[87] This fundamental structural idea, to be progressively elaborated throughout the present book, is touched on by Bryan Magee, *Wagner and Philosophy* (Allen Lane, The Penguin Press, 2000), p. 85: "It is possible to see the various characters of *The Ring* as multifarious aspects of a single personality, so that the whole gigantic work becomes a presentation of what it is to be a human being, from the first stirrings of our awareness out of primal unconsciousness to its final dissolution and return to its origins."

The peculiar formulations of the text suggest further that the erection of Walhall is unconsciously equivalent to the tumescent penis. The grandiose fantasy of Wotan's rising fortress stands in for the quotidian male experience of waking with an erection. The god equates Walhall with "Manly honor" and "Eternal power," which "Tower to perpetual fame."

Wotan rhapsodizes in his sleep, so Fricka verbally shakes him again. Appropriately, her first command is "Up!" though she urges him to abandon his "dreams of delightful deceit." But awake, Wotan is just as rhapsodic. The intimation of the German is rendered only awkwardly in English. "*Prächtig prahlt der prangende Bau!*" might be translated (word by word), "Magnificently glitters [but *prahlen* carries the meaning of boastfulness or ostentation] the resplendent building." In the next line, Wagner uses the verb *tragen* (to carry) idiomatically to mean "bear, bring forth." "*Wie im Traum ich ihn trug,*" suggests the equivalent pun, "As I bore it in my dream . . . strong and fair it stands to behold, lordly, majestic construction [or, but a short step removed, *erection*]." ("*Stark und schön steht er zur Schau: hehrer, herrlicher Bau!*").

The newly erected fortress frightens Fricka. "You only create delight for yourself with that which frightens me," complains the woman whose fear of the erect penis is transformed into castrating frigidity. Just as Alberich's burning passion was mocked into perversion by the Rhinemaidens, Wotan's "manhood," his newly erected "Walhall," is belittled by Fricka as an indulgence. Wotan is a child with a toy. "O laughing, mischievous frivolousness! Selfish gaiety . . . What is holy and of value to you hard-hearted men, when once you are greedy for power?" And a few lines later: "For the frivolous toy of power and glory would you in outrageous mockery play away love and woman's worth?"

"Fricka harbored the self-same greed, when you yourself begged me for the construction [*Bau*]," Wotan counters. But Fricka's intent in humoring her husband's whims was to tie him to domesticity and fidelity. The frigid woman indulges a husband's sexual demands not for pleasure, but for power. The sexual manipulation that characterized the relation between Wagner and Minna inverts the value of the erect penis. No longer the potent symbol of manhood, it reverts to the toy of childhood. The frigid wife gains power by assuming the double role of indulgent mother, humoring the boy's frivolous demands and, by thus infantilizing him, of punitive mother, agent of the dreaded castration.

The husband, however, is unmanned because he allows himself to be. Wotan, as he defensively reminds his wife, yielded one of his eyes to win her. Blinding in fantasies is often regarded psychoanalytically as symbolic (by the principle of "displacement upwards") of castration—the eyeballs, surrogates for the testicles. Accordingly, Oedipus's punishment is blindness. Wotan submits to his wife's domination as willingly as he has given his eye to win her. Infantilization is at once a resolution of Oedipal conflict by regression to the stage of monopoly over mother, and self-inflicted punishment by exchanging the erect adult penis for a boy's flaccid one.

This Oedipal strategy *requires* a frigid woman who is repelled by the erect penis. Fricka has hoped that by indulging Wotan in Walhall, she can curb his waywardness (reflecting Wagner's own numerous flirtations and extra-marital affairs in a grandiose search for the "ideal"). To her horror, it only stirs his passion all the more. "Lordship and power you wish it to increase for you," she says scornfully. "Only to stir up restless storm was the towering fortress erected for you." Here too, the peculiar syntax and vocabulary of the German is inadequately represented by any English equivalent: *"nur rastlosern Sturm zu erregen, erstand dir die ragende Burg."*[88]

Wotan stipulates their contract. For his commitment to the marriage, Fricka must indulge his wanderlust and thirst for change by allowing him the companionship of fallen warriors. He himself characterizes it as an amusement, a game. *"Wandel und Wechsel liebt wer lebt: das kann ich nicht sparen!"* The economy of the marriage is a closed circle. Wotan's marriage with Fricka (as Wagner's with Minna) allows him to monopolize mother in the person of her surrogate. That monopoly, the tabooed Oedipal victory over the father, requires the punishment of castration, symbolized by blinding and accomplished through Fricka/Minna's fear of passion, of the erect penis, manifesting itself as frigidity, which in turn drives Wotan/Wagner into puerile infatuations with other women. These affairs temporarily satisfy his sexual requirements, deflate his erections, and lead predictably to remorseful reunion with his frigid wife. The autoerotism implied by the imagery of Walhall as plaything represents a parallel course. In the economy of the sexually frigid

---

[88] For the sake of consistency, I have retained the line as rendered in the overall English translation of the libretto. A more accurate translation of the German, however, would be "Only to stir up restless storm, did the towering fortress *rise for you.*"

marriage, masturbation is simply a strategy more ready to hand (so to speak) than the affair. Wotan acknowledges the inescapable guilt. "With wicked price I paid for the construction!" he says gloomily to Fricka at the end of *Rheingold*. One would expect him rather to be rejoicing. *"Mit bösem Zoll zahlt' ich den Bau!"* The chief of the gods suffers from the "success depression" that characterizes modern man.

Wotan has awakened with the inflated equivalent of a matutinal erection. Alberich likewise entered the scene with an erection — in effect — which the repulse of the Rhinemaidens made wilt in shame and chagrin. And Fricka shames Wotan into detumescence. The central action of the opera is the parallel forfeiture of Alberich and Wotan; for their self-indulgence, they are each in turn required to yield up the Rheingold. As Wotan has seized the hoard from Alberich, the giants then extort it from him. Moreover, the giants' motive for accepting the gold in Freia's stead is that they begrudge Alberich its power. The Nibelung has done them much evil, and with this new power, the giants reason, he is bound to do more. They are just as bent on rendering Alberich powerless as on extracting rightful payment from Wotan. These two motives merge in the gold, and make Alberich's and Wotan's relinquishing of it appear all the more clearly parallel.[89]

The twin giants, Fasolt and Fafner, despite their guise as brothers, stand (as giants often do in dreams and fantasies) for parents. The murder of Fasolt at his brother's hand in the

---

[89] This expiation, yielding the gold, parallels (from the psychoanalytic viewpoint) the infant's experience of toilet training, when, held captive on the throne of cleanliness, it is compelled to yield the contents of its bowel to demanding parents.

dispute over division of the hoard (leaving Fafner sole guardian of the hoard where once a pair of giants lived together) may be informed by Wagner's repeated childhood experience of losing his father (his legal father at six months, Geyer at eight years). His mother survived as sole parent. Wagner may unconsciously have fantasized his mother as having killed the husbands she twice survived, a speculation buttressed by the transformation of the lone Fafner into a devouring dragon.[90]

Melanie Klein testifies to the commonplace nature of this idea. "The child also has phantasies in which his parents destroy each other by means of their genitals and excrements which are felt to be dangerous weapons. These phantasies have important effects and are very numerous, containing such ideas as that the penis, incorporated in the mother, turns into a dangerous animal or into weapons loaded with explosive substances; or that her vagina, too, is transformed into a dangerous animal or some instrument of death, as, for instance, a poisoned mouse-trap. Since such phantasies are wish-phantasies and since his sexual theories are largely fed by sadistic desires, the child has a sense of guilt about the injuries which, in his phantasy, his parents inflict on each other."[91]

Klein's statement lends phallic valence to the staff with which Fafner clubs his "brother" to death. For in the childish imagination, mother also possesses a penis. Ruth Mack Brunswick explains that, "Whereas both the active and the

---

[90] An image of the archetypal "terrible mother."
[91] Melanie Klein, *The Psychoanalysis of Children* (Delacorte Press, 1975), p. 132.

castrated mother exist in point of fact, the phallic mother is pure fantasy, a childish hypothesis elaborated after the discovery of the penis and the possibility of its loss or absence in the female. It is a hypothesis made to insure the mother's possession of the penis, and as such probably arises at the moment when the child becomes uncertain that the mother does indeed possess it. Previously . . . it seems more than probable that the executive organ of the active mother is the breast; the idea of the penis is then projected back upon the active mother after the importance of the phallus has been recognized. Thus it is a fantasy of regressive, compensatory nature."[92]

The phallic mother comprises both parents in one. Fafner kills Fasolt with the phallic staff, but the struggle is over the vaginal (and anal) ring, symbolically, over sexual roles. The victorious mother demands both. This struggle characterizes the relation between Fricka and Wotan, as well as that between Minna and Richard. In *Siegfried*, Mime similarly claims to be "father and mother at once" of the heroic boy. The image here is inverted, to be sure; dwarf Mime is the parental androgyne, but the castrated one, i.e., the parents deposed.

The disguise of the parents as brothers (i.e., both male) has another meaning. The female is the nurturing parent. The stern demand for regulation of bowel movement, on the other hand, emanates from the father, just as the superego "takes its

---

[92] Ruth Mack Brunswick, "The Pre-oedipal Phase of the Libido Development," *Psychoanalytic Quarterly* (1940), p. 304.

severity from the father."[93]   Thus, both parents assume the posture of the male in toilet training. To extort the gold, the giants threaten to withhold Freia, whose golden apples the gods require to maintain their eternal youth. Freud associates fruit in dreams and fantasies with the breasts and their contents.   Should the child refuse to comply with their demands for regulation, the parents withhold their love. The most palpable form of parental love is mother's breast, on which the infant's life entirely depends.   The parents, who function as male when they demand regulation, threaten to withhold their nurturing, female aspect.

Toilet training and withdrawal of the breast are connected even more crucially.   In Freud's view both function to convince the infant of the reality of the castration threat, whose acceptance allows the passing of the Oedipus Complex and entry into latency. His description of the process suggests that the theme of castration informs the giants' demand to surrender the gold and their threat to Freia's apples.   There are, he writes, "two experiences which all children go through, by which it is thought that they become prepared for the loss of a valued part of the body — the withdrawal from them of the mother's breast, at first intermittently and later finally, and the daily demand made on them to give up the contents of the bowel."[94]

Toilet training itself is experienced as a castration. "Since the column of faeces stimulates the erotogenic mucous membrane of the bowel," explains Freud, "it plays the part of an active

---

[93] Sigmund Freud, "The Dissolution of the Oedipus Complex," *Standard Edition*, vol. XIX, p. 176.
[94] *Ibid.*, p. 175.

organ in regard to it; it behaves just as the penis does to the vaginal mucous membrane, and acts as it were as its forerunner during the cloacal epoch. The handing over of faeces for the sake of (out of love for) someone else becomes a prototype of castration; it is the first occasion upon which an individual parts with a piece of his own body in order to gain the favour of some other person whom he loves."[95] Freud's final sentence recalls Wotan's sacrifice of his eye to win Fricka. The requirement that he yield the eye parallels Fricka's demand (for she sides with the giants) that he surrender the gold. Both demands epitomize the castration implied in the wife's infantilization of her husband.

If the giants Fafner and Fasolt are parental figures in one aspect, the appearance of Erda, (whose name and domain identify her as earth-mother: *Erde* is German for "earth") presents the parental figure in another. Female, in contrast to the male giants, she rises out of the earth only to her waist, only enough, that is, to reveal her breasts (her "executive organ," to use Brunswick's terminology). Wagner's stage direction is provocative.[96] Why only to her waist? Would exposing more of her body reveal possession of a male organ? Breasts signify the feminine, but Erda also rises, like a tumescent penis. In this context, her warning to Wotan to surrender the last of the gold hoard, the ring, may bear a

---

[95] Sigmund Freud, "Anal Erotism and the Castration Complex," p. 84.
[96] The *mise en scène* could easily serve as an emblem of the unconscious: "*Wotan wendet sich zürnend zur Seite. Die Bühne hat sich von neuem verfinstert. - Aus der Felskluft zur Seite bricht ein bläulicher Schein hervor; in ihm wird plötzlich Erda sichtbar, die bis zu halber Leibeshöhe aus der Tiefe aufsteigt; sie ist von edler Gestalt, weithin von schwarzem Haar umwallt.*"

double meaning.   Fricka has berated him as, "Hard god!" ("*Harter Gott!*"). Erda commands,"*Weiche, Wotan! Weiche!*"

The German imperative *weiche* means "yield," or "withdraw." But *weich* means "soft." The infant refusing to yield its feces is perversely stiffening in defiance of the parental demand. Literally, the sphincter is constricted and hard.   When the child physically "softens," becoming pliant to its parents' will, the love provisionally withheld (mother's breast) will be restored.

When the god asserts his will, he is hard; when he yields, he softens. In over-riding Wotan's authority, Erda requires him to wilt like a flaccid penis. Only one of them can be powerful and male. To soften is to yield, but to yield is to lose the power of erection. In order to maintain the flow of love on which emotional life depends, the boy must submit to the psychic equivalent of castration.

"I think that the reason why the boy has in the deepest layers of his mind such a tremendous fear of his mother as the castrator," writes Melanie Klein, "and why he harbours the idea so closely associated with that fear, of the 'woman with a penis,' is that he is afraid of her as a person whose body contains his father's penis; so that ultimately what he is afraid of is his father's penis incorporated in his mother."[97] Klein's explanation suggests that Alberich's presence in "the bowels of the earth" is emblematic of a Wagnerian fantasy of Geyer inside his mother.

---

[97] Melanie Klein, *The Psychoanalysis of Children*, p. 131.

It remains to discuss Loge's role in *Rheingold*. Loge is fire, whose meaning, in the terms of the standard psychoanalytic literature on dreams and fantasy, is straightforwardly sexual. Freud, for example, writes that, ". . . primitive man could not but regard fire as something analogous to the passion of love — or, as we should say, a symbol of the libido. The warmth radiated by fire evokes the same kind of glow as accompanies the state of sexual excitation, and the form and motion of the flame suggest the phallus in action. There can be no doubt about the mythological significance of flames as the phallus. . ."[98] On the other hand, Loge's attributes in *Rheingold*, his cleverness in particular, suggest an identification with the mind. Thus, G. B. Shaw characterizes Loge as, "the god of Intellect, Argument, Imagination, Illusion, and Reason."[99]

But Shaw further identifies Loge, god of intellect, with falsehood, with the Big Lie, that compulsion to deceive inherent in the exercise of state power symbolized (in Shaw's interpretation of the allegory) by Wotan. Wotan, he tells us, "is trusting to another great world-force, the Lie . . ., to help him to trick the giants out of their reward."[100] Are these seemingly contradictory interpretations reconcilable: libido and intellect?

Also bemusing is Shaw's association of intellect with untruth. Why not, on the contrary, with truth? Why is the exercise of intellect shot through with guilt? The myths of Eve's sin in

---

[98] Sigmund Freud, "The Acquisition and Control of Fire," *Standard Edition*, vol. IX, pp. 213-214.
[99] G. B. Shaw, *The Perfect Wagnerite*, p. 225.
[100] *Ibid.*, p. 224.

tasting the fruit of knowledge, and Prometheus's sin in stealing fire (reason) from the gods provide the answer. Knowledge is guilty because it exposes what ought not be known, and therefore must be stolen. Forbidden knowledge is sexual knowledge, at once the object of the child's most intense curiosity, and the secret most jealously guarded by god-like adults. The myths concerning the acquisition of knowledge can be regarded as translations into phylogenic terms of the individual's passage from innocence to sexual enlightenment and guilt.

The gods' censure of Loge as a knave and liar is puzzling too. Loge is actually no more deceitful than most characters in *The Ring*, a good deal less than some. He is astonishingly and persistently true, for instance, to his promise to the Rhinemaidens. That he should be singled out as mendacious, then, requires some interpretation. In reality, guilty knowledge is not punished for being false; on the contrary, it is punished precisely for being true. But it is punished *as if* a smutty lie. The charge of falsehood is an act of denial, like ritually washing out a child's offending mouth, a wishful attempt to remake the world into a "nicer" place.

Parents, not the inquisitive child, are the deceivers. Freud was convinced that the conflict in the child's mind between the sexual truth it intuits and the sexual fairy tales offered up by parents represents a prototypic thought-blockage that permanently impairs intellectual functioning. "Where a child is not already too much intimidated, it takes sooner or later the shortest way by demanding answers from its parents or attendants, who signify for it the source of all knowledge. This way, however, fails. The child receives either evasive answers or a rebuke for its curiosity, or is dismissed with that mythologically significant information. . . : 'The stork brings the children. . . ' It appears to be from much evidence conclusive that children refuse to believe the stork theory, and that from the time of this first deception and rebuff they nourish a mistrust against adults, have the presentiment of something forbidden which is being withheld from them by the 'grownups,' and consequently conceal their further investigations by secrecy. With this, however, it comes about that they experience the first occasion of a 'psychical conflict,' in that ideas for which they 'by instinct' feel a preference, but which adults consider 'naughty,' come into opposition with others which are maintained by the authority of the adults without being acceptable to them themselves. Out of these mental conflicts there may soon arise a 'mental dissociation'; the one idea which is bound up with 'being good,' but also with a cessation of thinking, becomes the prevailing conscious one; the other, for which meanwhile the inquiries prosecuted have brought new evidence, which is not supposed to count, becomes suppressed and unconscious. The nuclear complex of neurosis is formed in this way."[101]

But the will to know prevails over the attempt to suppress knowing, to shroud the truth of the infant's own genesis. Moreover, in the unconscious there is no boundary between this will to know the sexual truth, and the drive to participate in it. Thus, Loge is at once intellect and passion, reason and libido. Knowing and doing are equivalent. Here is the psychological (rather than the ethical) sense of Christ's dictum

---

[101] Sigmund Freud, "On the Sexual Theories of Children," *Standard Edition*, vol. IX, pp. 213-214.

that a lustful glance is equivalent to the act of adultery.[102] The intellect is an instrument to probe the interior of things as much as the penis is.

Under the concept of "the Oedipus complex of the life of the intellect," Gaston Bachelard gathers, " . . . all those tendencies which impel us to know as much as our fathers, more than our fathers, as much as our teachers, more than our teachers."[103] Knowledge of fire is the crucial symbol in Bachelard's study *The Psychoanalysis of Fire*. He contradicts the notion that the child fears fire from being burned; fire, he argues, ". . . is more a *social reality* than a *natural reality*."

"The true basis for the respect shown to flame," Bachelard writes, is that,

> If the child brings his hand close to the fire his
> father raps him over the knuckles with a ruler.
> Fire, then, can strike without having to burn.
> Whether this fire be flame or heat, lamp or stove,
> the parents' vigilance is the same. Thus fire is
> initially the object of a *general prohibition*;
> hence this conclusion: the social interdiction
> is our first general *knowledge* of fire. What we
> first learn about fire is that we must not touch
> it. (pp. 10-11)

If this first knowledge of fire—that we must not touch it— effectively blocks the path to further knowledge through

---

[102] *Matthew*, 5:28.
[103] Gaston Bachelard, *The Psychoanalysis of Fire* (Boston, 1964), p. 12. Subsequent page references follow quotations in parentheses.

direct, empirical testing, how is the child to satisfy that not entirely rational will to know more? "Since the prohibitions are primarily social interdictions," answers Bachelard, "the problem of obtaining a personal knowledge of fire is the problem of *clever disobedience*. The child wishes to do what his father does, but far away from his father's presence, and so like a little Prometheus he steals some matches." (p. 11)

Thus is Loge labeled a liar. His eyes have seen, his ears heard what they should not. He has the wits to disobey and to trick truth from the gods. This theme is elaborated in *Siegfried*, an opera of questions and answers, beginning, of course, with Siegfried's inquisitive questions about his origin. An obedient son would acquiesce to ignorance. Only through clever disobedience does Siegfried discover truth that frees him from Mime's dominance. The gods' accusation that Loge is a liar is at once denial and projection to justify the taboo against acquisition of sexual knowledge. It is on the contrary the "higher" psychic processes that tell lies in order to repress socially unacceptable wishes. Libido is truthful. Loge retorts quite accurately that the gods revile him only to conceal their own shame: *"Ihre Schmach zu decken schmähen mich Dumme."*

Wagner championed sexual emancipation. A major aspect of Siegfried's heroic character is that, unfettered by social taboo, he revels in his sexuality. In this sensual hero, Wagner fancied himself reflected, for he flouted social convention in the bohemian life of the theater, in amorous affairs, in open cohabitation with Cosima Liszt, whose children he fathered even though she was the wife of another man—his friend and conductor, no less. As his increasing dependence on aphrodisiacs, fetishistic costumes, and perfumed baths attested, though, Wagner's sexual emancipation was less than complete. Ensnared in neurotic compulsions himself, he recognized nonetheless that the sexual mores of his time were hypocritical and destructive of human freedom.

Loge represents libido, spurred on by the pleasure principle to discovery of erotic "truth." To this end, he explores the world "high and low," as he is driven by whim ("*zu Tiefen und Höhen treibt mich mein Hang*"), seeking a substitute for Freia, a substitute acceptable to man "for the delight and worth of woman" ("*Ersatz . . . für Weibes Wonne und Wert*"). This search parallels the infant's exploration of its own body for an erotic replacement of its mother's increasingly unreliable attentions. Loge has sought such a substitute in vain. Nothing can replace woman. Everyone laughs at his question. Except one, "the Nibelung, Night-Alberich," who, having wooed the Rhinemaidens without success, has declared gold "sublimer than the favors of woman" ("*hehrer als Weibes Huld*").

Underlying Loge's researches is the infantile discovery of the anus as a source of erotic gratification. Libido, first centered at the mouth on sucking and feeding impulses, continues the infant's attachment to mother's body after the shock of birth. Thus, libido is focused on the upper body, just as Loge begins in the clouds with the gods. To discover the erotic potential of the anus, libido explores the lower body. Loge searches *high* and *low* before finding Alberich and the gold in the bowels of the earth. Since erotic gratification at the anus is found to be independent of mother, libido shifts its focus from her body (specifically, her breasts) to the infant's own body. Anal gratification compensates for oral deprivation.

Loge's loyalty to the Rhinemaidens represents libido's urge to redeem the eliminative function from shame and loathing, from the sterile defiance of retention (what Erda calls "*des Ringes Not*"), and restore it to the realm of the polymorphously perverse. He explains to the gods that in the depths of the water gold is a toy, "for the pleasure of laughing children; but forge it into the round of a circle and it helps one to highest power, wins for man the world." What is but a toy for the child is the basis of power for the man. Defecation is similarly a source of erotic gratification for the infant, but later the focus of his struggle for control and mastery. Technically, Loge promises the Rhinemaidens only to inform Wotan of the theft of their gold, and convey their plea for the god's intervention. "Now I've kept my word," he says, implying that having discharged his obligation, he means to forget about it. Yet he does nothing of the kind. He continually (tactlessly, in Wotan's view) recalls the Rhinemaidens' supplication, and though Wotan would like to ignore their song, the mournful tune persists to the end of the opera. At the conclusion of *Götterdämmerung*, through Loge's agency in the form of universal conflagration, the Rhinemaidens repossess their ring.

To capture the gold, Loge guides Wotan into Nibelheim. Emblematically, this episode shows libido guiding the self from deprivation (Freia's absent apples) to the discovery of anal erotic gratification. "Shall we climb directly down through the Rhine?" asks Loge. ("*Steil hinab steigen wir denn durch den Rhein?*") "Not through the Rhine!" exclaims Wotan. Wotan's vehement avoidance of the Rhine is ostensibly designed to circumvent the Rhinemaidens' suit to recover their stolen gold. Loge's response, however, suggests a disguised motive. "Then we'll swing around through the sulfur cleft: slip in that way with me!" ("*so schwingen wir uns durch die Schwefelkluft: dort schlüpfe mit mir hinein!*")

Earth is the maternal body; entrances are orifices. Wotan cannot enter directly, through the waters of the Rhine, that is, the female genital orifice (which serves for urination also). Instead he must "slip"[104] through that sulfurous cleft reeking of Alberich. Wotan in effect becomes Alberich when he enters the symbolic anus of mother earth. What may appear a confusion in this symbolism between infantile and maternal bodily parts is actually logical since mother is introjected. In the infantile mind there is in any case an identification of its body with hers.

Wotan's avoidance of the vagina in preference for the anus is less a perversion of sexual aim than a reflection of the infantile theory of anal birth. The way out is also the way in. The child does not recognize the vagina as having any sexual function. Indeed, it may represent the *absence* of sexual function, since in the child's view the vagina is the place where once a penis was. The "wound" that remains serves — in the infant's mind — for urination only. To the extent that the male child is under the dominance of the castration complex, he identifies with mother — in particular, his anus is identified with his mother's. This identification may go so far in connection with the negative Oedipus Complex as to provoke fantasies of anal

---

[104] Loge's verb *schlüpfen* is a word otherwise reserved for the gait of the Nibelungs.

intercourse with the father, as in Freud's celebrated case of the Wolf-man.[105]

Freud clarifies this sexual confusion in his explanation of the sadistic-anal organization that follows the oral. "Here the contrasts which run through the whole sexual life are already developed, but cannot yet be designated as *masculine* and *feminine*, but must be called *active* and *passive*. The activity is supplied by the musculature of the body through the mastery impulse; the erogenous mucous membrane of the bowel manifests itself above all as an organ with a passive sexual aim."[106]

In this light, the anal-erotic orientation of *Rheingold* appears more clearly in terms of passivity, the mode we have seen was Wagner's major tactic with women. Wagner seduced by reversing normal sexual roles; he typically made himself the helpless receiver of the woman's attention. Wotan is likewise a remarkably passive figure. He sleeps while the giants build Walhall. Loge must search the world in the god's place, and must advise him how to acquire the gold. Loge must lead him into Nibelheim, and contrive to snare Alberich, while Wotan, exclusively the beneficiary of the exertions of others, stands by laconically commenting on the activity swirling around him.

G. B. Shaw correctly associates the metallic din of the anvils in Nibelheim with the factories of the industrial revolution. "This gloomy place need not be a mine: it might just as well be a match-factory, with yellow phosphorus, phossy jaw, a

---

[105] Sigmund Freud, *From the History of an Infantile Neurosis, Standard Edition*, vol. XVII.
[106] Sigmund Freud, "Infantile Sexuality," p. 198.

large dividend, and plenty of clergymen shareholders. Or it might be a whitelead factory, or a chemical works, or a Pottery, or a railway shunting yard, or a tailoring shop, or a little gin-sodden laundry, or a bakehouse, or a big shop, or any other of the places where human life and welfare are daily sacrificed in order that some greedy foolish creature may be able to hymn exultantly to his Plutonic idol: 'Thou mak'st me eat whilst others starve . . . '"[107] But coupled with these topical themes of entrepreneurial greed and oppression is the image of machinery inside mother's body, symbolically the female sexual apparatus, characterized by cyclical regularity and productive output.

The maternal body as combination factory and mine belongs to a familiar class of oral-sadistic fantasies arising, as Melanie Klein shows, from the child's "ideas that he gets possession of the contents of his mother's breast by sucking and scooping it out. This desire to suck and scoop out, first directed to her breast, soon extends to the inside of her body . . . An early stage of development . . . is governed by the child's aggressive trends against its mother's body and in which its predominant wish is to rob her body of its contents and destroy it."[108]

The twin dwarves Alberich and Mime who operate this subterranean factory/mine are like opposing aspects of the introjected father. Alberich, brandishing his whip, pinching his brother's ear, acts the role of punitive superego. The Tarnhelm lends him this power by making him invisible, as

---

[107] G. B. Shaw, *op. cit.*, p. 227. See also Ruth HaCohen, *The Music Libel Against the Jews*, (Yale, 2011), p. 204, who suggests that the Nibelungs' hammering is redolent of the Jewish "noise" (*"Lärm"*) of the Synagogue.
[108] Melanie Klein, *op. cit.*, p. 128.

the development of the superego makes father invisible by internalizing his interdictions and commands, which are subsequently obeyed even in father's absence.[109]

In the psyche, emotionally, father is ever-present, for he is within. "Where are you? I can't see you," whimpers Mime. "Well, feel me then, you lazy scoundrel! Take that for your scheming to steal!" answers Alberich, invisible under the helm. Not only deeds but forbidden thoughts are punished. There is no escaping the watchfulness of the internalized parent. "No one sees me though he searches; but I am everywhere, hidden from sight," gloats Alberich. "He lingers everywhere now to guard you; peace and rest are fled from you; for him you must produce, though you see him not; though never aware of his presence, you must expect him always! To him are you subjugated forever!" If, as Bachelard says, fire can strike without burning, father likewise can punish *in absentia* through the agency of the superego.

The wretched, compliant Mime for his part represents the father as alien, as Jew, the negative ideal (as Wotan, third of this paternal triumvirate, is the positive ego-ideal). Mime is an

---

[109] Margaret Mahler-Schoenberger, "Pseudoimbecility: A Magic Cap of Invisibility," *Psychoanalytic Quarterly*, vol. XI, no. 2, (New York, 1942), pp. 149-164, employs the symbol of the *Tarnkappe*, the cloak of invisibility, whose source is the *Niebelungenlied*, to represent the feigned ignorance, even stupidity, beneath which the sexually curious child pursues his researches. Though this symbolism differs substantively from the present interpretation of Alberich's use of the *Tarnhelm*, it is in fact quite pertinent to Siegfried's use of the same magical garment in *Götterdämmerung*, see footnote 196, p. 240, below. Note, by the way, that Mahler-Schoenberger mistranslates — not uniquely — *Tarnkappe* as "cap of invisibility." *Kappe* actually means "cloak," cf. "cape." This error does not materially affect her use of the symbol.

artist; he forges both ring and Tarnhelm. He aspires to power. Yet he fails — caricature of the versatile Geyer.

The third major theme of *Rheingold* is anxiety.   Anxiety overshadows the gods' triumphal entry into Walhall; it is the tension that persists (triple forte brass and tympani notwithstanding) and bridges the gap to the next segment of the drama, *Walküre*. For even as he strides across the rainbow, consort on his arm, Wotan knows that trouble has not been resolved by payment of the gold. Trouble has only just begun. More than the Rhinemaidens' plaintive song, his own sense of having paid the giants in wicked coin, his revulsion at the brutal murder of Fasolt, his anxiety that Erda has buried with her some crucial piece of wisdom, oppress him as an inarticulable prescience of doom.

If the psychic conflict of the opera is centered in the Oedipus Complex, its anxiety arises from the fear of castration. The parental demand for the product of the bowel is (as we have seen, above) a prototype of castration in a physical sense. Beyond the immediate, physical sense, toilet training is emotionally castrating in that obeying parental power impresses the infant's own powerlessness on him; his illusion of omnipotence suffers yet another blow. Toilet training is a requirement of growing up — a step toward adulthood. Appropriately, Alberich consoles himself with the thought that "the discipline" of surrendering the Tarnhelm is "a sharpening of my wit that makes me wise," and "a lesson" worth the price.   (*"Witzigung wär's, die weise mich macht; zu teuer nicht zahl' ich die Zucht, lass' für die Lehre ich den Tand."*)

Sphincter control is a mixed blessing, a double bind. While it means acquisition of mastery through training, it also requires submission to a superior will. Though the sphincter represents the child's control over his bowel, his parents wrest control from him (as the ring is extorted from Alberich/Wotan) by insisting that it function according to their schedule. Adulthood thus paradoxically entails infantilization.

An exactly parallel contradiction attaches to the penis, focus of adult male power. For if the power of the penis is realized in the state of erection when it is employed in copulation, the inevitable consequence following this exercise of power is detumescence and impotence. Masculinity may be experienced as undone in the very act of asserting it. In actuality, of course, detumescence is not castration, for potency returns. Sexual life is cyclical, passing from activity to passivity, and back again. Freud mythologized this rhythm as the struggle between Eros and Thanatos, indicating how closely castration anxiety is allied to death anxiety.

Castration anxiety seems to underlie the capture of Alberich by the clever Loge. "Make me speechless with amazement," he challenges the dwarf. And Alberich obligingly grows into a giant snake, as it were, an erect penis. In that form, Loge and Wotan cannot snare him. But inevitably following erection is flaccidity, and accordingly Loge asks Alberich next to make himself so small "That the narrowest cleft could hold you, where fearfully the toad hides." Turned to a toad (a penis gone limp) Alberich is captured, and lies bound like an infant in swaddling clothes before Wotan who gloats over the megalomaniacal dwarf. "Caught you are, fettered fast, just as you already imagined the world, whatever lives and stirs, in your sole power; you lie in bonds before me!"

The dilemma, then, is how to maintain erection "eternally," to cling to masculine power. Wotan's first words in the opera express this fantasy with respect to Walhall: "Manly honor, eternal power, rise to everlasting fame!" (*"Mannes Ehre, ewige Macht, ragen zu endlosem Ruhm!"*) And a moment later: "Finished, the eternal work!" (*"Vollendet das ewige Werk!"*) Walhall is nothing of the kind, of course. The entire tetralogy spirals towards Walhall's destruction and the death of the gods. This knowledge is contained in the pronouncements of Erda and Loge. But the audience is aware of it even before the curtain rises, as the audience of the Greek dramatic festival were perfectly conversant with the outcome of the Oedipus story. Suspense is not the issue.

On the contrary, *The Ring*'s over-arching subject is the inexorable machinery of doom. Wotan's obsession with everlasting power is obviously hopeless. Alberich's pretensions to immortality are equally hopeless. If the claims made for the Tarnhelm are true, Loge flatters the dwarf ironically, "then your power will last forever!" (*"Deine Macht wahrt dann ewig!"*) Alberich indulges in a reciprocal sarcasm when he calls the gods "Eternal revelers," (*"ewige Schwelger"*), and labels Wotan with the simple epithet *"Ewiger,"* ("Eternal one").

Mortality is after all the overt question posed by *The Ring*'s narrative. Can the fortress of Walhall, with its resurrected warriors, reverse the inexorable? All the plot's cycles and epicycles revolve around that fateful question, whose answer is apparent in advance. Let the giants build ever so stoutly, the fortress must crumble. The demise of Walhall may be seen as an emblem of mortality. That it is emblematic also of that more quotidian mortality of the penis, detumescence, is underscored by the parallel occurrence in *Parsifal*. Klingsor's castle, bastion of the self-castrated sorcerer, crumbles when Parsifal recovers the holy spear. The same fate befalls the Hall of the Gibichungs.

Castration anxiety is the *angst* that attaches to Alberich's terrible renunciation of love. For it is a renunciation of the penis, like Klingsor's. The dwarf paints himself as "ill-fated," and "lacerated by anxiety," and rails that Wotan should profit from the terrible price he has paid for the ring. *"Des Unseligen, Angstversehrten fluchfertige, furchtbare Tat, zu fürstlichem Tand soll sie fröhlich dir taugen? zur Freude dir frommen mein Fluch?"*

The theme of Alberich's curse is anxiety. The ring will be purchased only at the price he himself has paid. "Whoever possesses it, let anxiety consume him, and whoever possesses it not, by envy be gnawed!" (*"Wer ihn besitzt, den sehre die Sorge, und wer ihn nicht hat den nage der Neid!"*) The curse is constructed on the pattern of the double-bind, paradigm of anxiety. In asserting his virility, a man must lose it. Likewise, man is compelled to struggle against mortality even though he knows there is no possibility of evading it.

When Erda counsels Wotan to yield the anxiety-fraught ring, her mission is to persuade him to renounce both the childish dream of omnipotence, and the infantile tactic of defiant retention. She wants him to grow up. Her admonition to let the ring go applies to Wotan's desire for Erda herself. He wishes to know more than he ought. "Stay," he pleads (*pleads*, for though chief of gods, he is a child in Erda's presence), "that I might know more." But Erda replies darkly that he knows enough. Enough for what, though? Surely growing up entails learning. In the realm of sexual knowledge alone does the child manifest obedience to the parental injunction to mature not by learning, not by submitting to education, but by renouncing rational inquiry.

But cessation of thought and suppression of knowledge go hand in hand with anxiety, and to anxiety Erda accordingly condemns Wotan. "*Du weisst genug: sin' in Sorg' und Furcht!*" ("You know enough: meditate in anxiety and fear!") Actually, Erda has given Wotan a significant clue to the nature of her knowledge. Her three daughters the Norns, she has said, tell him each night what she knows. The Norns spin fate. That they speak to him each night means that Erda's knowledge is the substance of Wotan's dreams — what only the unconscious knows, the repressed.

Wotan instinctively thrusts to the heart of the matter when he attempts to follow Erda into her cleft. "If I am to meditate in anxiety and fear, I must seize you, learn everything!" ("*Soll ich sorgen und fürchten, dich muß ich fassen, alles erfahren!*") Here too, English inadequately renders the double sense of *erfahren*: not only "come to know, learn," but also, "experience." The concreteness of Wotan's intention, to seize Erda, and experience her secret knowledge, points to the Oedipal fantasy underlying the scene.

Equally revealing is the reaction of the other gods. "What do you wish, madman?" cries Fricka. "Restrain yourself,

Wotan!," shouts Froh, "Keep away from the noble woman, heed her word!" There is no obvious reason why the chief of the gods should not pursue Erda into the ground if he so wills. The vehemence of their reaction gathers force, however, in light of the incest taboo. The German of Froh's warning is "*scheue die Edle*," literally, "Fear, shun, or shrink from the noble one," and implies the horror attached to the incest wish. Wotan's wishes are not, in the event, suppressed by the social pressures of the taboo. The underlying sexual meaning of this scene ostensibly concerned with "secret knowledge" is made clearer when one learns that between *Rheingold* and *Walküre* Wotan overcomes his self-restraint, descends after all to Erda, and begets with her his "wishmaiden," Brünnhilde. Knowledge is carnal knowledge.

"How I am fettered by fear! Anxiety and fear bind the soul: how to end them, may Erda teach me: to her I must descend!" ("*Wie doch Bangen mich bindet! Sorg' und Furcht fesseln den Sinn: wie sie zu enden, lehre mich Erda: zu ihr muss ich hinab!*") The fantasy is that Oedipal tension, anxiety, can be ended by flaunting the incest prohibition and acting out the sexual wishes by which one is driven.

Wotan's sudden determination to end anxiety by pursuing Erda is mirrored in Donner's dramatic hammer blow, which clears away the mists that have gathered around the gods, symbolizing the oppression of anxiety. "Sultry mist hangs in the air; I feel oppressed by its gloomy weight!" Donner's solution is to gather the dispersed energy of the mists into one mighty thunderclap and sweep the heavens clear. This musical thunderclap climaxes the crescendo of an ascending scale in the orchestra with the passionate intensity of the orgasm it surely represents. Donner's hammer blow is another of those episodes in the opera that by their very senselessness (or the appearance of it) invite interpretation. Unfettered orgasm as the resolution of anxiety is an Alexandrian attempt to sever the knot of the Oedipus Complex. It fails, inevitably, and the unnerving anxiety lingering as the opera ends intimates as much.

As they cross the illusory Rainbow bridge, the gods speak reassuringly about the security of the fortress, which though won from the giants "in trouble and anxiety," ("*in Müh und Angst*"), is—in Wotan's words—"safe from fear and dread" ("*sicher vor Bang und Grau'n*"). But they are whistling in the dark, like Wotan when he defies the giants' demand for the ring with the myopic boast, "Without anxiety I'll keep it for myself!" ("*ohne Bangen wahr' ich's für mich!*"). His bravado is doubly false: Wotan will neither keep the ring, nor elude its anxiety *even in yielding it.*

So the gods are piped across the bridge to the Rhinemaidens' nagging song. "Rhinegold! Rhinegold! Purest gold! Oh that your sterling bauble shone yet in the deep!" Theirs is the last word, and it gives the lie to the gods above. "It's secure and true only in the deep: false and mean, what revels up there above!" ("*traulich und treu ist's nur in der Tiefe: falsch und feig ist, was dort oben sich freut!*") The Rhinemaidens' counterintuitive words foreshadow Wotan's subterranean intercourse with Erda after the fall of the curtain. The ostensible surface of life is a lie, at best a symbolic distortion of the truth, which dwells only in the depths of the unconscious.

Chapter III

Walküre: Melancholia

Anxiety is the thematic bridge from *Rheingold* to *Walküre*, belying the rainbow's hopeful promise. The pompous music of triumphal entry into Walhall cedes to *Walküre*'s agitated prelude: an incessant tremolo in the violins hovering over ascending and descending scales in the cellos, like the pacing of a caged animal. The nervous energy of this music depicting the storm outside Hunding's dwelling climaxes with a subdued recapitulation of Donner's hammer blow, thudding tympani representing thunder, but without the ringing lightning stroke that clears the air in *Rheingold*—not an arbitrary musical echo, for *Walküre* will spell out the consequences of severing the knot of desire and repression with the sword of unfettered orgasm, more pointedly, of incest. Incest achieves in this opera what Donner's hammer blow did in *Rheingold*, for as brother and sister declare their love, Hunding's door blows open to reveal that the storm has passed, leaving in its wake the tranquility of a moonlit spring night. The hounded melancholic trades his old identity Wehwalt ("Lord of Sorrow"), for Siegmund[110] ("Protector of Victory"). But peace and victory prove ephemeral.

Otto Rank sketched out the nexus between Wagner's relations with women (beginning with his mother) and the incest motif in his operas, principally in *Walküre*.[111] He focuses on the pattern of the unavailable woman in Wagner's fictions — a pattern to which Sieglinde, doubly unavailable as the hero's sister, and wife of another — obviously conforms. The loss of mother to father, which would normally precede a child's birth[112], Rank suggests, was experienced by Wagner directly when his mother married his "step-father" Geyer six months after his birth.

"The mature artist ever again seeks compensation through poetic fantasy for the loss, suffered in earliest infancy, of the mother to the step-father. It is as though to achieve revenge for the fact that his father at that time took away his mother, the beloved woman, that he now, in the persons of his heroes, seduces the women beloved of others. This predilection for the wife or the betrothed of another, for a woman no longer free, was traced by Freud to infantile incestuous roots: it is the result of infantile jealousy of the father."[113] Wagner pursues this fantasy compensation in each of his music dramas beginning with the abortive opera, *Die Hochzeit* (*The Wedding*),

---

[110] Old Norse *Sigmundr*, from *sigr* ("victory") + *mundr* ("protection").
[111] Otto Rank, *Das Inzest-Motiv in Dichtung und Sage* (Leipzig and Vienna, 1912), pp. 639-648.
[112] And thus be experienced only indirectly, in retrospect and fantasy.
[113] *Ibid.*, p. 640, my trans.

in which a melancholic, love-struck knight invades the bridal chamber of a woman betrothed to his kinsman, through to *Parsifal*, in which the hero must liberate Kundry from Klingsor's evil power. Many of the dramas combine winning the unavailable woman with the death of the father at the hero's birth, most obviously in *Siegfried*, *Tristan* and *Parsifal*. Rank argues that Wagner's repeated emphasis on these themes has its origin in the central issues of the Oedipus Complex. His study does not, however, proceed from the question of genesis to meaning.

The narrative function of *Walküre*'s first act in the overall scheme of *The Ring* is to depict Siegfried's conception. Yet much more occurs. The first act, lyrical and tender without a trace of that oft decried Wagnerian bombast, is a musical world apart from the rest of *The Ring*, not just because it departs the mythological realm of gods, dwarves and giants, and comes completely down to earth, for that happens also in *Götterdämmerung*. The music marks the act with a different stamp, so that (as Shaw said of the awakening scene in *Siegfried*) it could stand as a little lyric opera on its own.

In this fantasy of sibling romance, the veil of allegory is drawn gossamer thin, allowing the artist vicariously to indulge openly incestuous wishes. True to the paradigm of his relation to the "motherly" Rosalie, the incest wish is displaced onto a more available sister, and though displacement is itself a type of allegory, it is allegory that modifies the character of affect less than the transformation of symbolism, whose function often is to disguise the character of affect, not just redirect it. No energy is expended on disguise — none on the decorous overlay of "civilization." The idyll of *Walküre*'s first act inset into the otherwise heavier textures of *The Ring* strikes us, if not quite as out of place, at least as markedly different from the rest of the mythologically invested tetralogy.

But how do the incest idyll itself, and its expository function of establishing Siegfried's conception, work together towards the meaning of *The Ring* beyond the merely narrative? After all, Wagner selects only isolated episodes of *The Ring*'s sprawling saga for depiction onstage. The four operas are like widely spaced windows affording fragmentary views of the story, the long and complex connecting segments between which are related only in exposition. Some more compelling reason than simple appropriateness must explain why just this episode, or that one, is presented, to the exclusion of others. Recalling that *The Ring* (which appears to take place in an external world peopled with distinct characters) represents the inner world of the psyche, we see that the author has selected from Norse mythology and the *Nibelungenlied* those episodes that serve him emblematically as aspects of the self.

Though appropriate that a hero be son of a hero, more to the point is that both heroes, Siegmund and Siegfried, represent aspects of essentially a single personality. *The Ring*, I argue, is a self-reflexive fantasy, in which the characters are either elements of psychic structure, or the introjected or otherwise incorporated forms of some emotionally significant person.

For that matter, Wotan is equally involved in this picture since he is Siegmund's father, as Siegmund is Siegfried's. In fact, one has to go beyond even this sequential triad, Wotan-Siegmund-Siegfried; not to be omitted is the figure of Wehwalt before his amorous transformation into Siegmund.

Thus, the cluster Wotan-Wehwalt-Siegmund-Siegfried may be seen as a psychic entity, identified in the foregoing chapter as the ego ideal.

What is the effect of splitting the ego ideal into these four figures? We can distinguish two kinds of relations among them. First is the father-son relation. Second is the sequential relation, of time, which, as noted in chapter 1, is as fictional an element as plot or character, and so subject to interpretation. Under the first of these categories falls not only the familiar Oedipal project of usurping father's place by identifying with, emulating, and eventually replacing him. For splitting the ego ideal into four figures yields a succession of fathers procreating sons, each a reflection of the author, beginning with Wotan, introjected figure of the father. The effect of this succession is to reveal the ego as comprising father and son jointly. In Freud's formulation, the Oedipal project is to become father of oneself.

Commonly accompanying what Freud called the "family romance" is the child's fantasy of rescuing his parents, both to repay their gift of life, and to achieve independence, to escape the burden of indebtedness. "By a slight change of meaning . . . rescuing the mother acquires the significance of giving her a child or making one for her — one like himself, of course . . . The son shows his gratitude by wishing to have a son by his mother that shall be like himself; in the rescue phantasy, that is, he identifies himself completely with the father. All the instincts, the loving, the grateful, the sensual, the defiant, the self-assertive and independent — all are gratified in the wish to be the father of himself."[114]

In *Walküre*, both occur; Wotan's son rescues Sieglinde from the loveless marriage with Hunding (a fantasy with numerous analogues in Wagner's own erotic life), and gives her a son "as like himself as possible." Sieglinde is his sister, not his mother. Yet she displays maternal aspects too, notably her bestowal of the name "Siegmund," an obviously parental function. There is evidence of a similar confusion of roles in Wagner's relation to his mother (manifested in his relation to other women too). The twenty-one year old composer writes to her:

> Ah, how far, though, above all others stands the love of a mother! I belong admittedly to those who cannot always say outright how they feel at heart, otherwise you would often have come to know a tenderer side of me. But the feelings remain the same — and see, Mother, now — now that I am away from you, I am overwhelmed by the feelings of thankfulness for your wonderful love for your child, which you again lately revealed to him so sincere and warm, so that I would like to write to you and speak to you of it in the tenderest tone of a lover to his beloved.[115]

In *Walküre*, linking rescue with Siegfried's conception accords with Freud's clinical observation that the rescue fantasy

---

[114] Sigmund Freud, "A Special Type of Object Choice Made by Men," *Standard Edition*, vol. XI, p. 173.
[115] *Familienbriefe von Richard Wagner*, 1832-1874 (Berlin, 1907), nr. 4 (my trans.).

contains the meaning of impregnating the mother. He goes on to note that, "Even the element of danger is not lost in the change of meaning; the experience of birth itself is the danger from which he was saved by the mother's efforts. Birth is in fact the first of all dangers to life, as well as the prototype of all the later ones we fear; and this experience has probably left its mark behind it on that expression of emotion which we call anxiety."[116]

If Siegmund and Siegfried (father and son) are projections of the same ego, the dangers of Sieglinde's rescue (to which Siegmund succumbs) equally threaten the alter-ego Siegfried in the womb. In the third act, Brünnhilde will implore the desperate Sieglinde to rescue the child in her womb. "Live, Oh woman, for the sake of love! Rescue the pledge that you received from him: A Volsung grows in your womb!" Sieglinde, who a moment before has begged for death, is suddenly inspired by maternal instinct. "Rescue me, bold one!" she cries to Brünnhilde. "Rescue my child!" A few lines later: "Rescue me maid! Rescue the mother!" Finally, she assumes the role of rescuer herself: "For his sake, whom we loved, I rescue the most beloved."

Sieglinde flees the dangers of Wotan's wrath eastward towards Mime's cave, where the mortal dangers of birth finally overcome her too. Though Sieglinde is provisionally rescued, she dies in childbirth[117] (as the ego ideal in the person of Siegfried survives conception and birth through mother's sacrifice, but dies in the person of Siegmund), stark evidence of how grave the dangers really are.

---

[116] Sigmund Freud, *op. cit.*, p. 173.
[117] Thematically, that is, she *both* is rescued *and* dies.

An episode from Wagner's infancy, intriguing for its several parallels, presents itself as perhaps the thematic germ of Sieglinde's flight to escape Hunding. Only weeks after Wagner's birth, his mother Johanna (like Sieglinde, carrying Siegfried in her womb, fleeing the chaos of battle under threat of Wotan's wrath) fled with her infant son a hundred and fifty miles through occupied territory in the upheaval of the Napoleonic War, from her legal husband in Leipzig to the infant's putative father, Ludwig Geyer, in Teplitz.

Ernest Newman asks rhetorically, "What reason could there be for exposing a few-weeks old baby to the dangers and discomforts of several day's journey through a war area in which transport must have been difficult and food and decent lodging none too easily obtainable? And of all places and people in all Germany to which she might have gone, why was it imperative that she should go nowhere but to Teplitz, and to no one but Geyer — a struggling actor who could hardly keep himself and could offer her no protection of any kind from the perils of the time? Is it not difficult to resist the conclusion that, in some degree or other, her journey was, in fact, a flight from a home that had all at once become impossible for her, and that in taking only her recent baby with her she was taking from Carl Friedrich something for which he may have believed he had no call to feel any paternal enthusiasm? Taking all the facts into consideration, and looking at them from every possible angle, do they not seem to suggest that the putative father of the child had hinted she had better betake herself and it to its real father?"[118]

---

[118] Ernest Newman, *The Life of Richard Wagner*, vol. III, appendix 1, pp. 561-562.

Johanna and Sieglinde are both fleeing loveless marriages. Johanna's husband, Carl Friedrich Wagner, is a Leipzig police official; Hunding, just returned from a mission to avenge injured kinsmen, represents himself likewise as an agent of justice. More explicitly, Fricka deputizes him to punish the violators of the incest taboo, and Wotan too, though he initially indulges the siblings' joyful, forbidden act, is compelled to mete out retributive justice. Johanna flees east through the fog of war from Leipzig to Teplitz; Sieglinde flees eastward to Mime's cave, evading the chaos and perils of Siegmund's fatal battle with Hunding. Johanna flees to Geyer, the impoverished (perhaps Jewish?) actor; Sieglinde finds refuge with the Nibelung Mime, whose name means "actor." Carl Friedrich dies six months after Richard's birth; Siegmund and Hunding die a day after Siegfried is conceived.[119]

It follows from these parallels that, though the motif of loveless marriage in *The Ring* is conventionally seen as mirroring Wagner's marriage with Minna, the particular marriage of Hunding and Sieglinde seems a reflection rather of the relationship of Wagner's mother and legal father. Geyer rescued Johanna from that marriage, as Siegmund rescues Sieglinde from Hunding, but in the fantasy of *Walküre*, the rescuer is split into two figures, Siegmund, the father with whom the son identifies positively, and Mime (who shelters Sieglinde, rescuing her unborn child as well), the father whom the son envies and despises for preceding him into his mother's womb. The Oedipal solution in the *Ring* fantasy is to have the good father killed off, and deny the paternity of the

---

[119] As an infant of 6 months, Wagner would have had no conscious memory of this adventure. It is plausible, though, that the family tale had been recounted (and registered) during his childhood.

bad father (eventually, to kill him too in the subsequent opera)—a solution that achieves magically becoming "father of oneself."

The second category of relation among the father-son figures, the temporal, pertains primarily to Wotan's epic scheme to produce by sleight of hand a hero not beholden to him for his power. Wotan lays this scheme before Brünnhilde (and us) in the long and important monologue midway through Act II. Wotan must regain the gold ring he has paid the giants to ward off demise of the gods. But he is fettered by the very laws that give him power; he cannot wrest by force what the law has forced him to surrender. To do so would destroy the law and his power with it. He has not fooled Fricka with the transparent argument (when she demands Siegmund's destruction) that this human son is independent of him, has won the magic sword for himself, and fights his own battles. Fricka knows Wotan has imbued the sword with magic and left it embedded in the tree for Siegmund to find, and has guided his son into these straits to win both sword and tabooed bride. "How did I hope slyly to deceive myself?" asks Wotan in self-reproach, like a boy caught in a fib. "How easily Fricka unmasked my deceit: to my ultimate shame she saw through me quite! To her will must I yield."

As she did in *Rheingold*, Fricka, not Wotan, wields the power. Though it seems chimerical, Wotan clings to his project to bring forth, "a hero, whom I never stooped to help, who, stranger to the god, free of his favor, unconsciously, not under command, but out of his own necessity, with his own weapon, might accomplish the deed that I must shun, that never my counsel counseled him to, even though it be the only wish of my desire!" That deed is to wrest the ring from Fafner. But this project conceals another — to be father of oneself. Father Wotan must no longer be manifest in his son; his son must create himself. "To my disgust I find always only myself in whatever I accomplish! The other, for whom I long — the other I never catch sight of: for the free one must create himself; I mold only slaves!"

The goal of the procession of fathers and sons is Siegfried's self-creation. Siegfried is to be free of Wotan, and with reason, for he represents the power of the sadistic superego to punish incestuous wishes with castration, witness Siegmund's fate. But one can see in the Wotan-Wehwalt-Siegmund-Siegfried sequence progressive solutions to Oedipal conflict. On the surface, this progression moves forward in time, from the Ur-god Wotan in the first opera through two generations to the young hero Siegfried in the third. One might express the sequential solutions as follows: Wotan (or, as he calls himself in this phase, "Wolfe," or, alternatively, "Wälse") and Wehwalt pursue a life of manly comradeship in arms. Under the guardianship of father Wotan, Wehwalt the son renounces Oedipal wishes. In the story, mother has been killed and sister stolen away. The fantasy corresponds to the latency solution of repression and identification with the father, the former adversary. In latency, the desired mother is *as good as* dead; she and any sister who might substitute for her are unavailable as love-objects even in fantasy.

Wehwalt accordingly tells Sieglinde and Hunding sadly that though born a twin, "Early in my life mother and maid disappeared; hardly ever did I know either her who bore me, or her whom she bore with me." When one day Wolfe and

Wehwalt were out hunting, the Neidings attacked the defenseless women, killing the mother and abducting the sister. This ascetic life apart from women, particularly mother and sister, reflects the solution of latency, and corresponds in Wagner's life to those periods of his boyhood when he was sent away from home, away from mother and sisters, to live as alien in the households of strangers. Alienation is reflected in Wehwalt's very name, which he has chosen because, though driven to seek the society of men and women, "However many I met, wherever I found them, whether I sought them as friend or as wife, always was I despised: Evil lay upon me. Whatever I judged right seemed wrong to others, whatever appeared bad to me got the blessings of others. I fell into feuds wherever I found myself; anger greeted me wherever I went; whenever I sought pleasure I only awakened woe: therefore I had to call myself Wehwalt; for woe only was I lord of."

Wehwalt's alienation from the social world is the emblem of his alienation from his own instinctual wishes. His avowal of love for his sister, and his adoption of her name for him, Siegmund, represents a new level of solution over the outworn, now discarded solution of repression. It is a short step of displacement from the underlying desire for mother. This new solution is made possible by the disappearance of father, and with him the threat of castration. But the removal is imperfect. Wehwalt explains that he was separated from his father in the heat of battle; "I lost his track the more, the longer I searched for it: only a wolf's skin did I find in the forest; empty it lay before me; my father I never found." If the father is gone, his traces (the wolf's skin), like the introjected father, the superego, remain. Fear of the father results in displacement of incest wishes onto the sister, and even those substitute wishes are punished with castration (the splintering of Siegmund's magic sword) and death. The tragic conclusion to Act II reflects the truth that beyond infancy, the individual carries his father embedded inescapably within him.

The incest theme assumes graphic form in the image of Wotan's sword thrust into the tree growing through Hunding's hut. It is a commonplace to regard the sword as a phallic symbol. If Wotan's sword is father's penis, the tree where he has left it (logic suggests) is mother's body. This interpretation parallels Freud's analysis of the childhood hallucination of a celebrated patient, who reported, "'When I was five years old, I was playing in the garden near my nurse, and was carving with my pocketknife in the bark of one of the walnut-trees . . . Suddenly, to my unspeakable terror, I noticed that I had cut through the little finger of my (right or left?) hand, so that it was only hanging on by its skin. I felt no pain, but great fear. I did not venture to say anything to my nurse, who was only a few paces distant, but I sank down on the nearest seat and sat there incapable of casting another glance at my finger. At last I calmed down, took a look at the finger, and saw that it was entirely uninjured.'" In a footnote, Freud adds the patient's later "correction" of the hallucinatory experience: "'I don't believe I was cutting the tree. That was a confusion with another recollection, which must also have been hallucinatorily falsified, of having made a cut in a tree with my knife and of blood having come out of the tree.'"

Freud comments: ". . . This hallucination belongs to the period in which he brought himself to recognize the reality of castration and it is perhaps to be regarded as actually marking this step. Even the small correction made by the patient is not without interest. If he had a hallucination of the same dreadful experience which Tasso, in his *Gerusalemme Liberata*, tells of his hero Tancred [who unwittingly slashed a tree in which his beloved Clorinda was imprisoned, causing her blood to flow from the cut], we shall perhaps be justified in reaching the interpretation that the tree meant a woman to my little patient as well. Here, then, he was playing the part of his father, and was connecting his mother's familiar haemorrhages with the castration of women, which he now recognized, — with the 'wound.'"[120]

The tree dominating the Act I set, with Wotan's sword embedded to the hilt, constitutes an emblem of parental intercourse.[121] That primal act has brought all others in its train, for it was the act by which Siegmund and Sieglinde were conceived. The role of the father consists in training the son for manhood, which means to be like the father, to do all that father does — with one single, terrible exception. The son must not repeat the paternal intercourse with mother. Yet the wish is primordial and overwhelming, and Wotan, colluding in the act he will later punish, has left his sword in the tree for his son to retrieve. The collusion flows naturally from the role Wotan plays in the overall fantasy: an element of the image complex representing the whole (we might well say *gesamt*) Wagnerian psyche. Thus he is torn by both the son's desire, on the one hand, and the superego's imperative to punish on

---

[120] Sigmund Freud, "Anal Erotism and the Castration Complex," *Standard Edition*, vol. XVII, pp. 85, 86.
[121] A parallel fantasy of incest between father and daughter is adumbrated in Wotan's thrusting his sword home on the occasion of Sieglinde's wedding to Hunding.

the other. The sword cannot fail because it possesses magic that doubtless stands for the magic ability of the penis to become erect. But Wotan's punishment of Siegmund's incestuous act is to withdraw that magic just at the critical moment, so the weapon shatters in combat with Hunding. Alongside the central theme of castration as punishment of Oedipal wishes, there is the fear (noted in the foregoing chapter) that the normal detumescence of the penis after orgasm amounts itself to a type of castration.

The final levels of solution are embodied in the life of Siegfried. First he will forge (or re-forge) the sword that has shattered in Siegmund's grasp, so that (at least according to the internal logic of Wagner's narrative, which we are obliged to accept) he creates himself by establishing his own sexuality. Not Wotan's "magic," but Siegfried's revolutionary skill as smith makes the sword strong. This could mean that Siegfried maintains erection by virtue of his own strength, and his lack of fear. He is no longer vulnerable to castration (though he can be stabbed in the back). Thus, Siegfried's fearlessness represents the liberation of the self from the strictures of the superego. Siegfried can accomplish what Wotan cannot, since his father's law means nothing to him. He can awaken the Brünnhilde Wotan has been obliged to put to sleep.

The progress from father to son in the temporal flow of the plot appears as a movement forward in time. Wotan brings forth Siegmund, who in turn fathers Siegfried. But the hope that the ultimate Oedipal solution, overthrow of the superego, lies in the future is an illusion. *The individual begins life free of a superego, while the future brings him ever more under its domination. Moral freedom is found only in a return to infancy.*

Thus, the figures of Wotan, Siegmund and Siegfried represent a sequence of progressively younger projections of the self. Wotan's wish to recreate himself as Siegfried is the regressive wish to return to the infancy in which he enjoyed omnipotence, free from the strictures of "law." Beneath the movement forward in time on the surface of the plot is the deeper wish to return to a liberated past.

To the extent that the forward-looking project to create (to become) Siegfried contains the backward-looking meaning of regression to infancy, future is equivalent to past. Wagner, profoundly dissatisfied with the hollow, bourgeois, commercial (in his view "Judaic") present, was obsessed with an inflated vision of the future. Siegfried represented the "man of the future," free of the strictures binding modern man. *The Ring* was the music of the future, the artwork of the future, that *Gesamtkunstwerk* whose mission was to reintegrate the arts and re-fuse mankind into a harmonious social whole. As a concept and a movement, Wagnerism in the second half of the 19th Century was synonymous with a kind of futurism. If the present was given over to exploitation and Philistinism, the Wagnerian future promised economic, artistic and sexual liberation.

It is striking that, with the exception of *The Flying Dutchman*, all Wagner's operas — the canon of his futurism — depict the Middle Ages. Wagner shared the fashionable Romantic nostalgia for the medieval world. Even Marx regarded the medieval economy as something of a lost ideal, contrasting the human interdependence and mutual obligation on the feudal manor to the exploitative and alienating "cash nexus" to which human relations had degenerated in modern times.

Wagner's futurism arrayed in medieval garb with all the trappings appears less paradoxical in light of the thematic idea that regeneration entails a circular return to a remote past. Wagner looks forward only to find what was once possessed but now is lost.

Typically Romantic, he bemoans the loss of "nature." Redemption lies in the future, but necessitates a return to nature, our connection with which has been sundered. "He who longs to return to nature," Wagner writes in *The Artwork of the Future*, "and who is hence unsatisfied in the modern present, finds not only in the totality of nature, but above all in man's nature, as it presents itself to him historically, those images which, when he beholds them, enable him to reconcile himself to life in general. In this nature he recognizes an image of all future things, already formed on a small scale; to imagine this scale expanded to its furthest compass lies within the conceptual limits of the impulse of his need for nature." [122] Past and future thus are identical.

The paradox of this equivalence is explained by Norman O. Brown. The ultimate return to nature would be regression to the animal state. "The difference between men and animals," Brown explains, "is repression. Under conditions of repression, the repetition-compulsion establishes a fixation to the past, which alienates the neurotic from the present and commits him to the unconscious quest for the past in the future. Thus neurosis exhibits the quest for novelty, but underlying it, at the level of the instincts, is the compulsion to repeat. In man, the neurotic animal, the instinctual

---

[122] Trans. in Oliver Strunk, *Source Readings in Music History: The Romantic Era* (New York, 1965), p. 138.

compulsion to repeat turns into its opposite, the quest for novelty, and the unconscious aim of the quest for novelty is repetition."[123] Time itself, which one assumes not to exist for animals, who experience life only in the eternal present, is the product of man's neurotic essence. "Repression generates historical time by generating an instinct-determined fixation to the repressed past, and thus setting in motion a forward-moving dialectic which is at the same time an effort to recover the past. In that perspective on man's history the crucial psychoanalytic concept is fixation to the past."[124]

Just as the Wagnerian future lies in return to what he perceived as the "natural" past, the future of art lies in return to the principles of the art of the Greeks. "To this, to this art of all-loving Mother Nature's favored children, those most beautiful human beings whose proud mother holds them up to us, even in these nebulous and hoary days of our present fashionable culture, as an undeniable and triumphant proof of what she can do — to the splendid art of the Greeks we look, to learn from intimate understanding of it how the art work of the future must be constituted! Mother Nature has done all she could — she has borne the Hellenes, nourished them at her breasts, formed them through her maternal wisdom; now she sets them before us with maternal pride and out of maternal love calls to us all: 'This I have done for you; now, out of love for yourselves, do what you can.'"[125]

[123] Norman O. Brown, *Life Against Death* (Wesleyan University Press, 1959), p. 92.
[124] *Ibid.*, p. 103.
[125] Trans. in Strunk, *op. cit.*, p. 139.

Not coincidentally, this paean to Greek naturalism is pitched mythologically. The return urged is to *mother nature*. The way forward is return to the past, and each person's ultimate past is mother's womb. Wagner's representation of sexual liberation in his man of the future, Siegfried, embodies the wish to return to the polymorphously perverse mode of infancy, the human being in the "state of nature." Futurism thus veils regression. Interest is displaced from what *is* (the present) onto what *is not* (past or future). In this sense, the essence of the Romantic is denial — denial of the temporal present through either nostalgia or hope, denial of the ordinariness of life through grandiose fantasy of the heroic. Otto Rank explains, "The true hero of the romance is, therefore, the ego, which finds itself in the hero by reverting to the time when the ego was itself a hero, through its first heroic act, i.e., the revolt against the father. The ego can only find its own heroism in the days of infancy, and it is therefore obliged to invest the hero with its own revolt, crediting him with the features which made the ego a hero."[126]

Heroic inflation, nostalgia, and futurism thus equally deny reality. Reality is the instinctual wish. But reality is also repression — i.e., the impossibility of acting out instinctual wishes. Act I of *Walküre* is a crucible of the imagination in which are tested the consequences of throwing off the strictures of taboo and acting out incestuous desires. Although this "reality" is itself a fantasy, it constitutes a provisional lifting of repression in that the incest wish rises into consciousness, undisguised. But the imagined

---

[126] Otto Rank, *The Myth of the Birth of the Hero*, Nervous and Mental Disease Monographs (New York, 1910), pp. 81, 82.

consequences of incest only reinforce the original repression. Siegmund's sword shatters and he dies at Hunding's hand. Sieglinde must flee to give birth in suffering that ends in her own death. Wotan is humiliated by his submission to Fricka and the disobedience of his daughter Brünnhilde. Brünnhilde, in turn, is punished with dismissal from Walhall, loss of divinity, loss of consciousness, and ignominious defloration by the first mortal to wake her. This horrendous chain of consequences justifies the anxiety haunting the prelude to *Walküre*, and forms the thematic bridge between the first two operas of *The Ring*.

In his later writings Freud relates his surprising discovery that, contrary to his earlier assumption, anxiety gives rise to repression, and not *vice versa*.[127] This distinction is for the present discussion more than a fine point of psychoanalytic theory; it offers a rationale for *Walküre*'s plot. We think of anxiety as a mental state, but it is characterized first of all by physiological symptoms, notably, constricted breathing and palpitation. This physiological reaction and its attendant mental state are the organism's response to perceived danger. Whereas in the case of realistic anxiety the perceived danger is external, in neurotic anxiety the perceived danger is internal. "What the neurotic is afraid of is evidently his own libido."[128] Freud adds that, "an instinctual demand is, after all, not dangerous in itself; it only becomes so inasmuch as it entails a real external danger, the danger of castration."[129] *Walküre*

---

[127] Sigmund Freud, "Anxiety and Instinctual Life," *New Introductory Lectures, Standard Edition*, vol. XXII, pp. 81-111; *Inhibitions, Symptoms, and Anxiety, Standard Edition*, vol. XX, pp. 87-175.

[128] Sigmund Freud, "Anxiety and Instinctual Life," p. 84.

[129] Sigmund Freud, *Inhibitions, Symptoms, and Anxiety*, p. 126.

begins with anxiety produced by the Oedipal wishes adumbrated in *Rheingold*, which culminated in Wotan's project to follow Erda underground between the first and second operas. Anxiety calls forth repression of the dangerous wishes so that the discomfort of the anxiety itself may be avoided, and repression, in turn, results in symptom formation.

In the figure of Wehwalt, the symptomatology produces a classic Romantic melancholy: that apparently aimless and baseless sense of oppression, *Weltschmerz*, and dissatisfaction with the reality of modern life. Karl Abraham explains how anxiety leads to melancholy. "Anxiety and depression are related to each other in the same way as are fear and grief. We fear a coming evil; we grieve over one that has occurred. A neurotic will be attacked with anxiety when his instinct strives for a gratification which repression prevents him from attaining; depression sets in when he has to give up his sexual aim without having obtained gratification. He feels himself unloved and incapable of loving, and therefore he despairs of his life and his future."[130]

Freud pursued Abraham's argument in "Mourning and Melancholia." Melancholia is, he concluded, a chronic state of mourning for an unconscious loss, moreover a loss which, by the unconscious process of identification, is an internal one. "The melancholic displays something else besides which is lacking in mourning—an extraordinary diminution in his self-regard, an impoverishment of his ego on a grand scale. In

---

[130] Karl Abraham, "Notes on the Psycho-analytic Investigation and Treatment of Manic-Depressive Insanity and Allied Conditions," (1911), *Selected Papers* (London, 1942), p. 137.

mourning it is the world which has become poor and empty; in melancholia it is the ego itself. The patient represents his ego to us as worthless, incapable of any achievement and morally despicable; he reproaches himself, vilifies himself and expects to be cast out and punished. He abases himself before everyone and commiserates his own relatives for being connected with anyone so unworthy."[131]   It is easy to see Wehwalt in this portrait of self-castigation. For him life is inexplicably bitter. Things go wrong. He is despised and abandoned. What he approves, others hate; what he hates, others love. Whatever he puts his hand to withers; where he looks for love, he finds only rejection. He is Wehwalt, Lord of Sorrow.

But the description fits Alberich in *Rheingold* as well. Alberich has had to renounce the erotic gratification that is the universal infantile aim; his very physical characteristics embody the consequences of his rejection by the Rhinemaidens.   Here is Freud's "diminution in his self-regard" with a vengeance: Alberich is a dwarf. He has been emptied of worth, his ego "impoverished," and he can fill his emptiness only with the gold he seizes and hoards, symbolic feces he refuses stubbornly to relinquish. Wehwalt's diffuse, puzzling melancholy in *Walküre*, then, achieves a sharper focus in relation to Alberich's unambiguous and catastrophic loss in the preceding opera.   The figure of Wehwalt is Wagner's first step along the path of heroic transformation. Before *The Ring* has concluded, Alberich will become Siegfried, despised dwarf metamorphosed to exuberant hero.

---

[131] Sigmund Freud, "Mourning and Melancholia," *Standard Edition*, vol. XIV, p. 246.

Freud came to a surprising conclusion about the melancholic's representation of himself as worthless and despised, an extreme example of which is Wagner's characterization of Alberich. "If one listens patiently to a melancholic's many and various self-accusations, one cannot in the end avoid the impression that often the most violent of them are hardly at all applicable to the patient himself, but that with insignificant modification they do fit someone else, someone whom the patient loves or has loved or should love. Every time one examines the facts this conjecture is confirmed. So we find the key to the clinical picture: we perceive that the self-reproaches are reproaches against a loved object which have been shifted away from it on to the patient's own ego."[132] Melancholy (or depression) is, then, mourning the loss of a loved person, or the loss of love, but it is also an attack against the beloved for causing such pain. Repression turns the unconscious reproach inward against the self as surrogate. As Freud puts it, "The shadow of the object fell upon the ego, and the latter could henceforth be judged by a special agency, as though it were an object, the forsaken object. In this way an object-loss was transformed into an ego-loss and the conflict between the ego and the loved person into a cleavage between the critical activity of the ego and the ego as altered by identification."[133]

Freud's clinical observations suggest that the source of Wehwalt's melancholy is parental neglect, and that his self-accusations have as their real objects the mother and father who have abandoned him. Self-castigation is inappropriate

---

[132] *Ibid.*, p. 248.
[133] *Ibid.*, p. 249.

for an epic hero. And behind Wehwalt stands the melancholic Wagner, expressing in letter after letter the same depression, the same sense of himself as misfit, as alien, as rejected man of sorrows, just as inappropriate in a man who considered himself a messianic genius. Wagner's periodic depression appears to have been masking profound anger at his sense of abandonment by his mother and both his fathers.

The self-accusation of Wehwalt as consistently failing where he most wishes to succeed, combined with the dwarvish image of Alberich, appears in this light as Wagner's unconscious anger at Geyer turned inward against himself. For Wagner was enormously successful as an artist, even if his talents were insufficiently recognized. Geyer, however, the hack, had abandoned the boy (by dying) when he most needed his father, at the beginning of latency, with its goal of replacing Oedipal ambitions with paternal identification. Wehwalt's mother is dead; in the life of the psyche, when Oedipal wishes are renounced, mother is as good as dead. This is how Wagner must unconsciously have experienced that aloofness of his mother's about which he speaks so nonchalantly in *Mein Leben*. Melancholy, then, which is a condition of mourning for the lost object, is also a mourning for renounced and repressed instinctual wishes. Thus Wotan, a melancholic on an even grander scale than Wehwalt, in his long farewell mourns the loss of Brünnhilde, embodying the Oedipal wish he must put to sleep, and *Walküre*, which began in restless anxiety, ends in brooding (if rapturous) melancholy, a progression that parallels Abraham's theoretical scheme.

Since the figures of Wehwalt and Wotan are fictional projections of the Wagnerian psyche, they are not to be diagnosed like psychoanalytic patients. Real persons differ from fictional projections fundamentally in their relation to symptoms. Whereas a real person *displays* symptoms, whose function is to mask and substitute for a concealed inner conflict, and which can therefore serve the analyst as a system of clues to that concealment, the fictional projection *is itself* a symptom. In fact it is *only* a symptom, since there is no reality behind the image, whether in words, pictures, or actors on a stage. "Wehwalt" is wholly contained in Wagner's text. There is nothing else to him. Likewise, nothing more can be discovered about Wotan than appears in the text. He cannot lie on a couch and give up more of himself. He has no psyche to reveal; he consists only of the words on the page. It makes sense to describe Wehwalt not so much as melancholic, but *as melancholia*. The application of either clinical term, however, is an analogy, not a diagnosis.

This analogy illuminates the transformation of Wehwalt into Siegmund. Incestuous love for his sister, one might say, transfigures melancholic Wehwalt into manic Siegmund, for melancholia appears typically as half of an alternating cycle of depression and elation—a syndrome known as the manic-depressive, or cyclothymic.[134] It is obvious enough why Wehwalt's mood might change from glum to gay at the prospect of his first successful seduction. That the transformation is not simply of mood, however, but of character is signaled by his change of name. He is reborn. Yet the circumstances of his life do not warrant optimism. They

---

[134] Or currently, *bipolar.*

have not (the seduction excepted) changed for the better. Quite the reverse. He makes his entrance pursued by enemies, and he exits the same way, his flight destined this time to end in death. Wehwalt's luck, so bitterly belabored earlier in the act, has not changed with his name. But his outlook has. Winter storms give way to spring, enmity gives way to love, defeat gives way (in his mind) to victory. Since the audience of *Walküre* knows the unhappy outcome, Siegmund's enthusiasm is made poignant by the certainty of his doom.

Wehwalt lives in the shadow of Wotan (the empty Wolf's skin), and his melancholy is directly connected with Wotan's disappearance, experienced as abandonment. Reborn as Siegmund, however, he escapes the dictates of his father, which forbid incestuous love for his sister, and threaten castration. How much Siegmund's exuberance resembles the manic phase of *cyclothymia* is apparent from Abraham's characterization of the symptomatology: "We see that the manic patient has thrown off the yoke of his superego, which now no longer takes up a critical attitude towards the ego, but has become merged in it. The difference between ego and superego has now disappeared. For this reason Freud takes the view that in the manic condition the patient is celebrating a triumph over the object he once loved and then gave up and introjected. The 'shadow of the object' which had fallen on his ego has passed away. He is able to breathe freely once more, and he gives himself up to his sense of regained freedom with a kind of frenzy."[135]

---

[135] Karl Abraham, "Development of the Libido," *Selected Papers*, p. 471.

Siegmund's unrealistic optimism and the sense of invincibility his magic sword lends him also display the typical attitude of the manic phase. "The patients often have an excessive feeling of power, measuring it not by actual performance but by the violence of their instincts, which they are now able to perceive in an unusual degree. Fairly frequently there appear grandiose ideas which are very similar to children's boasts about their knowledge and power."[136] The manic personality derives its exuberance by a return to the childish state of freedom from inhibitions of the superego. "The removal of inhibitions renders accessible once more old sources of pleasure which had been suppressed; and this shows how deeply mania is rooted in the infantile."[137] The reunion of brother and sister bears in itself the meaning of a return to childhood. Siegmund's erotic relation to his sister acts out that wish Alberich was compelled to renounce.

Siegmund's "Winter Storms" aria builds on the parallel between his own and spring's rebirth. The extended and provocative metaphor of "brother" Spring united ecstatically with "sister" Love signals that "Frosty Winter's suspension" (as Sieglinde puts it) has reference to the lifting of the repression under which this instinctual incestuous love has lain dormant. It is liberated by regression and rebirth. "This manic state, in which libidinal impulses of both kinds have access to consciousness, once more establishes a condition which the patient has experienced before — in early childhood. Whereas in the depressive patient everything tends to the negation of life, to death, in the manic patient life begins

---

[136] Karl Abraham, "Notes on . . . Manic-Depressive Insanity . . .," p. 151.
[137] Ibid., p. 150.

anew. The manic patient returns to a stage in which his impulses had not succumbed to repression, in which he foresaw nothing of the approaching conflict. It is characteristic that such patients often say that they feel themselves 'as though newborn.'"[138] The regressive nature of Wotan's project is clearer still in the ultimate case of the childlike Siegfried.

But Wotan, too, regresses. With Fricka, he plays the role of naughty boy. His interest in Siegmund's affair (vicarious and pandering, not to say voyeuristic) bears out Abraham's observation that in the manic phase the superego is merged in the ego. It is Wotan's sword Siegmund uses, after all. It is Wotan's plan that brother and sister find one another. It is Wotan's wish that they consummate their love, and do so with impunity. The incestuous wish, "Wotan's innermost mind," is embodied in the figure of Brünnhilde, whose own childishness is given voice in her celebrated gibberish, "Hojotoho! Hojotoho!" Wotan's total identification with Siegmund is clear to the perceptive Fricka, who dismisses the claim that his son is independent of him. "In him," she replies, "I find only you, for only through you is he defiant."

Siegmund has accomplished what Wotan longs for: open, shameless acting out of the incest wish. For if Wotan has had intercourse with Earth Mother Erda, he has done so furtively, in the dark underground, between operas. A burden is lifted when his son accomplishes directly what he cannot, a relief expressed movingly in the sudden shift from intense, strident music leading to Fricka's indignant question *"Wann ward es*

---

[138] *Ibid.*, p. 149.

erlebt, daß leiblich Geschwister sich liebten?" ("When have we ever lived to see blood brother and sister as lovers?") to the idyll (the "Winter Storms" motif) accompanying Wotan's disarming and lapidary reply, *"Heut' — hast du's erlebt!"* ("Today — you've seen it!").[139] The rhetoric and the tender music lull us (and Wotan) momentarily into an illusory sense of triumph.

But Fricka carries the day. Stridency is redoubled in her rejoinder, for she in effect sounds the gods' death knell, and so anticipates the fiery conclusion of *The Ring*, twilight of the gods. "Is it then all over for the eternal gods, since you conceived that wild breed of Volsungs?" Incest, not just the theft of the Rheingold, sows the seeds of their ruin. "Laughing stock of men, shorn of our power, we gods would meet our destruction, were the bold maiden to fail to avenge today my sacred, glorious right."

When Fricka demands Wotan's pledge to remove divine protection from Siegmund — which he yields only grudgingly, like a sulking adolescent — Wagner's stage directions describe in essence a grieving melancholic. "Wotan: (throwing himself in terrible depression and inner rage onto a rocky seat) 'Take the pledge!'" As Brünnhilde enters, he maintains this attitude of melancholy, like Dürer's allegory, head on hand, "sunk in dismal brooding." He expresses the melancholic's inflated conviction that no shame matches his, no wretch has ever been more down-cast than he. "Oh holy shame! Oh ignominious sorrow! Suffering of Godhead! Suffering of

---

[139] My trans. The colloquial effect of the two contractions in *"Heut' — hast du's erlebt!"* sheds a sudden, humanizing and sympathetic light on the character of Wotan at this juncture.

Godhead! Endless wrath! Eternal grief! I am the saddest of all!" ("*O heilige Schmach! O schmälicher Harm! Götternot! Götternot! Endloser Grimm! Ewiger Gram! Der traurigste bin ich von allen!*") Though this speech borders on incoherence, it is certainly grandiose. Wotan plays the grieving melancholic because Siegmund, the alter ego who has accomplished his secret wish, is doomed, "walking dead" as it were, and with his demise, Wotan relinquishes his last illusion of power. Most pathetic are those curt, bitter words cited above, "Take the pledge!" ("*Nimm den Eid!*"), which the god utters in abysmal dejection, like the muffled beat of a funeral drum.

Incongruously (or should we say pathetically?), only moments later he scruples to confide in Brünnhilde for fear of losing the power he has just relinquished unconditionally to Fricka. "Father! Father! Tell me what troubles you . . . Trust me!" implores Brünnhilde.

"Were I to give it breath, would I not loosen the mastering grasp of my will?" Wotan muses.

Brünnhilde reassures him; since she is an aspect of his own psyche — his will — speaking to her is no more than speaking to himself. That Brünnhilde's true signification is Wotan's unconscious Oedipal wishes is suggested when Wotan concludes that his words are as good as unspoken under these circumstances, and shall remain so. "Let that which I've said openly to no one, then, stay unexpressed forever: I take counsel only with myself, talking with you." ("*Was keinem in Worten ich kunde, unausgesprochen bleib' es denn ewig: mit mir nur rat' ich, red' ich zu dir.*") Wotan's reticence here is at odds with his character, for at no other point in *The Ring* does he hesitate to express his thoughts. The inconsistency is resolved, though, if we take "the unexpressed," "the unspoken," "*das Unausgesprochene*," to signify the repressed. The Oedipal fantasy, unspoken, but embodied in the figure of Brünnhilde standing beside him, is to be realized through the plan on which Wotan's second-act monologue focuses—the self-creation of the hero, the project to become father of oneself.

What does Wotan's monologue accomplish? Ostensibly, the god is filling Brünnhilde in on the background of the dilemma forcing him to intervene against Siegmund on Hunding's behalf. But since Brünnhilde—as both agree—is an aspect of Wotan's mind, the fictional device of monologue represents the process of Wotan's thought.[140] What appears as a

---

[140] Dismissing the validity of such an interpretation, Michael Tanner, *Wagner*, (Princeton University Press, 1996), p. 125, writes " . . . Wagner uses his ever-developing powers to portray someone who has to recognize that the fundamental issues with which he is confronted are all within himself . . . This is not to say, as has been claimed, that the *Ring* is the anatomy of a single psyche: to see the other characters as projections of elements in Wotan is to effect a disastrous simplification and, in the end, de-dramatisation of the work." Tanner's assertion, made in this single sentence, and neither supported here, nor further developed elsewhere in the book, is vulnerable on several counts. 1.) It ignores Wagner's own suggestion to this effect implied in Brünnhilde's rationale, "*Zu Wotans Willen sprichst du, sagst du mir, was du willst; wer bin ich, wär' ich dein Wille nicht?*" ("You are speaking to your will when you tell me your will: Who am I if not your will? "), and in Wotan's concurrence, quoted above. 2.) In the present study, it is not Wotan's psyche whose constituent elements are seen as projected in the various characters of the drama. Rather, Wotan *himself* is such an element. The psyche thus represented (whether construed as Wagner's or a fictional, generalized one) comprises Wotan as well as Brünnhilde and other characters of *The Ring*. 3.) The conclusion

narrative of past events is really the *memory* of those events. But in memory, facts are suspended in a medium of feeling permeated with significance beyond the facts themselves.

"As the pleasure of youthful love paled for me," he begins, "my spirit longed for power: driven by the rage of impetuous wishes, I won for myself the world." Repressed libido is displaced from erotic aims to power aims. Wotan's phrase "driven by the rage of impetuous wishes" (*"von jäher Wünsche Wüten gejagt"*), points to irrational, unconscious, instinctual energy, not rational choice. If he is driven by unconscious impulses, it is no wonder he also incurs unconscious guilt. "Unknowingly false, I practiced falsehood, brought about through covenant that which concealed evil: cunningly Loge enticed me, who then wanderingly vanished." Wotan is referring to his contract with the giants to build Walhall in exchange for Freia — an expedient bargain urged by Loge, who promised in the meantime to find a substitute for Wotan's sister-in-law in order to free her from the giants. But how was Wotan "unknowingly false?" Perhaps he placed unwarranted trust in the fire god, but he certainly entered the agreement with eyes (one eye, at least) open to the risk. Wotan's words, however, are provocatively vague — abstractions and circumlocutions: "falsehood," "covenant," "that which

---

that such an interpretation "effect[s] a disastrous simplification and . . . de-dramatisation of the work," ignores the intricate complexities of the human psyche, and indeed, the intense *drama* going on continually within it. On the contrary, if anything effects an oversimplification, it is viewing characters of *The Ring* as if they were real, individual people, with passions and personal motives, for with the exception of the figure of Wotan, whose character *is* drawn with depth and complexity, *The Ring*'s *dramatis personae* tend frankly to be two-dimensional.

concealed evil." We are left to infer he means the bargain struck with the giants.

If Wotan's words do not quite fit the overt situation, though, they are on the other hand applicable to a covert one. Meanings taken loosely, the words suggest the unconscious guilt of Oedipal wishes. The wish for intercourse ("covenant," "contract") with the mother is desired, yet conceals evil. Thus, Wotan gives a sexual coloring to Loge's trickery: enticement, seduction (*Verlockung*)—appropriate, since Loge embodies libido. He has "wanderingly vanished" ("*schweifend . . . verschwand*") only in that libido is repressed. For Loge (fire, passion) is in reality ever-present.

Ever-present and inextinguishable, as Wotan bears witness. "I didn't wish, however, to renounce love; powerful, I yet longed for love." This contradiction of his earlier statement that when youthful love had paled he had substituted power-lust is resolved by Freud's concept of "the return of the repressed," a normal phase of neurosis. Wotan's ascribing his troubles to Loge's trickery is reminiscent of Freud's description of the mechanism. "A return like this of what has been repressed," he writes, "is to be expected with particular regularity when a person's erotic feelings are attached to the repressed impressions—when his erotic life has been attacked by repression. In such cases the old Latin saying . . . 'You may drive out Nature with a pitch-fork, but she will always return' . . . does not describe the highly remarkable manner of that return, which is accomplished by what seems like a piece of malicious treachery. It is precisely what was chosen as the instrument of repression—like the 'pitchfork' of the Latin saying—that becomes the vehicle for the return: in and behind the repressing force, what is repressed proves itself victor in the end."[141]   Wotan's return of "longing for love" refers, as he goes on to say (after briefly recounting his extortion of the ring from Alberich), to his intercourse with Erda, which constitutes the carrying out of the Oedipal wish. In keeping with Freud's observation, the Oedipal fantasy is inextricably mixed with Wotan's drive to power. To illustrate his principle, Freud cites a well-known etching that depicts, "An ascetic monk [who] has fled, no doubt from the temptations of the world, to the image of the crucified Saviour. And now the cross sinks down like a shadow, and in its place, radiant, there rises instead the image of a voluptuous, naked woman, in the same crucified attitude."[142]

Here is how Wotan tells it: "She who knows all, what once was, Erda, the sacredly wisest Vala, counseled me off from the ring, warned of the everlasting end. Concerning the end I wished to know more; but saying nothing, the woman disappeared." This is double talk, of course, but significant double talk. Knowledge and *carnal knowledge*, that is, are the same. "To know was the god's desire; into the womb of the world I swung myself down, with love-magic forced the Vala, disturbed her pride of knowledge, so that she yielded me speech." The interchangeable sense of *knowledge* and *carnal knowledge* is reflected in the location of the encounter, "the womb of the world." "Erda" is the earth; "the womb of the world" and her womb are symbolically identical. Wotan *forces* Erda with "love-magic" to *yield* him speech, knowledge. And — indeed — the episode leaves her with child. "I got

---

[141] Sigmund Freud, "Delusions and Dreams in Jensen's *Gradiva*," *Standard Edition*, vol. IX, p. 35.
[142] *Ibid.*, p. 35.

knowledge from her;" and, adds Wotan waggishly, "from me, though, she got something left in pledge: the world's wisest woman bore me, Brünnhilde, you."

Wotan's shadowy encounter with Erda in the womb of the earth ("*in den Schoss der Welt*") is the Oedipal wish acted out in fantasy in contrast to the overt incest of Siegmund and Sieglinde. Consider the logic of Wotan's scheme for Walhall. He has raised Brünnhilde and her eight sisters, he explains, to help him fend off the disaster Erda has foretold. "Through you Valkyries I wished to avert that which the Vala gave me to fear: an ignominious end for the eternal ones" ("*Durch euch Walküren wollt' ich wenden, was mir die Wala zu fürchten schuf: ein schmäliches Ende der Ew'gen*"). The word *schuf* (imp. of *schaffen*) — translated above simply as *gave* — has a double meaning: "to provide, furnish with," but also, "create, produce." So Wotan's formulation may suggest that Erda has not merely informed him of the ignominious end of the gods, but is herself implicated in that dénouement, the destruction of Walhall, the "*Götterdämmerung*." The Oedipal wish calls forth castration. Walhall bears the meaning of the erect penis. It is a logical nicety that erection is maintained by Brünnhilde, the Oedipal wish, while acting out that wish entails castration. Brünnhilde gathers fallen warriors to man Walhall against the foretold onslaught of Alberich's army of darkness. Brünnhilde's mode of maintaining Walhall's (the erection's) potency — raising fallen warriors — hardly requires further comment. So long as the wish remains a fantasy, so long as mother remains a longed for, rather than a possessed object, erection is maintained. Here, the mere wish gets out of hand. Wotan assumes he controls it. But Brünnhilde (Wotan's will, as she has declared), swayed by Siegmund's passion, defies his command and promotes the incestuous *act*, not just the wish. The wish itself must now be repressed; Brünnhilde must be made to sink into the unconsciousness of sleep.[143]

Wotan experiences his dilemma metaphorically as fetters. He is caught between countervailing forces, the threat of Alberich on the one hand, and on the other the compacts, *Verträge*, he has made in the framework of the law that lends him his power. But Brünnhilde sees to the heart of the matter. Wotan's dilemma is not external.

He is torn by inner forces. *Zwiespalt* ("conflict") is the word she employs here, and in Act III. This is why Wotan fears not Alberich's army of the night itself, but the possibility that Alberich might corrupt his own warriors in Walhall to rebel against him. "The end threatens us through Alberich's horde: with envious fury the Nibelung threatens me: yet not his nocturnal host do I fear now; my heroes would procure me a victory. Only if ever he won back the ring, then Walhall would be lost: he who cursed love, he alone would enviously employ the ring's runes to the endless disgrace of all who are noble; he would steal from me the spirits of the heroes; the bold ones themselves he would compel in battle; with their strength he would war against me."

Wotan's fear of rebellion masks the fear that his own impulses will betray the conscious strictures (in the allegorical scheme we are here pursuing) dictated by the superego. Instinctual forces are the source both of his strength (sexual desire, erection) and his downfall. But the grandiosity of his fear arises from the overvaluation typically assigned cathected

---

[143] See *Appendix*.

objects: the longed for mother, inflated to omniscient goddess, the earth itself; the penis magnified into a fortress, its detumescence the equivalent of universal conflagration, *"Götterdämmerung;"* the controlling power of the anal sphincter, exalted in the symbol of the Nibelung's ring to magical omnipotence.

By virtue of overvaluation of the anal sphincter, Wotan perceives his life as hanging by the thread of possession of the ring. For control of the anal sphincter means control of the forces that betray from within. If Alberich possesses the ring, these forces, the army of darkness, the nocturnal horde, impulses, can overwhelm the superego and inundate the world with filth. Alberich is but the obverse of Wotan. Overvaluation of the ring's power is underscored in the next opera when Siegfried, *whose project Wotan has intended to be acquiring the ring, in fact treats the ring with indifference*, and focuses his attention on Brünnhilde. Siegfried thrusts instinctively to the essential matter, although it costs him his life. Death is not to be avoided; only its form is in doubt. Timorous, morbid clutching to life constitutes the ultimate form of anal retention. The twilight of the gods *will* come.

Divided against himself, Wotan is ambivalent toward his rebellious impulses. Though he has just expressed apprehension, in the next breath he makes it clear he means to liberate those same impulses in producing the self-created hero. If impulses are Alberich, they are also Siegfried.

"Only one could do what I dare not: one hero, whom I never condescended to help; who, stranger to the god, free of his favor, unconscious, uncompelled, of his own necessity, with his own weapon, might accomplish the deed that I must shun, that I never counseled him to, even though my wish wished for it alone." Despite his horror of Alberich's horde and his fear it might corrupt his own warriors, Wotan longs for this enemy to oppose his conscious will. "Him who would fight for me against the god, the friendly enemy—how shall I find him? How might I create the free one, whom I never shielded, who in his own defiance is yet dearest to me?" In spite of himself, Wotan recognizes what Brünnhilde never doubts— that the god's authentic self is allied against the strictures of godhead.

The consequence of this emotional schism is that Wotan's authentic self seems alienated from his conscious self, and can only appear objectified in external figures: Siegmund, Brünnhilde, Siegfried. "How should I create the other, who would be no longer I, and would of himself accomplish that which alone I wish for?" Wotan longs for the free scope of shameful impulses. In others, sexual impulses, particularly Oedipal wishes, seem desirable and free from guilt. He defends as wholly natural the instinctual union of Siegmund and Sieglinde: "Was it so terrible what that couple did, united in love by spring? The magic of love enchanted them: whom should I punish for the power of love?" (*"Was so Schlimmes schuf das Paar, das liebend einte der Lenz? Der Minne Zauber entzückte sie: wer büßt mir der Minne Macht?"*) His own impulses, however, are hateful and disgusting to him. "Oh divine anguish! Terrible shame! I loathe finding ever only myself in everything I create!" To avoid the shame of his own desires, he must project them onto another.

This strategy has begotten Siegmund. "But the Volsung, Siegmund, does he not act for himself?" asks Brünnhilde obligingly. Wotan's reply seems oblique at first. "Freely I roamed the forests with him; I provoked him boldly to act against the counsel of the gods: against the vengeance of the gods now only the sword protects him that a god's favor granted." Wotan's answer, though veiled, is finally clear enough. No, Siegmund does not act freely, since Wotan has taught him rebellion and put the sword in his hand. A similar relation exists in *Götterdämmerung* between Siegfried and Brünnhilde. In the "prologue" to that final opera, where Siegfried takes leave of Brünnhilde, the hero self-effacingly attributes all his glories to her. "Shall I still do deeds through your virtues alone?" he asks. "You choose my battles, my victories redound upon you: on your horse's back, in the shelter of your shield — I consider myself Siegfried no longer: I am only Brünnhilde's arm!" If Siegfried is Brünnhilde's arm, and Brünnhilde in turn Wotan's inner most will, then Siegfried, too, is only a part of Wotan. Siegfried is Wotan's infancy.

Logically, Siegfried is no freer of Wotan's will than Siegmund. Yet Siegfried accomplishes what Siegmund and Wotan cannot. The watershed is Brünnhilde's sleep. Siegmund is on one side, Siegfried, on the other. Siegfried is free only because he acts unconsciously, for Brünnhilde's sleep represents repression. Thus, he is a critical distance further from Wotan's consciousness than Siegmund. Specifically, Siegmund who acts out the displaced incest wish with sister corresponds to the adolescent; Siegfried, who acts out the primal incest wish with mother disguised in the person of Brünnhilde, corresponds to the infant on the far side of that impenetrable curtain of infantile amnesia concealing the unrestrained impulses of earliest life. His lack of fear is the result of this distance from Wotan, infancy's freedom from the as yet undeveloped superego.

"Are you then taking the victory from Siegmund?" Brünnhilde asks. Wotan's answer is once more oblique. "I touched Alberich's ring; greedily I held the gold! That curse, which I fled, now flees not me: what I love I must abandon, murder whom I love, deceivingly betray him who trusts me!" But now Wotan launches into a bitter nonsequitur whose illogicality raises an important question. In his despair, not only does he resign himself to but actually embraces the downfall of the gods, whose rescue was the only purpose of surrendering the ring in the first place. Röckel complained to Wagner of much the same inconsistency in the first opera. Newman paraphrases Röckel's objection: "When . . . in the *Rheingold*, Erda warns Wotan that *unless* he gives up the Ring the Gods will go down to destruction, surely the implication is that *if* he gives it up the Gods will be saved. Yet although Wotan surrenders the Ring the Gods are still doomed!"[144]

Newman considers this apparent contradiction a flaw, and attributes Wagner's "confusion" to his attempt to combine the *Siegfried* material with the downfall of the gods, which are unrelated in Teutonic mythology. Yet in his reply to Röckel, Wagner evinces no confusion. "I feel that, at a good performance," he writes confidently, "the most simple-minded spectator will be in no doubt as to that point." He concedes that the plot does not require the gods' downfall in

---

[144] Ernest Newman, vol. II, p. 359.

any legalistic sense. "No," he continues, "the necessity of this downfall springs from our innermost feelings, as it does from the innermost feelings of Wotan. It was thus important to justify this necessity by feeling: and this happens of itself when the feeling follows the total action, with all its simple, natural motives, in complete sympathy from beginning to end. When finally Wotan gives expression to this necessity he only says what we ourselves already feel must needs be."[145]

Newman comments: "It is manifest enough from this confused statement that the reason why Wagner does not give a plain answer to Röckel's plain question is that he cannot do so."[146] Newman's usually sound common sense abandons him here. Wagner's statement cannot accurately be characterized as "confused," though it may not be a model of Aristotelian logic either. Wagner is clear and determined on this point. Though logic says one thing, feeling says another. ". . . Anyone who has followed this prelude [i.e., *Rheingold*] sympathetically," Wagner declares, "not cudgeling his brains over it but letting the events themselves work on his feelings, must agree . . ." that the *inner* logic of the tetralogy, the logic of feeling, dooms the gods.

The logic of feeling speaks in the language of ambiguity and ambivalence, the ambivalence that Brünnhilde recognizes in Wotan's order to destroy Siegmund. "*Dein zwiespältig Wort,*" she calls it. It is the ambiguity and ambivalence of Wotan's surrender of the ring, simultaneously a victory and a shattering defeat. It is the ambiguous interplay of life and death, Eros and Thanatos. Ultimately, the triumph of

---

[145] Richard Wagner, letter to Röckel, quoted in Newman, vol. II, p. 359.
[146] Newman, vol. II, p. 360.

Thanatos is inevitable, and we alternately dread and long for it, as Wotan has armed Walhall against the downfall he now embraces. "Go your ways, then, imperious glory, glittering disgrace of godly pomp! Fall apart, what I have built! I abandon my work; only one thing do I still wish for: the end, the end!"

A pregnant pause ensues while Wotan meditates on what he has said. "And the end," he concludes, "will be seen to by Alberich!" The implication is that downfall will come of itself inexorably; whoever wishes it need but wait. Yet if Wotan and Alberich are doubles, in attributing the end to Alberich, Wotan attributes it logically to himself. Alberich is the dark, alienated portion of the self that openly renounces love to clutch at power. Love is freely spending and — without regret — yielding to the natural force of death. But power is the illusion of immortality, and the illusion of immortality has its foundation in the denial of life,[147] so that the will to power is wedded to morbidity.

Wotan's accusation that Alberich will see to destruction of the world is in essence a self-accusation; this equivalence is graphically manifest when the god threatens Brünnhilde for daring to resist Siegmund's downfall. "Ha, insolent one! Do you outrage me?. . . Do you, child, know my wrath?. . . In my bosom I harbor such rage as would throw into terror and chaos a world that once laughed for my delight." "Chaos," incidentally, translates the German *Wust*, which means also "rubbish," "filth," "dirt," "disgusting object," recalling the excremental aspects of Alberich's power. The rage stirring

---

[147] I.e., denial of its mortality.

inside Wotan can reduce the world to rubble and filth. His threat expresses the infantile fantasy of covering the world with feces (harbored not in his bosom, but his bowels). It is consistent that Wotan's furious threat is logically connected with filth, since, as Freud showed, sadism derives from the erotism of the anal stage. And as sadism and masochism are two sides of a single coin, Wotan's fury, directed against Brünnhilde and Siegmund, is inflicted (unconsciously, as it were) upon himself. "*Siegmund falle!*" Wotan's final command to Brünnhilde, is in reality a decree of self-castration.[148]

Ambivalence towards death—obsessive anxiety (exemplified in Wotan's building and manning of Walhall) and morbid longing—leads logically to the themes of the conclusion to Act II. Obviously, one theme is death. Brünnhilde is death's herald. Siegmund dies. But the keynote is sounded before Brünnhilde's annunciation of doom. In likening her own defiled body to a corpse, Sieglinde introduces a necrophiliac theme that will become even more pronounced in *Siegfried*.

Sieglinde's metaphor occurs in a passage surprising for another reason. She has, namely, just committed incest with her brother. She might be expected, in the wake of that act, to feel shame. And she does, though perversely. "Away! Away!" she urges her brother. "Flee the desecrated one! Impiously her arm clasps you; dishonored, shamed, this body is wasted: flee the corpse, let it go!"

Is her body a wasted, dishonored corpse because she has committed incest? On the contrary, her body is shamed in ever having yielded to the entirely lawful embraces of

---

[148] Cf. Klingsor in *Parsifal*.

Hunding, a man who never loved her. "May the wind blow her away who gave herself without honor to the noble one! [Siegmund] Since he, loving, embraced her, since she found most blessed pleasure, since totally she was loved by the man who totally awakened her love — in light of the sweetest delight of holiest consecration, that coursed totally through her soul and senses, horror and shuddering must grip the disgraced woman with terror over most horrible shame, that ever she obeyed that man [Hunding] who held her without love! Leave the lost soul; let her flee from you! I am cast out, devoid of honor! I must run from you, purest man; I must never belong to you, glorious man. I bring shame upon my brother, disgrace upon the wooing lover."

Although this passage is less clumsy in Wagner's artful German, it is just as tortuous and overblown. Through his mouthpiece Sieglinde, the unhappily married composer here vents his own rage and frustration at the loveless marriage in which he is trapped. The extreme and repetitive nature of the statement is rendered more emphatic by inversion of the conventional moral prohibition of incest. Even so, the spluttering quality of Sieglinde's speech does not ring true to her ostensible meaning. She protests overly; her topsy-turvy falls clearly into the category of denial. For the vehemence of her feeling is more appropriate to the incestuous act, than to the loveless marriage. Her denial here resembles Wotan's attempt to convince himself and Fricka that incest is harmless. Sieglinde puts more feeling into it, but the gist of her argument is the same. And destiny is equally unmoved. Sieglinde's inverted take on incest voices once again the son's wishful fantasy not only that he is the rightful possessor of his mother, but that mother is appreciative of father's displacement.

Later, Sieglinde falls into a swoon that mimics death, to all appearances actualizing what began as a metaphor. Siegmund notices the likeness when he wonders whether it was not Brünnhilde, herald of death, who with this death-like sleep intended to spare his sister the terrors of battle. "Lifeless she seems," he says, "who nevertheless lives." That the state of unconsciousness approximates death is indicated in Wagner's stage directions, which specify that Siegmund "listens for her breathing and convinces himself that she still lives." Siegmund holds her in his arms; sitting down, he lets her body sink with his, her head coming to rest in his lap. The stage directions continue: "Long silence, during which Siegmund bends with tender care over Sieglinde and kisses her forehead with a long kiss." This tableau — Siegmund bending over and kissing the unconscious Sieglinde — anticipates Brünnhilde's awakening in the next opera.

There are other parallels. Just before Sieglinde's swoon, she relays her hysterical fantasy of Hunding's vengeance, in which Siegmund is torn to pieces and devoured by her husband's dogs. The very howling of the dogs bespeaks the outrage of incest. "Boldly goaded the pack howls, barking wildly to heaven over the broken vows of marriage! . . . Listen, Oh listen! That is Hunding,s horn! His pack nears in powerful force: no sword avails against the horde of dogs: throw it away, Siegmund! . . . Terrible sight! The hounds bare their teeth after flesh; they care nothing for your noble appearance; the powerful teeth grip you by the feet — you fall — your sword is knocked in pieces. The ash-tree crashes down — its trunk splits!"

Sieglinde's fantasy in which Siegmund is devoured by dogs parallels Siegfried's battle with the dragon Fafner, the devourer. The fantasy of being devoured, followed by a love scene with a woman in a death-like state of unconsciousness, is an emblem of necrophilia. This perversion represents a psychic solution to the fear of coitus rooted in castration anxiety.

Ferenczi explains the general meaning of necrophilia. "Many neurotics unconsciously regard coitus as an activity which, either directly or subsequently, is calculated to injure life or limb, and in particular to damage the genital organ, i.e., an act in which are combined gratification and severe anxiety. Murder then at any rate partly sub-serves the purpose of avoiding anxiety by rendering the love-object incapable of inflicting injury; gratification can then be enjoyed undisturbed by castration anxiety. In these phantasies of aggression the woman is attacked in the first instance with external weapons (knife, dagger, or, in the case of throttling, with parts of the body which are not usually protected, i.e., the hand), following on which coitus is performed, that is to say, the penis is employed as weapon against a now harmless object."[149] Ferenczi associates neurotic anxiety over coitus

---

[149] Sandor Ferenczi, "On Unconscious Phantasies of Sexual Lust-Murder," section 3 of "Psychoanalysis of Sexual Habits," in *Selected Papers of Sandor Ferenczi: Further Contributions to the Theory and Technique of Psychoanalysis*, vol. II (New York, 1952), p. 279.

with the common fantasy of the *vagina dentata*, the vagina as a devouring mouth armed with teeth.[150]

The same elements occur in the disguised (and unconscious) fantasy of necrophilia of *The Ring*. Coitus is fraught with mortal dangers. One danger is the ferocious beast with teeth. The other is the fragility of the hero's sword. And if Sieglinde's prophecy of the shattering of her brother's sword does not adequately convey castration, she adds the otherwise gratuitous vision of the ash-tree, its trunk broken, crashing to the ground. The quiescent, unconscious woman, however, is no threat. In *Siegfried* the hero undoes Brünnhilde's breastplate with his sword, a gesture suggesting that (to use Ferenczi's words) "the penis is employed as weapon against a now harmless object." When the breastplate falls away, Siegfried steps back in amazement. "That is no man!" he cries, a line whose gentle humor may conceal a more potent meaning. The hero heaves an unconscious sigh of relief at the discovery that this is no man. After all, he is looking for a woman in the flames; why should he be surprised to find one?

---

[150] This is apparently the anxiety informing Isolde's likeness of herself to a corpse, while Tristan fearfully avoids so much as her glance. Isolde tells Brangäne scornfully that the hero, who is making himself scarce as their ship nears the Cornish coast "timidly flees the blow [of my glance] wherever he can, since he has won a corpse as bride for his lord! . . . Ask him yourself, this noble man, whether he dares approach me." Later in the act, Brangäne picks up a related thread when she asks rhetorically, "Where lives the man . . . who, seeing Isolde, would not happily, wholly die in Isolde?"

Brünnhilde appears *armed* like a man. Perhaps his reaction derives from the infantile theory that mother has a penis, a fantasy related to the *vagina dentata*, for the penis is a threat just as teeth are. The necrophiliac fantasy functions to disarm the woman of her ability to castrate. Siegfried's wry *"Das ist kein Mann!"* says, in effect, "Ah . . . this is, after all, only a harmless, castrated woman, whose penis I need not fear."

Of course Siegfried does come to fear Brünnhilde, and with good reason. That is the point. Unconscious, she need not be feared. But he learns the fear no one else could teach him the moment she awakens. Obviously, although Siegmund's scene with the unconscious Sieglinde *parallels* Siegfried's awakening of Brünnhilde, the scenes have opposite outcomes. In fact, Siegfried's awakening of Brünnhilde is like a reverse necrophiliac fantasy, although as such it only reaffirms the *need* for the fantasy. For Brünnhilde proves Siegfried's nemesis. Coitus harbors these mortal dangers after all.

Brünnhilde is Siegmund's nemesis also. Her very appearance heralds death. "Only those consecrated to death are served by my glance; whoever looks on me must depart the light of life." The Oedipal wish is like the face of the Gorgon: merely looking at it, consciously acknowledging it, is fatal. Brünnhilde's annunciation of Siegmund's imminent death and Siegfried's discovery of the sleeping Brünnhilde correspond to the alternatives inherent in the necrophiliac fantasy. The woman must be killed or she will kill.

All the themes of necrophilia are now repeated as Brünnhilde expatiates on the death she has come to announce. Siegmund will have the pleasurable company of "wish-maidens" —

maidens who, in fulfilling the wishes of fantasy, pose no threat to the anxious male. Siegmund seems willing enough. Will he meet Sieglinde there? Siegmund bridles when Brünnhilde tells him he will not, and reproaches her, "so youthfully and beautifully you shimmer in my gaze: yet how cold and hard I see you in my heart!" Brünnhilde becomes metaphorically his devourer. "Yet if you must feast on my pain, may my sorrow delight you; may my woe refresh your envious heart." ("*Doch mußt du dich weiden an meinem Weh, mein Leiden letze dich denn; meine Not labe dein neidvolles Herz.*") Conscience-stricken, Brünnhilde replies, "I see the pain that gnaws at your heart!" ("*Ich sehe die Not, die das Herz dir zernagt!*")

Sympathy does not placate Siegmund. He threatens to make actual Sieglinde's mere semblance of death. "None other than I shall touch the pure one while she lives: if I have fallen prey to death, I will kill the unconscious one first!" Drawing his sword to commit the act that would certainly bear resemblance to rape/murder, Siegmund voices the castration anxiety that underlies the fantasy. "This sword, that a deceiver fashioned for the faithful one; this sword, that would like a coward betray me against my enemy — if it will not avail against the enemy, at least it avails against the friend!"

His impulse to kill Sieglinde only because he must die — though it pretends to the nobility of saving her from defilement — is a bizarre idea. Sieglinde echoes the rape/murder fantasy when she pleads later in the act with both Siegmund and Hunding, "Murder me first!" Seeing Siegmund die when Wotan withdraws his protective magic, Sieglinde "sinks with a scream as though lifeless." Though

Brünnhilde has acquiesced to Siegmund's threat, it has failed in the long run. If the anxious son is not castrated and destroyed by the phallic mother, he is castrated and destroyed by the avenging father.

We see a similar necrophiliac theme implicit in *Rheingold* where "mother" earth's body swarms with Nibelungs, an image we encountered in "Judaism in Music," where Jews are pictured as maggots infesting the corpse of music. It is plausible that Wagner had fantasized Jews as maggots by association with his father's name, Geyer (vulture — i.e., carrion feeder). We noted in the foregoing chapter Wagner's concern that this bird be identifiable as the emblem on his autobiography. Like his father, Wagner was (to the age of 13 at least) a "Geyer," a vulture.[151]

H. Segal[152] offers a rationale for this fantasy. It proceeds, she argues, from profound emotional deprivation in early

---

[151] As noted, above, lacking his spontaneous associations, Wagner cannot be psychoanalyzed *in absentia*. The putative association of vulture and maggots is admittedly conjectural. Cf. Chapter II, p. 73, n. 78.

[152] H. Segal, "A Necrophiliac Phantasy," *International Journal of Psychoanalysis*, vol. 34 (London, 1953), pp. 98-101. Necrophilia gives the appearance of a tabooed subject, since it is barely touched in the psychoanalytic literature. Among the few items the bibliography comprises, most suggestive by far is Segal's paper, which while restricting itself to a single case history, and a fragmentary one at that, nevertheless outlines a general interpretation of the perversion. Ferenczi's contribution cited above adds an important theoretical dimension to Segal's clinical observations. Aside from these brief discussions, deserving mention are Ernest Jones, *On the Nightmare* (New York, 1951), which contains several pertinent comments, and Klaf and Brown, "Necrophilia, Brief Review and Case Report," *Psychiatric Quarterly*, vol. 32 (Utica, 1958), pp. 645-652. Although the reason for this psychoanalytic neglect may be that as an actual perversion necrophilia is encountered only infrequently in clinical

childhood (like that Wagner must have experienced). The deprived child feels there is neither love enough nor life to sustain both mother and infant as separate individuals. Normal separation anxiety is intensified to the point where separation means death for one or the other, since they cannot be alive simultaneously. Either mother or child must therefore be a corpse, and the child vacillates in his sense of who is the corpse and who the living Person. At times he is dead; at times his mother is. The childhood history of Segal's patient parallels Wagner's in several points. "Certainly the fact that my patient was the youngest of a biggish family, and remained the smallest when they grew up, as well as the fact that his parents were both poor and old by the time he was born, must have done a great deal to confirm this feeling that there was not enough life left for him." Wagner was the next youngest of a "biggish" family, and was, as has been remarked, undersized, except for his conspicuously large head. His parents were old when he was born; his father died after six months, his step-father, eight years later. His mother, distant and undemonstrative, alternately sent him away and abandoned him throughout his childhood.

Segal continues, "I have the impression that M. must have suffered a severe deprivation at the very start of his life. This deprivation was felt to be, or maybe indeed was, a threat to his very existence." Besides the general deprivation Wagner suffered at his mother's hands, one must add his legal father's putative rejection of him at birth that led his mother to that dangerous war-time journey, "a threat to his very existence."

---

practice, Segal's paper implies its prevalence as a theme in fantasy — which is our interest here.

Segal once more: "It must have led to an overwhelming destructiveness and greed. He felt that in phantasy he emptied his mother of all life and she became the corpse; this corpse he introjected and identified with himself. He said once, 'If I could remember so far back, I know what my first memory would be: I would remember realizing my mother's existence and feeling, *It is either you or I.*' And to this day this emotional situation persists in the form of his necrophiliac phantasy."

It is perhaps incorrect to speak of Wagner's character as essentially greedy, but he was, with his incessant begging and dependency and indebtedness, insatiably *needy*. "Overwhelming destructiveness" is manifest in the fantasy of cosmic annihilation to which the whole of *The Ring* is devoted.

Annihilation connects the theme of deprivation (the self as corpse) with the aggressive and sadistic responses to deprivation (transforming the other into a corpse in order to live oneself). Ernest Jones explains the sadistic element in necrophilia: " . . . the person obtains gratification . . . either by performing some kind of sexual act on the corpse or, more characteristically, by biting, tearing and devouring its decaying flesh. It evidently signifies a reversion to the most primitive aspects of sadism, both of the oral and anal kind; the latter is indicated by the close association that is often found in the unconscious between the ideas of faeces (or the babies supposed to arise from them) and of any kind of decomposing material, particularly human corpses."[153]

---

[153] Ernest Jones, *op. cit.*, p. 111.

The music of the third act of *Walküre* is stirring and voluptuous enough to mask an otherwise obvious fact, that the story is on its face disturbingly morbid. The act opens with the mimetic music depicting the ride of the Valkyries. Who are these women, though, and what are they up to? They are "wish-maidens," gathering corpses to appease their father's all-consuming anxiety. What extenuates the morbid character of this activity, so that audiences not merely tolerate, but idealize it? Primarily it is the glorious music, but also the sanctimonious gloss of the sacred, the sense that this is mythology and these are gods, and merely human criteria do not apply here. Yet Wagner was an outspoken free-thinker. The behavior of his gods and goddesses have meaning only insofar as they represent *human* actions, values, and obsessions.

Provisionally resisting the music's powerful seduction, however, we need to confront the unvarnished plot, with its mannish ladies of necrophiliac inclination. Their categorization as "wish-maidens," and Brünnhilde's hints of the pleasures they lavish on slain warriors suggest a straightforwardly sexual function. Their ultimate purpose is that assigned by Segal to the necrophiliac fantasy — to infuse with their life the body of the one deprived. Their mission is to garrison Walhall against the threat to the life of the gods posed by Alberich and his nocturnal hordes. Segal writes of her patient's transference, "As we progressively unraveled his phantasies and fears, it became clear that the basic situation was that in any relation either he or I had to be a corpse. There was one life between us and one death, as it were, represented by the concrete form of the corpse, and we were constantly identified with one another by projection and introjection. The various complicated relations we had on various levels were endless attempts at solving the problem of how to share one life between the two of us."

This ambivalence illuminates Wotan's curious passivity. The chief of the gods seems immobilized. Everything is done for him by others. What little he attempts goes awry. His passivity, his dependence on others, is his deadness. In his relation to the rest of the world, Wotan is a "corpse galvanized"[154] only by sucking life from others.

If Wotan is the passive side of the ambivalence, Alberich, his nocturnal double, is the active side. Alberich is the threat against which Wotan builds and mans Walhall. Alberich is the living body; Wotan, the corpse. The identity of Alberich and Wotan accords with Wotan's fear that the power of the ring will enable Alberich to corrupt the god's own warriors against him. Their rebellion is manifested in fact in the form of Brünnhilde's defiance. The personality that morbidly defends against its own impulses will always in the end be betrayed by them. Return of the repressed.

The principal subject of Act III is Wotan's punishment of this defiance. He puts Brünnhilde to sleep. So far this act has been interpreted as the repression of the incest wish. Necrophilia appears now superimposed on this underlying theme. Wotan's transformation of Brünnhilde into the semblance of a corpse has as object that her lifeless form be ravished by the

---

[154] Cf. Letter to Liszt (Nov. 20, 1851), quoted above, Chapter II, p. 38, in which Wagner speaks of "a corpse . . . unwittingly galvanized." This letter proposes the surprising idea — surprising in that it appears to anticipate the Freudian concept of sublimation — that culture is a symptomatic efflorescence of morbid somatic processes.

first man (as it happens, Wotan's alter-ego, Siegfried) to come along. Alongside the patently sadistic component, a strong element of promiscuity pervades this fantasy, corresponding to the Oedipal fantasy of the mother as prostitute, available to anyone, *even the son*. Brünnhilde pleads for a hedge of fire. But the sexual symbolism of the fire that will protect her confirms what both the music and the text of this act also reveal — that Wotan's punishment and farewell is a rapturous love scene.

It is a love scene that, like many, begins in a lovers' quarrel. But it concludes in the voluptuous music of Wotan's farewell. Everything but the stage action indicates that this is not so much a leave-taking as a sexual act — or perhaps, that the leave-taking sub-serves the love-making. That is, since the impulse to the sex act is undergoing repression, it must adopt a displaced form. Putting Brünnhilde to sleep represents not only the repression of the Oedipal wish, but also the necrophiliac fantasy that substitutes for it — of love without anxiety. Segal's patient, "started extolling the virtues of a corpse as a sexual object. He described with relish the feeling of power and security that he could enjoy in making love to a corpse: it is there when wanted, you put it away when finished with it, it makes no demands, it is never frustrating, never unfaithful, never reproachful; persecution and guilt, he said, could be quite done away with." How different is the unconscious, corpse-like Brünnhilde from the icy, nagging, relentless Fricka; how different, too, from the demanding, plaintive Minna to whom Wagner was legally bound!

Love object as corpse reappears as a theme in *Parsifal*, where Klingsor stores his love-slave Kundry in the deep-freeze of a coma.   Moreover, Klingsor is already castrated — living testimony of the dangers the sex act harbors for the male genital, dangers necrophilia circumvents. Klingsor boasts of his unique immunity to Kundry's seductive powers, but lapses into uncontrolled rage when she taunts, *"Bist du keusch?"* ("Are you, then, chaste?") Klingsor, like Alberich, has renounced love in favor of eroticized power. To the safety of necrophilia he adds the defensive distance of voyeurism, whereby he continues vicariously to enjoy Kundry's charms.

Wotan kisses Brünnhilde unconscious, as Siegfried will kiss her awake, lending the life-taking and the life-giving acts a distinctly oral character.   Segal explains the deprivation underlying the necrophiliac fantasy. The infant senses there is but one life to share. Transforming the lover into a corpse repeats the experience of sucking mother dry of life as well as milk.   Conversely, the necrophiliac inflates his ego with the fantasy of the godlike ability to breathe life back into his mother's corpse. This fantasy is related to the rescue fantasy of the Oedipus complex. Segal's patient, "drew [her] attention to the pleasures of giving and withholding life. He likes to feel that he infuses life into people as though he were animating corpses. He will lend them money, set them up in business, look after them, console them, feel that he gives them life. But to feel secure he must have the conviction that the moment he withholds his love, interest, money, they must again become lifeless, inert; when he withholds his wish to see them they will disappear."

Wotan kisses Brünnhilde's eyes; the farewell reaches its climax in his long celebration of them. "This pair of shining eyes, that often I have smilingly caressed, when a kiss rewarded your battle ardour, when childishly babbled heroes' praises flowed from your sweet lips: this pair of radiant eyes, that often gleamed through the storm to me, when hopeful longing burned my heart, when out of wild weaving fears my desire yearned for earthly delight: for the last time let it refresh me today with my farewell's final kiss! . . . For thus the god turns from you, thus he kisses away godhead from you!"

The image of Wotan caressing (or fondling)[155] Brünnhilde's eyes is logically somewhat incoherent; he means, we suppose, that he has caressed them, as it were, with the beams of his own eyes. Or we might regard his daughter's eyes as unconscious surrogates for another part of her anatomy. Such an abundance of light, ardour, babbled praises, radiance, gleaming, refreshment, and ultimately godhead flows from Brünnhilde, which Wotan, in turn, imbibes by kissing (and following the logic of his conceit, sucking from) her eyes. Wotan's vague but provocative recollection that "out of wild weaving fears my desire longed for earthly delight" bears erotic overtones that tinge also the "refreshment" in which the god indulges "for the last time . . . with [his] farewell's final kiss." This imagery is pervaded by an oral motif hinting that Brünnhilde's eyes stand for breasts disguised by sublimation upwards. Her maternal aspect has already been underscored in Wotan's declaration that "She herself was the creative womb of my desire." *"Sie selbst war meines Wunsches schaffender Schoss."*

Brünnhilde's defiance threatens Wotan's autonomy. They cannot both exert the power of divinity; Wotan must derive

---

[155] The German is *kosen*.

his godhead from kissing away (sucking out) godhead from Brünnhilde. In essence, he secures his life by rendering her a corpse. The embodied Oedipal wish, the introjected mother, animates the son, yet in being repressed, denied, it yields up its own life to sublimation. For Wotan has not renounced his Oedipal wishes; he has merely put them out of sight and mind. "You are banished from my sight!" he tells Brünnhilde. "I must avoid you; no longer may I whisper counsel together with you; separated, we must no longer act in common and in trust; so long as he lives and breathes, the god may never more encounter you!"

Brünnhilde, sensitive to Wotan's ambivalence, recognizes that though he puts her out of his sight, he cannot undo the role she plays in his essence. "Must I then depart and shyly avoid you; must you split up what formerly was encompassed as one, hold distant from you half of your own self? — that it once belonged wholly to you, Oh God, forget it not!"

But Wotan wills ignorance. "I turn away from her who already is absent; I may not know what she wishes for herself; only the punishment must I see exacted." Wotan dares not know what Brünnhilde wishes, very simply, because her wishes are his own. Yet the role Wotan plays, the role corresponding to Freud's super-ego, demands that he punish the ardent wishes of the self. He bitterly resents Brünnhilde's freedom to act on impulse. "So you did," he berates her, "what I so longed to do myself, but what necessity doubly compelled me not to do. So easily, you imagined, were won the joys of love, while searing pain erupted in my heart, while terrible anguish — for the sake of a world — begot in me the fury to confine the well of love in my tormented heart? While turning violently against myself, seething, I shot up out of the anguish of impotence ("*aus Ohnmachtsschmerzen schäumend ich aufschoss*"), while raging desire, ardent wish begot in me the terrible will to end my eternal sorrow in the wreckage of my own world — blissful pleasure sweetly delighted you; you drank laughingly the blissful feeling of voluptuous ecstasy from the love draught, while divine necessity mixed gnawing gall for me?" The bitter envy of this spluttering reproach offers a glimpse of the fury of the impulses repressed. Wotan's almost graphically ejaculatory imagery, and his violent tableau of inner turmoil and self-laceration displays here the obverse of that more lyrical union of deity and daughter shown us in Act II.

Wagner's music overlays Wotan's speech with voluptuous grandeur. But in their rage, his words lapse nearly into incoherence. What comes through the chaos of image and epithet, however, is the primitive character of the instinct struggling for expression. Even the "anguish of impotence" is represented in a violently sexual image. Rage and semen are confused. The penis is transformed from an organ of pleasure, love, and generation into an instrument of self-punishment. "Whosoever fears my spear's point" — declares Wotan in the final words of the opera, "never stride through this fire!" ("*Wer meines Speeres Spitze fürchtet, durchschreite das Feuer nie!*") His prohibition conceals the idea that the penis is a weapon, and trades on the classic fear of castration administered by an avenging father. Yet as he is the father introjected, the self must fear its own penis. The penis is a rebel; it betrays its master; it is turned against the self by the self's own avenging superego.

Die Walküre, which has opened in the agitation of anxiety, concludes in the calm of repression. Wehwalt's melancholia recurs now as the dominant mood of Wotan, mourning for what he must lose, for her whom he bids farewell, for her who is as good as dead. Yet his dilemma's loophole is the entrance to Sieglinde's womb, through which, between this opera and the next, Siegfried will squirm to act out what Wotan has only seemingly renounced. For repression affirms even as it denies. The audience knows of this loophole in Wotan's strictures, and knows that if this opera has ended in mourning and melancholia, the next will begin in laughter and end in triumph.

Chapter IV

Siegfried: Family Romance

1.

"Moderately agitated," *mässig bewegt*, is the tempo indication Wagner gives the *Siegfried* prelude, and the music does express Mime's agitation over his inability to forge a weapon equal to his perverse foster-son's strength and boundless energy. But "brooding" better describes the initial fifty measures, containing the ponderous contrabass tuba theme of Fafner turned dragon. Fafner *broods* over the gold horde in the cave Mime calls the dragon's "nest," as though he were indeed hatching eggs. And if the music of the prelude becomes more agitated with the futile ringing of Mime's dwarvish hammer on his anvil, brooding nonetheless remains the undercurrent. No wonder. This opera's action springs from brooding—Mime, racking his brains how to forge a sword that will withstand Siegfried's grasp; Siegfried, tirelessly researching his origins and his inexplicable connection to the loathsome dwarf.

The pun that links Fafner on his nest with the "brooding" Mime and Siegfried is not merely ingenious.[156] In *Rheingold*, we saw Fafner the club-wielding giant as a parental figure in dream-work disguise. When bludgeoning giant becomes a devouring dragon, its guise is more clearly that of the "terrible mother," so that Siegfried's task at the center of this opera — slaying the dragon — is pervaded by the theme of matricide.

It is not, in other words, by virtue of an arbitrary metaphor that Fafner is seen as a nesting mother. That the dragon's metaphorical young are a heap of gold is consistent with the common infantile equation of feces and babies, and leads to the alternative meaning of brooding. Siegfried is "brooding" over his genesis, his connection with his true as well as his false parents. Though these are not — in the text — overtly sexual researches, we surmise what the child who inquires where babies come from wants to know.

The pervasive mode of interaction in *Siegfried* is questioning. Siegfried interrogates Mime about his origin; Wotan and Mime duel with questions; Siegfried questions the forest bird about Brünnhilde; Wotan asks Erda about anxiety, and Siegfried about waking Brünnhilde; Siegfried, finally, inquires of no one in particular about the armor-clad person he finds

---

[156] Brooding is used in this double sense in the text of the opera. In Act I, Siegfried says of birds in springtime, "*Sie bauten ein Nest und brüteten drin*" ("They build a nest and brooded in it"). In Act II, Fafner asks Siegfried who put him up to his heroics: "*Dein Hirn brütete nicht, was du Vollbracht?*" ("Your brain surely didn't hatch what you have accomplished?").

asleep inside the circle of fire. Questioning is so pronounced in *Siegfried* as to constitute a formal theme.

In a 1947 introduction to *Hamlet*, Ernest Jones remarks that verbal dexterity like that of the moody Prince of Denmark reflects the displaced sexual curiosity of childhood.[157] In *Hamlet and Oedipus*, Jones compares Shakespeare's text with the original saga. "The fine irony exhibited by Hamlet in the play, which enables him to express contempt and hostility in an indirect and disguised form—beautifully illustrated, for instance, in his conversations with Polonius—is a transmutation of the still more concealed mode of expression adopted in the saga, where the hero's audience commonly fails to apprehend his meaning. He here combines a veiled form of speech, full of obvious equivocations and intent to deceive, with a curiously punctilious insistence on verbal truthfulness."[158] Jones identifies verbal dexterity employed to deceive as part of a syndrome (constituting Hamlet's "feigned madness") that he calls *simulated foolishness*. It is related to the affected inanities of the hero of the saga, who rides into the palace seated backwards on a donkey, imitates a cock crowing and flapping its wings, and the like.

"The complete syndrome comprises the following features: foolish, witless behaviour, an inane, inept kind of funniness and silliness, and childishness."[159] The saga hero's "peculiar riddling sayings," Jones goes on, "obviously aping the innocence of childhood, his predilection for dirt and for smearing himself with filth, his general shiftlessness, and

---

[157] Ernest Jones, "Introduction," *Hamlet* (Vision Press, 1947).
[158] Ernest Jones, *Hamlet and Oedipus* (New York, 1949), p. 163.
[159] *Ibid.*, p. 165.

above all the highly characteristic combination of fondness for deception . . . with a punctilious regard for verbal truth, are unmistakably childish traits."[160]

In this regard, the Shakespearean *Hamlet* and its source, too, resemble *Siegfried*, although in the latter, the behavior in question is divided between two characters. Mime is the verbally dexterous deceiver, withholding information from Siegfried, matching wits with Wotan, his hypocrisy undone finally by the candid twittering of the forest bird and the taste of dragon's blood. Siegfried is the childish hero, entering the stage inanely driving a bear before him to terrorize his foster-father, petulantly smashing his soup bowl and splintering his swords. His childishness is the quality that allows him to achieve what his wiser parents despair of. These two facets of behavior are appropriately split in *Siegfried* since Mime here takes the role Alberich played in *Rheingold*: the putative Jew Geyer, introjected — the paternal aspect of the self that Siegfried (the self, idealized as infant hero) complements.

The object of *simulated foolishness*, Jones asserts, is "demonstrated beyond any doubt" by psychoanalysis. Behind a mask of innocence and childishness, the clown or fool or prankster deludes elders into disregarding his presence, thinking him too young to understand what he may see or hear in their company. "The purpose of the artifice is that by these means children can view and overhear various private things which they are not supposed to. It need hardly be said," Jones adds, "that the curiosity thus indulged in is in most cases concerned with matters of a directly sexual nature;

---

[160] *Ibid.*, pp. 165, 166.

even marital embraces are in this way investigated by quite young children far oftener than is generally suspected or thought possible."

These three major themes of *Siegfried*, *questioning*, *verbal dexterity*, and *childishness*, all point to a basis in infantile sexual curiosity, a conjecture borne out by what actually occurs in the opera: Siegfried seeks and finds sexual enlightenment in the embraces of (as Anna Russell archly informs us) his aunt.

Jones' description of Amleth, Hamlet's precurser in the saga, suggests the meaning of Mime's behaviour. "The core of Amleth's attitude is secrecy and spying: secrecy concerning his own thoughts, knowledge, and plans; spying as regards those of his enemy, his stepfather. These two character traits are certainly derived from forbidden curiosity about secret, i.e., sexual matters in early childhood. So is the love of deception for its own sake, a trait which sometimes amounts to what is called pathological lying; it is a defiant reaction to the lies almost always told to the child, and always detected by him. In so behaving the child is really caricaturing the adult's behaviour to himself, as also in the punctiliousness about verbal truth that is sometimes combined with the tendency to deceive; he is pretending to tell the truth as the parent pretended to tell it to him, deceiving going on all the while in both cases."[161] Mime is himself a caricature — a caricature, like Alberich, of Jewishness, but also of the father's hateful aspects, as Wotan represents an idealization of his admired ones. If Mime is a projection of the infantile self, he is precisely that inner caricature of the parent's deceptive

---

[161] Ibid., pp. 166, 167.

behavior described by Jones. His essence is secretiveness. Huddling in his cave, he plots and schemes; he conceals the truth from Siegfried gratuitously, even when to reveal it would not threaten his exploitative intentions; he is "characterologically" hypocritical. Spying, meanwhile, is the predominant behavior of Mime's double, Alberich, camped outside the dragon's hole awaiting an opportunity to regain the ring. The prototype of the spy is the child with ear tuned to the alluring noises of his parents' bed room.

The underlying curiosity in Siegfried resolves itself into two questions, Mime's and Siegfried's. Mime must discover how to forge Siegmund's shattered sword; Siegfried needs to learn his origin. Regarded symbolically, these questions complement one another. Siegfried's is the problem of childhood: what is the nature of sexual activity? It is, initially at least, an intellectual problem. Mime's is the practical problem of adolescence: how can the son employ the erect penis for its intended purpose, yet escape castration? Mime's very ugliness embodies the adolescent's typical feelings about his burgeoning sexuality.

Freud, also based adult questioning and research in infantile sexual curiosity. He shows, for instance, that much of what children ask are actually surrogate questions. "The curiosity of small children is manifested in their untiring love of asking questions; this is bewildering to the adult so long as he fails to understand that all these questions are merely circumlocutions and that they cannot come to an end because the child is only trying to make them take the place of a question which he does *not* ask . . . Many, perhaps most children, or at least the most gifted ones, pass through a period, beginning when they are about three, which may be called the period of infantile sexual researches . . . Researches are directed to the question of where babies come from, exactly as if the child were looking for ways and means to avert so undesired an event. In this way we have been astonished to learn that children refuse to believe the bits of information that are given them—for example that they energetically reject the fable of the stork with its wealth of mythological meaning—that they date their intellectual independence from this act of disbelief, and that they often feel in serious opposition to adults and in fact never afterwards forgive them for having deceived them here about the true facts of the case."[162]

Although questions are answered in *Siegfried*, questioning is ceaseless until the curtain falls at the end of Act III, when Siegfried answers bodily for himself the unspoken question for which the others have stood as surrogates. Intellectual curiosity is thus of a piece with physical sexual awakening, and is not satisfied until desire is. Knowledge is carnal knowledge, the sex act.

Freud's discussion stresses the intimate connection between the sexual curiosity of the child and his need to protect selfish interests *vis-a-vis* siblings. The parallel to *Siegfried* is clear, for Act II caricatures sibling rivalry in the encounter between the dwarf brothers Alberich and Mime, a rivalry all the more hateful and pitiable as they bicker over what they never will possess: the gold hoard Siegfried has just won from Fafner. Some suggest that in Alberich's name and character Wagner

---

[162] Sigmund Freud, *Leonardo da Vinci and a Memory of his Childhood, Standard Edition*, vol. XI, pp. 78, 79.

concealed his brother Albert. Rather—I would argue—we see in Alberich/Mime a distorted portrait of step-father Geyer. To be sure, these meanings are not necessarily mutually exclusive in the unconscious process of association. Whatever the case, the scene between the brothers *means* sibling rivalry.

This less savory concomitant of sexual enlightenment is shifted onto the rejected part of the self, leaving the ego-ideal, Siegfried, free to achieve his martial and sexual heroics unencumbered by greed. In fact, his pose of nonchalance concerning the gold that everyone else covets is a major component of his heroic stance. The dichotomy between dwarvish greed and heroic ignorance of (or indifference to) the value of gold corresponds to Wagner's own ambivalence toward money. While he felt himself above concerns as crass as financial prudence, and spent prodigally on himself and others, he boxed himself continually into the necessity of worrying about and coveting money, which his detractors understandably deplored as mercenary (not to say "Judaic").

Both Freud and Jones emphasize the pervasive deception that characterizes the adult response to children's sexual curiosity. For his part, the child learns by outwitting secretive parents with deceptions that caricature theirs. Mime resists answering the simplest of Siegfried's questions about his origins. The young hero extracts answers from him only grudgingly. Apparently in contrast, Wotan ridicules Mime's foolishly defensive strategy that loses him the opportunity in the contest to ask the essential question—how to forge a sword from Notung's splinters. Yet it is improbable that Wotan would supply Mime such information should it ever occur to him to ask. The god is prevented by the very logic that compelled him to let Notung shatter — namely that he could not participate in the hero's overthrow of his own binding agreements. Wotan's pretense that, had Mime only asked the proper question, he would have revealed the secret is the kind of deception all parents employ when they respond to children's sexual inquiries with, say, the story of the stork. Such an answer conceals the truth more impenetrably than silence. Mime is rightly suspicious of Wotan.[163] The superego cannot supply instructions for use of the penis — the very employment for which it threatens castration. Wotan's apparent even-handedness is a disingenuous pose.

As the opera opens, Mime formulates his dilemma. A skilled smith, he is accustomed to forging swords strong enough to withstand the battles of giants. Yet every sword he fashions shatters in Siegfried's "childishly" powerful grasp. Mime does know of one sword Siegfried would not be able to shatter, one sword equal to the singular deed ("*die einzige Tat*") the dwarf has set his heart upon, the slaying of Fafner. Unfortunately, this unique sword destined to accomplish the singular deed lies in fragments the master smith is helpless to fuse whole.

What is the meaning of this singularity? Why is the slaying of this particular dragon unique? Why should ordinary swords suffice in the hands of giants, but not in this particular hero's, with his "childish strength" ("*kindischer Kraft*")? If the sword

---

[163] It is not inconsistent to regard Mime at one moment as the withholding parent, and as the inquisitive child at the next. Similarly, in the discussion of *Rheingold*, Alberich appeared in one scene as the embodiment of *id*, and in another as punitive *superego*. These figures are fluid in meaning because introjection is a mechanism of identification. Self and other are merged, and thus become more or less interchangeable.

is invested with symbolic phallic value, what is so special about it? First, Notung is Siegmund's sword, that is, father's penis; for every child, father and mother are unique. Second, the sword has been shattered for violation of the incest taboo, the uniquely terrible transgression. The uniqueness of Fafner's slaying lies in its symbolic meaning as incest with the mother.[164] If the shattered penis can be made whole (i.e., invulnerable to the punishment attached to incest) it can be used for that unique purpose — thrust into mother's body. That this symbolic disguise of intercourse also contains the meaning of matricide will emerge from further analysis of Act II. Suffice it to say for the moment that the slaying of Fafner and the "awakening" of Brünnhilde are parallel episodes — if not equivalent in meaning, then complementary, and equally tinged with the aura of necrophilia. The slaying of Fafner is Mime's project; the "awakening" of Brünnhilde is Siegfried's.

Enter Siegfried, pursuing a bear. Modern theatrical practice often omits the bear, whose farcical presence onstage seems to embarrass the serious Wagnerite, and whose vestiges in the text are probably assumed to go unnoticed in the brisk tempo, and the commotion of the young hero's entrance. The omission is an error. Siegfried's pointedly childish antics with the bear serve him (symbolically) as a blind behind which to spy out the secret of sex. Moreover, Wagner deliberately set out to write in *The Young Siegfried* a comic counterpart to the tragedy of *The Death of Siegfried*. Comedy completes the circle tragedy initiates by ending happily, conventionally in marriage. *Siegfried* conforms to this pattern. But Wagner's

---

[164] Recall that Fafner is one of the giants of *Rheingold*, a parental figure, transformed into a dragon.

opera is also quite simply funny; Wagner intends his audience to laugh, not just smile — to laugh at Mime's grotesque futility and absurdly transparent hypocrisy; at Siegfried's outbursts and tantrums, his sour attempts to play a whistle like a bird, and his ingenuous surprise on discovering that Brünnhilde is a woman; at Fafner's aphoristic quips: *"Ich lieg' und besitz': lasst mich schlafen!"* and, encountering Siegfried, *"Trinken wollt' ich: nun treff' ich auch Frass!"* ("I wanted to drink; now I've also found feed!") We should smile indulgently with Wotan at the dramatic irony of Siegfried's unwittingly telling the "Wanderer" that Notung's fragments would have been useless had he not reforged them. *"Das mein' ich wohl auch!"* ("I think so too!"), is Wotan's good-natured reply. Siegfried's entrance with the leashed bear is slapstick, and ought to be played for laughs, not glossed over.

The inclusion of the bear, first of several devourers, is also thematically coherent. It prepares the way for the more monstrous dragon, and establishes Siegfried's fearlessness. He threatens Mime with the bear to torment him. *"Hau' ein! Hau' ein! Friss' ihn! Friss' ihn!"* ("Attack! Attack! Eat him! Eat him!") Siegfried's first words in the opera incite the bear to gobble up the hapless dwarf, though his raucous laughter assures us it is all in fun.

Thus, for all the boisterous humor of the scene, the bear represents another guise of the "terrible mother;" as a devouring monster it objectifies a critical aspect of that figure. Siegfried has brought it home because he was searching for some "companion better than the one who sits at home," (*"Nach bess'rem Gesellen sucht' ich, als daheim mir einer sitzt."*) Siegfried's word *Gesell* ("companion") is applied successively to the bear, Fafner, and ultimately Brünnhilde, asleep within the ring of fire. *"Jetzt lock' ich ein liebes Gesell!"* ("Now I'll attract a dear companion!") Siegfried cries in the penultimate scene as he strides through the fire towards his bride. His search for a "companion" is the fundamental plot of the opera, and corresponds to the normal adolescent project to achieve independence. But Siegfried is driven to seek a "companion" because his real mother and father are not "sitting at home." Thus his search for independence from Mime's pseudo-parental authority through a mother surrogate actually constitutes a regression.

In a short paper titled "Family Romances," Freud describes the necessary though painful process of the individual's liberation from the authority of his parents. Whereas, "for a small child his parents are at first the only authority and the source of all belief," intellectual growth and widening experience inevitably lead to a lower estimation of his parents' worth, wisdom and power. "Small events in the child's life which make him feel dissatisfied afford him provocation for beginning to criticize his parents, and for using, in order to support his critical attitude, the knowledge which he has acquired that other parents are in some respects preferable to them."

Dissatisfaction usually stems from the feeling that his parents do not adequately love him, occasioned by having to share their love with siblings. "His sense that his own affection is not being fully reciprocated then finds a vent in the idea . . . of being a step-child or an adopted child . . . But here the influence of sex is already in evidence, for a boy is far more inclined to feel hostile impulses towards his father than towards his mother and has a far more intense desire to get free from *him* than from *her*."[165]

As a fantasy of independence, then, *Siegfried* exhibits this typical element, denial that the father is genuine, insistence that the real father is a noble and heroic personage, in contrast to the ridiculous dwarf who pretends to the role. The question of Siegfried's getting free of his mother, who he soon learns is dead, is moot. On the contrary, independence from the father is achieved by winning the mother through the necrophiliac fantasy of killing her and restoring her to life. The ambiguity of Wagner's paternity lent substance to the typical fantasy that parents are actually only *step*-parents. But Geyer posed as step-father when he was most likely Richard's father in fact—a curious inversion of the normal pattern.

Freud sees the "family romance" developing in two stages. The first, during which the child in fantasy replaces both parents with others of higher birth, precedes knowledge of sexual procreation. "When presently the child comes to know the difference in the parts played by fathers and mothers in their sexual relations, and realizes that *'pater semper incertus est,"* while mother is *'certissima,'* the family romance undergoes a curious curtailment: it contents itself with exalting the child's father, but no longer casts any doubts on his maternal origin, which is regarded as something unalterable." This second stage of elaboration explains the connection between sexual enlightenment and independence in *Siegfried*. Siegfried accepts unquestioningly what he learns about Sieglinde, while at the same time he is obsessed with

---

[165] Sigmund Freud, "Family Romances," *Standard Edition*, vol. IX, pp. 237, 238.

denial of Mime's paternity. Behind this gossamer fantasy one sees Wagner unconsciously denying Geyer's paternity, though he regarded it as a fact.

The spinning of the family romance does not signify ingratitude or depravity on the child's part, though Mime decries it as such. "The faithlessness and ingratitude" Freud concludes, "are only apparent. If we examine in detail the commonest of these imaginative romances, the replacement of both parents or of the father alone by grander people, we find that these new and aristocratic parents are equipped with attributes that are derived entirely from real recollections of the actual and humble ones; so that in fact the child is not getting rid of his father but exalting him. Indeed the whole effort at replacing the real father by a superior one is only an expression of the child's longing for the happy, vanished days when his father seemed to him the noblest and strongest of men and his mother the dearest and loveliest of women. He is turning away from the father whom he knows today to the father in whom he believed in the earlier years of his childhood; and his phantasy is not more than the expression of a regret that those happy days have gone."[166]

The mode of the "family romance" is regression. The idea of father as hero returns the child in fantasy to the time when his real father appeared of heroic proportions. Wotan's project of self-fulfillment ultimately in the person of Siegfried is the same regressive fantasy, returning the self to the omnipotence of earliest infancy, when it was a hero. *Siegfried* thus displays contradictory tendencies, for its fantasy is both regressive and

---

[166] *Ibid.*, pp. 240, 241.

forward looking. On the one hand it expresses the desire to regress to the heroic era of infancy; on the other it expresses the desire to grow independent of parents and home. Freud's essay suggests in some measure how these contradictory tendencies function together. The adolescent must seek outside the family those idealized attributes he can no longer find at home. He can leave home only by growing up, yet what he seeks abroad are the vanished things of infancy.

Siegfried's search for a "companion" to replace Mime is a search for surrogate parents. He blew his horn in the woods to attract a companion, and when the bear answered his summons, he tells Mime, "I liked him better than you." Siegfried orders the bear to ask about the sword Mime has been working on: *"Brauner, frag' nach dem Schwert!"* His search for a "companion" may seem unrelated to the forging of a sword. Yet the adolescent's drive for independence is grounded in his ability to make his penis erect, and maintain it that way during use. Siegfried takes the sword Mime has made for him and exclaims, "Hey! What sort of a useless toy is this? You call this puny pin a sword?" In a tantrum he smashes the sword on Mime's anvil, and launches into a tirade against his foster-father's bungling: *"nehm' ich zur Hand nun, was er gehämmert, mit einem Griff zerqreif' ich den Quark!"*[167]

The imagery here of an adolescent's first, groping experiments with masturbation is graphic. A single grasp and the sword, as it were, spews "cottage cheese." The adolescent's self-initiation into the mysteries of sex proceeds to the problem of premature ejaculation — how to make the penis function in

---

[167] Literally, "If I take in my hand what he has forged, with a single grasp I'll crush the [piece of] rubbish!" But *"Quark"* also means "cottage cheese."

TOM ARTIN

intercourse.   The solution is control — a control Siegfried eventually achieves through the magic of necrophilia. At the moment, however, he displays the adolescent's typical lack of control. "Siegfried throws himself in a rage onto a stone bench," the stage directions specify. When Mime replies, he pouts and turns his back. When the dwarf offers him roast meat and broth, the impetuous boy knocks the food to the floor.

The ensuing dialogue consists of Mime's bitter complaint against his foster-son's ingratitude, and Siegfried's extortion of genealogical enlightenment from his foster-father. Siegfried first muses about his ambivalence towards the dwarf. Why — though he is disgusted by Mime and flees to the woods to escape him — does he always return?   Siegfried's disgust recalls Wagner's diatribe in "Judaism in Music"; the rage the mere sight of Mime provokes in the childish hero derives its murderous intensity from the closeness of the relationship, just as Wagner's irrational hatred plausibly proceeded from an unacknowledged fear of being Jewish himself. "When I see you standing, hobbling, walking, bending and nodding, blinking with your eyes: I would like to take the nodder by the neck, to kill the nasty blinker!" The sheer alliterative nastiness   of   Siegfried's   invective   cannot   properly   be translated. *"Seh' ich dich stehen, gangeln und geh'n, knicken und nicken, mit den Augen zwicken: beim Genick' möcht ich den Nicker packen, den Garaus geben dem garst'gen Zwicker!"*   This picture has   its   roots   in   the   same   anti-Semitism   that   generated Wagner's   description   of   Jewish   characteristics,   and   his argument that the Jewish race "naturally" inspires disgust. Even so, its gratuitous violence is stunning — rather less than "heroic," even if Mime does turn out to be a rascal.

190

All animals, Mime replies, long for their parental nest. This longing is love, and since Siegfried feels it, it follows that he must love his foster-father. Siegfried's ambivalence towards his foster-father is predictable in an adolescent boy, whose sexuality is reawakening from latency, his Oedipal impulses stirring once more. Thus, Siegfried's next question logically concerns his mother. Where is she? Siegfried has learned about love, he says, from watching mother animals suckling their young. "Where have you, then, Mime, your loving little wife, that I may call her mother?"

At this point, Mime's reluctance to answer the probing questions begins—appropriately, since they now touch the uniquely tabooed person. "What's the matter with you, idiot? Oh, how dumb you are! After all, you're neither bird nor fox!" But Siegfried is not so easily put off, naive though he may be. "Did you then make me without any mother?" he asks mockingly.

"Believe what I tell you," Mime commands him; "I am your father and mother in one." Siegfried rejects this answer and abuses Mime for lying to him. Yet in a real sense Mime has answered truthfully, just as Wagner's twice-widowed mother was obliged to be both father and mother for substantial periods to her children. Mime as androgynous parent also reflects the infantile fantasy termed by psychoanalysis "the combined parent concept," deriving from the child's speculations about intercourse. This fantasy of intercourse, in turn, stems probably from the still more archaic hypothesis of the "phallic mother."[168]

---

[168] Cf. the "beast with two backs," *Othello*.

But Siegfried insists it is impossible that Mime could be related to him, for his image in the stream looks nothing like the repulsive dwarf, whereas animals, he knows, resemble their parents. This denial may hold water in Siegfried's case, the Aryan stereotype. It is less convincing in Wagner's own, who attributed to the Jews, and to the Nibelungs his very own features: short stature, a bizarrely large head, and a beak-like nose. Wagner's vigorous denial of the Jewishness he feared Geyer had bequeathed him conforms to the pattern of the normal "family romance" outlined by Freud. The adolescent establishes independence by denying a relationship to his parents, particularly his father, whom he scorns and belittles.

Who are my *real* parents? Siegfried asks. "See, now it occurs to me by myself what before I wondered in vain: when I run off into the woods to escape you, how does it happen that I come home again? First I must learn from you who my father and mother may be!"

Only when threatened by violence does Mime yield up the truth about Siegfried's "real" parents. Mime's malicious recalcitrance caricatures the child's experience of his parents' conspiracy of silence and deception about sex. "So I have to lay hands on you to find anything out: I get nothing voluntarily! I have to bully everything out of you: I would barely have learned to speak, had I not extorted it by force from the villain! Out with it, mangy fellow! Who are my father and mother?"

Now Mime confirms what Wagner unconsciously wishes had been true of Geyer: he is neither father nor relative, "*Nicht . . . Vatter noch Vetter*," to Siegfried. Nevertheless, Siegfried owes him his life. Out of pity he took into his cave a moaning, abandoned woman. She bore a child in her womb—"*Ein Kind trug sie im Schosse.*" It was born in sorrow; the mother writhed in the agony of birth; Mime helped as well as he could: the pain was enormous; the mother died. "But Siegfried—he recovered."

Wagner seems to have been preoccupied with the fantasy of mother's death; it occurs repeatedly in the stories he chose for his operas. Parsifal's mother dies of shock when her son leaves her. Here the trauma of parturition is replaced with abandonment by the adolescent son, but the meaning is much the same. Its source is that infantile sense of deprivation (alluded to in the discussion of necrophilia), experienced by the child as a paucity of vitality. Separation apparently entails the death of mother or child, and since the child knows itself to be alive, it is the mother who must have had to give up life. At the same time, the fantasy serves the sadistic function of retaliation for the very deprivation it stems from. The mother has deprived the child; the child retaliates by killing the mother in fantasy. "*So starb meine Mutter an mir?*" ("My mother died, then, of me") asks Siegfried, taking on himself the responsibility for her death.[169] The tender melancholy of the music to which he sings these words papers over the underlying fantasy of matricide.

Now Siegfried presses Mime to name his parents. Each name must be forced from the dwarf. He tries to divert Siegfried's attention by returning constantly to his self-pitying song, "*Als zullendes Kind zog ich dich auf . . .*" ("I raised you from suckling

---

[169] The German idiom, namely, implies disease (e.g., *Er starb an Krebs*, "He died of cancer").

child . . . "). The song drives Siegfried into a rage, not only because it avoids his questions, but because he wishes to deny the care his foster-father claims to have lavished on him. He extracts his mother's name: Sieglinde. "I ask next, how was my father called?" he presses. Mime answers evasively that he never saw him; the mother said only he had been slain. Quickly, he takes up the song: ". . . And as you grew up I looked after you; made you a bed so you might sleep easily. "

"Stop that old starling's song!" cries Siegfried enraged; "*Still mit dem alten Starenlied!*" When Siegfried wishes to learn about his real father, Mime's song of evasion[170] — which states his claim to be Siegfried's *de facto* father — becomes a starling's song, the song of a black bird, an image plausibly (and just slightly) displaced from that of a vulture. Thus it is perhaps a *Geyerlied* Mime sings — the song of the impostor father.

"If I am to believe this story, if you haven't lied in anything, let me see some evidence! . . . I don't believe you with my ear;

---

[170] There may be an additional rationale for Mime's reluctance — not attributable to the dwarf, but to a conjectural unconscious association on Wagner's part. Mime's reluctance to name Siegfried's parents resembles Lohengrin's prohibition against asking his name. Otto Rank, *Die Lohengrin-Sage: Ein Beitrag zu ihrer Motivgestaltung und Deutung*, gen. ed., Sigmund Freud, *Schriften zur angewandten Seelenkunde*, no. 13 (Leipzig and Vienna, 1912), explains that the secret name conceals the crime of incest. If Lohengrin's name comes to light, Rank argues, his incestuous relation to his bride is (by being known) rendered impossible. In the charmed circle of ignorance he can safely commit incest. Lohengrin is not actually related to Elsa, of course. But in unconscious fantasy he is; the *meaning* of his relation to her is incest. Lohengrin fears and prohibits Elsa's asking his name *lest it turn out* that he is her brother. Hence his identification with the swan: he dare not reveal his own name, but his sobriquet "Knight of the Swan" covertly reveals the incestuous relation. For the swan is Elsa's brother bewitched.

I believe you only with my eye. What evidence supports you?" Parents pretend to answer children's questions about sex and birth, but they use words deceitfully. Only seeing is believing. So Mime exhibits the fragments of Siegmund's sword, whose successful forging will constitute the climactic action of this opening act.

Siegfried imperiously commands Mime to make these into the sword with which he will go into the world, free of his hateful foster-father forever. "You are not my father; I am at home somewhere far away; your hearth is not my home, nor is your roof my shelter." He rushes into the forest, leaving Mime to puzzle out how to fuse these fragments into a sword stiff enough for so rash a youth.

The question contest between Wotan (disguised as "The Wanderer") and Mime extends the theme of sexual researches. It seems a gratuitous competition because the vapid questions do nothing to advance the plot. Its only obvious function is to rub Mime's nose in the hopelessness of his situation, and add to his humiliation. The dwarf does not just narrowly and foolishly miss his golden opportunity to pick Wotan's brains. The god is not actually in a position to supply the information he tantalizes Mime with.

The contest reinforces the split between the image of the bad father and the good father, a dichotomy corresponding to mother as both devouring dragon and virginal love object. But another turn of the screw is added by the special circumstances of Wagner's birth. Because his paternity was ambiguous, Wagner could unconsciously attach the attributes of the good father to his officially "real" father, and the attributes of the bad father to his "step-father" Geyer. The split image of the father, that is to say, was ready-made for Wagner by circumstance, and easily transferable onto the figures of Mime (or Alberich) and Wotan.

The central problem of Act I is forging the sword inherited from father Siegmund. But the figure of Siegmund is very much in the background in this opera; the sword really derives from Wotan by way of Mime. The question whether Mime will discover how to forge it resolves itself symbolically to the question of legitimacy. Who is Siegfried's (Wagner's) *real* father? Mime (Geyer) pretends to be, but isn't. Wotan (Wagner the elder) appears in the guise of "the Wanderer," yet bears all the earmarks of the real father. Like a real father in the eyes of his child, he is omniscient. He has all the answers—in particular, the answer Mime vainly seeks. The question contest underscores the motive of denial behind Wagner's fantasy. Siegfried must not inherit his sword from Mime, but from Wotan. Wagner thus denies his is a Jewish penis, a paltry thing made from "pap," that turns into "cottage cheese" at a single grasp. *"Mit Bappe back' ich kein Schwert!"* ("I can't fire a sword with pulp!") Siegfried declares.

If questioning in the contest is imbued with the curiosity of infantile sexual researches, the inquiry seems to be: *Who is my father?* Each question but the last two, about the sword Notung, concern race or family—the German is *Geschlecht*, which covers both, and which also means "gender." Mime asks which race lives under the earth, which on the earth, and which in the heavens above. Wotan asks which family (though he afflicts them with pain) Wotan loves the most.

This concern with race, with family, with origins is a generalized or abstracted form of the question of paternity.

Legitimacy ultimately rests on each claimant's relation to the mother. Repeatedly, Wotan represents himself as a wanderer on "the earth's back," ("*auf der Erde Rücken*"), using a bodily metaphor whose connotations, considering Wotan's relations with Erda, are pointedly sexual. The earth is mother's body, and wanderer Wotan plays the infantile explorer on it. "*Viel erforscht' ich, erkannte viel.*" Mime employs a similar metaphor. Reflecting what Wagner would consider his essentially Jewish nature as rootless alien, Mime tells Wotan, "long ago I left my homeland, long ago I departed my mother's womb" ("*Lang' schon mied ich mein Heimatland, lang' schon schied ich aus der Mutter Schoss.*") Wotan has just identified the homeland of the Nibelungs as the bowels of the earth, so that mother's womb is mother earth's womb. The parallel structure of Mime's sentence suggests the metaphor too. Earlier, he has called the Nibelung's home "earth's navel-nest," an unavoidably clumsy rendering of the German: "*der Erde Nabelnest.*"

At stake in this contest is paternal legitimacy. Is earth-ruler Wotan the legitimate father? Or is the dwarvish Mime, who, though he does not rule, has possessed the earth by inhabiting it? Wotan forces Mime to wager his head against the god's. Decapitation, the terrible consequence of losing the question contest, at least the fantasy of it, is often equated in psychoanalysis with castration. The virility of Wotan, the "real" father, is preserved in his son's image of him, while the usurper is in fantasy castrated and set aside. In Act II, when Siegfried has slain the dragon, Mime wishes to save his own head by decapitating his foster-son. "*Ich will dem Kind nur den*

Kopf abhau'n," he cackles. And in Act III, although Wotan does not lose his head, the shattering of his spear is freighted with the same meaning. The son achieves manhood by castrating both his fathers, bad and good.

The final scene of Act I begins with an emblem of Mime's dilemma, the dwarf himself portraying the penis. He begins to imagine the flickering sunlight and rustling trees to be the horrible dragon coming to devour him. "There," he cries, "it's crashing through the wood, it's coming for me!" The stage directions now specify: "He rears up in terror" (*"er bäumt sich vor Entsetzen auf."*) Mime continues his delusion: "A terrible mouth gapes at me! — The dragon wants to catch me! Fafner! Fafner!" The stage directions again: "Screaming loudly, he sinks in a heap behind the anvil." The horror of the gaping mouth is exciting. Mime rises like a penis. Likewise, there is a distinctly erotic tenor to Mime's attempt, moments later, to excite fear in Siegfried. "Have you not then felt grisly horror take hold of your limbs? Glowing shudders shake the limbs; the hammering heart, quivering and fearful, bursts in your breast." Siegfried, who has not yet learned fear, replies, "Wondrously strange that must be! Hard and firm (*"Hart und fest"*), I feel, my heart remains. The terror and horror, the glowing and shuddering, the heat and the swooning, hammering and quivering — eagerly I desire such fear, longing, I look for such pleasure." The music of Siegfried's reply is marked, surprisingly, *piano* and *nachsinnend* ("meditatively"), and is set to the theme of the magic fire music and Wotan's farewell. In theme and tone, the music anticipates Siegfried's discovery of fear, not in the martial encounter with Fafner, but the sexual encounter with Brünnhilde. Fearless, the young hero remains "hard and firm" despite the threat of the "terrible mother," while Mime "sinks in a heap." The Oedipal project is at once uniquely desired and uniquely fraught with peril. If the project is to succeed, the penis has to defy the threat of castration.

"Stiffness" is achieved in the culmination of Wotan's plan, his hero's self-creation. Siegfried impatiently abandons hope that foster-father Mime can ever forge his sword, and takes matters into his own hands. He fashions the sword from his father's fragments by first reducing them still further to a pile of metal filings, then melting those on the coals of the brown ash (the text specifies) he himself has felled. Siegfried, that is, burns the tree from which Wotan's spear has been cut. The youth derives strength for his sexual-creation from castrating his father, and incorporating his father's strength. This emblem will reappear in Act III: when Wotan bars his way to Brünnhilde, Siegfried unsanctimoniously smashes the ashen spear of the god and pushes him aside.

The forging scene centers around three categories of action — filing, pumping the bellows, and hammering, all vigorous back and forth motions of the hand and arm. Siegfried fixes the fragments in a vise, and attacks them with the file. Intermittently, he pumps the bellows, an instrument whose phallic attributes are its shape (resembling scrotum and testicles as well as the penis) and its ability to inspire heat. Finally, Siegfried completes the sword by hammering it, the up and down motion emphasized by its incorporation as a rhythm of the music. The motion of masturbation dominates this scene — self-initiation into the mysteries of sex, trial ground of the penis's functioning. Autoerotism, ultimately, is the meaning of the grandiloquent notion of "self-creation," a logical absurdity of course. In his first acts of masturbation the youthful Prometheus steals "knowledge" from his father — or so he experiences his acquisition of sexuality. And if he has stolen, in fantasy he must have dispossessed his father of what he has acquired. How will father respond?

Siegfried's heroism, however, resides in his lack of fear. Fearlessness is the regressive fantasy. Fearlessness is the wish *The Ring* realizes, by magically attributing to the adolescent the lineaments of infancy. Siegfried, as it were, masturbates without guilt and castrates his fathers with impunity. In contrast, each paternal phallic attribute ends in a heap. Mime, risen in fear, sinks in a heap. The ash tree Siegfried felled "now lies heaped on the hearth." Notung is a heap of filings. In *Götterdämmerung* we learn that the World Ash, withered when Siegfried shattered Wotan's spear, has been cut into logs and heaped about Walhall. Brünnhilde begins her final elegy in *The Ring* with an order to heap wood for Siegfried's funeral pyre: "*Starke Scheite schichtet mir dort.*" The severed penis that ends in a heap is like the gold hoard around which the tetralogy revolves — symbolically a fecal heap, useless, barren, a curse.

Siegfried plunges Notung, newly molded from a heap of metal filings, into water, and over the violent hissing of steam says, "Rigid it is, and stiff , lordly, the hard steel!" ("*starr ward er und steif, herrisch der harte Stahl!*") Mime gladly relinquishes the forge, and starts cooking broth. Siegfried has unmanned him, made a housewife of him. "A smith has come to shame," confesses Mime, "the teacher tutored by his pupil; the old man is finished now with that art, and will serve his child as cook: if he melts down his iron to paste, the old man will cook him a broth of eggs" ("*mit der Kunst nun ist's beim Alten aus, als Koch dient er dem Kind. Brennt es das Eisen zu Brei, aus Eiern braut der Alte ihm Sud.*")

Mime's megalomaniacal dreams of glory now are comical and pathetic. He foresees Siegfried's victory over Fafner, and plans to usurp gold hoard and ring. "The despised dwarf, how he will be honored! Hero and god are driven to the hoard: the world will bow to my nod, tremble at my wrath! . . . Mime, the bold one, Mime is king, Prince of Nibelungs, Lord of the world!" Yet Mime's fate is foreshadowed rather in the dramatic climax to Act I. "Strike the false ones," Siegfried exhorts the newly forged Notung, "Cut down the knaves! Look, Mime, you smith: thus cleaves Siegfried's sword!" ("*Schau, Mime, du Schmied: so schneidet Siegfrieds Schwert!*") And crystalizing into a single dramatic gesture all the emblems of castration, Siegfried brings his sword down upon the anvil, slicing it neatly in two.

2.

Act II depicts Siegfried's encounter with Fafner, the sex act conceived in the childish imagination as a violent struggle. At *Neidhöhle* (the "Cave," or "Hollow of Envy"), Siegfried is to learn fear. "Believe me, dearest!" pipes Mime, "if you don't learn fear here today, you'll hardly learn it any other time or place." *Neidhöhle*, the Cave of Envy, is an orifice in the body of mother earth, the entrance to mother's womb, whose possession son begrudges father. Insofar as *Neidhöhle* is the repository of the gold hoard, it also corresponds in bodily terms to the anus. For Mime, however, it is a cavernous mouth, *"ein dunkler Höhlenschlund."* Erotically, particularly in the realm of fantasy, these orifices are often equivalent. The anus becomes a substitute vagina in the infantile theory of anal birth, and in autoerotic fantasies as well as in actual sexual practice. The mouth can function similarly. It is an imaginary route into mother's body: the child, expelled through the vagina, can regain the womb through the terrifying but wished for consummation of being swallowed.

"Do you see that dark cavernous mouth over there? Inside lives a horribly savage serpent: immeasurably cruel he is, and huge; he tears open his terrible jaws; at a single bite, the terrible one will doubtless swallow you, skin, hair and all," warns Mime. Siegfried, however, is unshaken. "It would be good to shut its mouth," he boasts, "so I'll just not offer myself to its jaws."

Mime tries next to frighten Siegfried with Fafner's poisonous slaver. Let it merely touch you, he warns, and it will waste both flesh and bones. Siegfried's off-handed reply is that then he'll step aside.

"A serpent's tail he lashes about," Mime returns, "whoever he embraces with it and firmly grasps—his limbs will shatter like glass!" Siegfried vows he'll keep a sharp eye out.

These three threats, devouring, poisoning, and crushing correspond to the child's most prevalent fantasies of the "terrible mother." Mother will eat him, her milk will poison him, or she will suffocate him in a crushing embrace or by sitting on him. He fears excessive love, being loved to death, which in the case of a child deprived of love is merely the projection onto the mother of the child's own desperate and insatiable longings.

"Has the serpent a heart?" asks Siegfried.

"A cruel, hard heart!" replies Mime.

" . . . I'll thrust Notung into the proud one's heart: is that perhaps what it means to fear?" the hero asks naively.

Mime leaves Siegfried to await Fafner alone. The youthful hero launches into another denial of Mime's paternity. "That he is not my father—how happy I feel about that! Only now does the fresh forest please me; only now does the joyful day laugh for me, now that the nasty one has left me, and I need never see him again!" What did father look like?, he muses. Why, just like himself, of course. Whereas a son of Mime's would resemble the dwarf, "just as nasty, coarse and grizzled, little and crooked, hunchbacked and hobbling, with long hanging ears, oozing eyes—away with the incubus! I want never to see him again."

Pondering his mother's appearance, however, he encounters an imaginative conundrum he solves with a metaphor of romantic extravagance. "Like a doe's her bright eyes must certainly have shimmered — only much more beautiful!" This rhapsodic hyperbole is followed by the heart-rending question, "When she bore me in pain, however, why did she die? Do human mothers all die of bearing their sons? That would be tragic, truly!"

The idea of death of the mother in childbirth merges the infantile fantasies of violent intercourse and birth, and shows traces of both matricide and necrophilia. It is thus in keeping with the event about to occur: the slaying of the "terrible mother" in a sadistic caricature of intercourse. The overly romantic image of the good mother with doe-like eyes is the complementary obverse of the "terrible mother." *Siegfried* enacts the fantasy that the son can possess his mother successfully and with impunity by splitting her, killing the "terrible mother," and assuming omnipotence over the good mother by awakening her, exercising the magical power over life and death.

As though to insist on Fafner's maternal associations, Wagner makes Siegfried next voice the wish to see his mother. "Oh! that I, the son, might see my mother! my mother! — a human woman!" (*"meine Mutter! — ein Menschenweib!"*) That last curious appositive, *"ein Menschenweib,"* suggests that Brünnhilde, the next *human* woman he will see, is the mother he longs for. In the event, however, Siegfried's fateful encounter with Fafner in the form of a dragon turns out to be the proximal answer to this wish.[171]

Siegfried hits on the idea of learning the language of birds because he surmises the forest bird twittering from a nearby branch can tell him something about his dear mother. Eventually the forest bird leads him to Brünnhilde, but first it leads him to Fafner, whom Siegfried awakens with his horn call after an abortive attempt to imitate bird song with a hastily cut reed pipe. These juxtapositions imply that Siegfried gets what he asks for — his mother. In waking Fafner from sleep, Siegfried further parallels the awakening of Brünnhilde. The comic figure of Siegfried coaxing nasal cacophonies from a reed pipe, as well as the more heroic figure cut when he tosses aside the pipe and takes up his horn, suggests an image of Wagner as youthful musician, as aspiring Orpheus in his early attempts at composition. These childish efforts must have aimed at eliciting love and approval from a mother whose attentions he was, rather, accustomed to doing without. Wagner's attraction to music that evoked the weird and fantastical — music that titillated with a thrill of terror — is understandable in this context. For him, such music was imbued with a maternal valance, mixed of terror and longing. Through music, young Richard must have looked for a more intense relationship with mother, like Siegfried, who summons Fafner with his horn in order to learn fear. From the beginning of the opera the hero has sought a companion. "Now let me see," he says setting his horn to his lips, "whom I now attract: will it be a dear companion?"

---

[171] Recall here too that Fafner, as he appears in *Rheingold* in the form of a giant, is recognizably a parental figure.

("... *ob das mir ein lieber Gesell?*") When Fafner appears, to the ominous notes in the contrabass tuba, Siegfried laughs, "Ha, ha! My song has blown me something dear! You would make me a pleasant companion!" ("... *du wärst mir ein saub'rer Gesell!*") Fear and longing are one; the terrifying is desired because intercourse is inseparable from both the fear of castration and the violent fantasy of matricide.

Siegfried transforms *Neidhöhle* from a nest into a grave when he tosses first Mime's corpse, then Fafner's into it. This transformation ties the conclusion of Act II to the opening of Act III, in which Wotan summons Erda to rise out of the earth to answer his question: "How may the god overcome anxiety?" ("*Wie besiegt die Sorge der Gott?*") — the focal problem of *Walküre*. The symbolism of the present scene tacitly answers the question. If the hole in the earth has been made a repository of the dead, the awakening of Erda is another representation of the necrophiliac fantasy — the fantasy that resolves castration anxiety. Corpses don't complain.

The "terrible mother" has been buried in *Neidhöhle*; Erda sleeps in a cave leading to the bowels of the earth. "Awake, Wala! Wala, awake!" commands the god. "I awaken you, slumbering one, from long sleep." This sleep is death-like; behind Erda's awakening is the fantasy of treating a mother's corpse as if it were alive. "I summon you: Arise! Arise! Arise out of misty cavern, out of the nocturnal depths." Here is the underlying motive in necrophilia — omnipotence. The necrophiliac uses the corpse at his convenience, returning it to coffin or grave when he is finished. So necrophilia has the same power as the ring, which rules the world that is mother's body. "Erda! Erda! Eternal woman! Arise out of the depths where you are at home! I sing your song of awakening, that you may awaken; I awaken you from your meditative sleep. All knowing! Primevally wise! Erda! Erda! Eternal woman! Wake, awake, you Wala, awake!"

Erda rises from the cave's mouth as though from her grave. "Powerfully calls the song; mighty is the enticement of the magic. I am awakened from knowing sleep. Who frightens away slumber from me?" she asks.

"I am the awakener" ("*Der Weckrufer bin ich*"), replies Wotan (a designation that equates him with Siegfried), "and I employ ways to waken from afar what is locked in deepest sleep." No one is wiser than Erda, Wotan avers. She knows what is hidden in the depths, and interwoven through mountain, valley, air and water. To imbibe her knowledge, Wotan has awakened her. The markedly necrophiliac fantasy expresses the wish for carnal knowledge without anxiety.

Wotan has wrested love from Erda. "The deeds of men throw mists around my mind." Ask someone else, she tells him. "Me, the knowing one herself, a ruler once forced. I bore Wotan a wish-maiden . . . She is bold, and wise too: why do you wake me and not ask what you wish of Erda's and Wotan's child?" The violence implied in Erda's memory of intercourse with the god stands mid-way between the rape-murder disguised as Siegfried's slaying of Fafner, and the sentimentalized seduction of Brünnhilde.

Brünnhilde has betrayed him, Wotan replies. He cannot ask her because he has renounced relations with her. Betrayed by Oedipal impulses, that is, he can no longer act on them since he has repressed them by putting them "to sleep."

"I grow dizzy since I have awakened: in wild confusion circles the earth!" Erda replies. She perceives it is his own impulses that have betrayed him. "He who taught defiance, punishes defiance? He who incited the deed is angered by the deed? . . . Let me sink again! Let sleep lock up my wisdom!"

But Wotan will not let her go. "You, Mother, I will not allow to depart, so long as I am empowered with magic." ("*Dich, Mutter, lass ich nicht ziehn, da des Zaubers mächtig ich bin.*") But Erda chastens him, as an angry mother a wayward child. "You are not what you call yourself! Why have you come, headstrong wild one, to disturb the sleep of the Wala?"

Wotan hurls in reply, "You are not what you think you are." Evoking the magical omnipotence of the necrophiliac fantasy he tells her, "The wisdom of the primeval mothers comes to its end: your knowledge is blown away by my will." He welcomes the destruction of the gods; he wills it freely. He bequeaths his power to Siegfried who has fearlessly won the ring, and is about to win Brünnhilde, redeemer of the world. "Therefore, sleep now, close your eyes; behold my end in your dreams! . . . Descend then, Erda! Terror of the primeval mothers! Primeval anxiety! Descend! Descend to eternal sleep!" Here is the necrophiliac strategy to allay anxiety: Wotan returns the corpse to its grave.

But the next scene answers Wotan's question in another way. In the guise of the Wanderer, he encounters Siegfried on his way to Brünnhilde's rock and perfunctorily bars his way, playing the role of jealous father to Siegfried's ardent wooer. Siegfried aptly cites Wotan's missing eye here, for the scene exemplifies the god's castration. "What do you actually look like? What sort of big hat have you got? Why hangs it over your face like that?

. . . **W**hy, you're missing an eye under it: someone no doubt knocked that out for you in whose way you stood too defiantly?" Wotan is in effect semi-castrated — self-castrated at that, like Klingsor in *Parsifal*. For castration itself is one solution (Pyrrhic, certainly) to castration anxiety.

Another solution, embodied in Wagner's idealization of the revolutionary Siegfried, is defiance (castration) of the prohibiting superego in fearless, exuberant, unrepentant sexual indulgence. Wotan's role as superego is epitomized in Siegfried's challenge, "Hoho! You prohibitor! Who are you that you wish to block me?" (*"Hoho! Du Verbieter! Wer bist du den daß du mir wheren willst?"*) In a profoundly emblematic gesture, Siegfried shatters Wotan's ashen spear, and proceeds to win Brünnhilde. Nevertheless, in the next and final opera, Hagen's spear will complete the circle of vengeance. The crime of Oedipus will, in the end, exact its price.

The circular, paradoxical irony is epitomized in Wotan's token resistance to Siegfried. Though all along he means for Siegfried to ravish Brünnhilde, as manifestation of the superego's prohibition he must ritually submit to castration, as Siegfried in his turn will submit to Hagen's spear. "Fear the guardian of the rock!" warns Wotan hollowly. "Locked within my power lies the sleeping maiden." Then — not merely resigned to the inevitable, but embracing it — he adds, "Whoever wakes her, whoever wins her, makes me powerless forever!"

When Fafner dies, Siegfried remarks contemptuously, "Nothing to be learned from the dead. So let my living sword be my guide!" His "living sword" leads him to intercourse with Brünnhilde. "Notung! Notung! Enviable sword!" as he earlier apostrophized the inert steel in the forging scene of Act I. "To life I wake you once more. You lay dead in fragments there; now you gleam defiant and majestic." The reanimated sword gives Siegfried power to slay Fafner, that is, to render mother's surrogate body an inert corpse. The necrophiliac fantasy, however, is not only of murder, but of magical power.

Siegfried's powers, that is, derive not just from brawn and audacity. As though supernaturally, he is also able to *restore* the surrogate mother to life in awakening Brünnhilde, whose armor he slices open with his "living sword." Cutting the armor reveals that she "is no man," but a woman. "Mother" is transformed from Fafner to Brünnhilde. Siegfried has castrated the phallic Fafner. This now harmless female "mother" can safely be restored to life in the person of Brünnhilde. Possessing both ring and sword, Siegfried exercises the power of life and death. In *Götterdämmerung*, Siegfried ingenuously yields the ring and its omnipotence to Brünnhilde as a love token, and becomes unwittingly vulnerable to the destruction she later devises. If the infant's problem is sharing one life with mother, the adult's problem is sharing one penis with mother surrogate.

The incestuous relationship between Siegfried and Brünnhilde is treated here nearly as overtly as that of Siegmund and Sieglinde in *Walküre*. To begin with, Brünnhilde is (as we have seen) Siegfried's aunt. That relationship — mother's sister — has the double meaning of mother *and* sister,[172] suggesting that the figure of Brünnhilde comprises both incestuous possibilities. Finding the sleeping warrior is "no man," Siegfried reflexively calls on his mother for help. Curiously, he applies masculine pronouns to her. *"Wen ruf' ich zum Heil, daß er mir helfe?"* ("Whom [masculine form] shall I call to aid, that *he* might help me?") he asks, and at once answers his own question, *"Mutter! Mutter! Gedenke mein'!"* ("Mother! Mother! Think of me!") This shift from masculine pronouns to feminine noun conforms to the transition from phallic to virginal mother, from Fafner to Brünnhilde.

"Oh Mother! Mother! your brave child!" he cries out again. This textual ambiguity (is he invoking his mother, Sieglinde, or addressing the sleeping woman?) intentionally confuses Brünnhilde with his mother. "In sleep lies a woman: she has taught him to fear! How do I end the fear? How seize the courage? That I myself may awaken, the maid must revive me!" he says, expressing with this hyperbolic inversion the life and death dependency that characterizes the infant's relation to its mother. Brünnhilde remains deaf to his appeals. "She does not hear me," he says. "Then will I suck life from sweetest lips — though I should thereby dyingly perish!" (" . . . *sollt' ich auch sterbend vergeh'n!"*)

Paradoxically, he will suck life from her lips (like an infant at mother's breast) though he should die from it.[173] Wagner's

---

[172] In Swedish, this double meaning is explicit in the word itself: the relation who is aunt by virtue of being mother's sister is called "*moster*," a contracted form of *mors syster*.

[173] Siegfried's figure of speech suggests the childish fantasy of poison milk. The idea of sucking life from the sleeping woman's lips echoes Wotan's farewell paean to Brünnhilde's eyes at the conclusion of *Walküre*.

stage directions specify further that, "He sinks, *as though dying*, onto the sleeping one" (my emphasis). He kisses Brünnhilde (metaphorically, "sucks life" from her lips) to awaken her. But his sunken attitude suggests that restoring her to life may entail his own dying. Either Brünnhilde can be alive (the emblem *en scène* proclaims) or Siegfried — not both.

Now Brünnhilde wakes, and gives overt expression to her maternal essence. "Oh Siegfried! Siegfried!" she exclaims, "blessed hero! You awakener of life, conquering light! Oh if you, joy of the world, knew how ever I have loved you! You were my thought, my worry! I nourished you, tender one, even ere you were conceived; even ere you were born my shield sheltered you: so long have I loved you, Siegfried!" These words voice a mother's anticipation of parturition and parenthood. Brünnhilde's "shield" accordingly is her womb. Siegfried's response is apt. "Did my mother then not die? Did the loved one but sleep?" ("*So starb nicht meine Mutter? Schlief die Minnige nur?*") Brünnhilde tells him laughingly, "You delightful child, your mother will not return to you."

"I am you yourself if you love me, happy one," she goes on. The merged identities of lovers is a conventional figure which reappears in *Götterdämmerung* (and notably in *Tristan und Isolde*). The trope is related to the theme of the devouring mother, for to be consumed is of course the ultimate merger of identities. Wotan had warned Siegfried ominously, "soon igniting flames will devour and consume you!" Now, Siegfried applies this idea figuratively to his own passion — though he has broken unharmed through the magic fire, "A devouring fire has been kindled within me." He will leap into Brünnhilde's "watery flood" and be devoured in her "waves."

"I love you: Oh, if you loved me! I am no longer myself: Oh, if I had you! A lovely pool billows before me; with all of my senses I see only it, the blissfully billowing waves . . . I burn to cool the searing fire in the flood; I myself, as I am, leap into the stream: Oh, that its waves might blissfully devour me, and my desire fade in the flood!"

Brünnhilde unwittingly[174] evokes Fafner the dragon. "Siegfried! Siegfried!" she cries, in her last, futile attempt to scare him off. "Do you not see me? As my gaze devours you, are you not struck blind? When my arm presses you tight, do you not burst into flame? As my blood surges toward you in streams, do you not feel the wild fire? Do you not fear, Siegfried, do you not fear the wild raging woman?" The typically mixed Wagnerian metaphors notwithstanding, these three threats correspond closely to Fafner's threats: infantile fears of devouring, smothering, and poisoning. And lest we miss the parallel, Wagner sets Brünnhilde's warning to the dragon's writhing motif.

The idea that Siegfried and Brünnhilde are symbolically a single person parallels *Walküre*, where the daughter Brünnhilde was father Wotan's innermost "thought." The identity forced the necrophiliac conclusion to that opera. In the same way, because the lovers are one, with only one life between them, one of the two must die as it were into union with the other. Either Brünnhilde must devour Siegfried, or Siegfried must destroy Brünnhilde. "Oh Siegfried," Brünnhilde pleads to the themes from the *Siegfried Idyll*, ". . . see my fear! . . . do not approach me with violent closeness!

---

[174] Though Wagner was not unwitting.

Do not force me with your destroying force! Do not shatter your beloved!"

The necrophiliac logic goes a step further. If the lovers are in truth a single entity, the death of one must entail the death of both. This final turn of emotional logic leads to the opera's consummation. *Liebestod*, whose definitive form is Isolde's apostrophe to Tristan's corpse, is also the basis of the closing duet of *Siegfried*, "*Leuchtende Liebe, lachender Tod!*" ("Radiant love, laughing death!"), as well as Brünnhilde's immolation in *Götterdämmerung*. In fact, the conjunction of love and death pervades most Wagnerian operas, including the youthful sketches. Only *Die Meistersinger* is an unqualified exception.

Love and death are inseparable in Wagner because love is linked with the anxiety informing the necrophiliac fantasy. Isolde's rapturous *Liebestod* and Brünnhilde's immolation reenact Wagner's childhood "seductions" by maternal females while asleep, experiences reflecting in turn a fixation on the earliest sexual seductions, real or fancied, by his mother. To repeat these seductions in fantasy, Wagner must become a corpse. Hence, Siegfried learns fear and love together. "Oh Mother! Mother!" he exclaims at this new sensation. "Your brave child! In sleep lies a woman: she has taught him to fear! How do I end the fear? How seize the courage?"

The alternative to seduction in the semblance of a corpse is to ravish mother by the same violence attributed to the father in the sex act. One of the lovers must die in the act of love; and if one, then both. Necrophilia thus contains not only the wish that the love object be safely dead, but the wish to be dead oneself. It is a perversion of passivity, whose ultimate form is death. This, finally, is the meaning of *"Götterdämmerung,"* Wotan's self-willed self-annihilation. Corpses feel no anxiety.

Thus is all the opera's brooding resolved. Mime learns how Notung may be forged. Siegfried gains carnal knowledge. And Wotan contrives to allay anxiety. Brünnhilde yields to Siegfried's importunities at last. "Laughingly I must love you, laughingly be blinded, laughingly go to ruin! Farewell, Walhall's glittering world! May your proud fortress crumble to dust! Farewell, splendid magnificence of the gods! End in bliss, you eternal race! Norns, sunder your rope of runes! Twilight of the gods—darken the heights! Night of annihilation—let the fog roll in!" (*"Nacht der Vernichtung, neble herein!"*) Thus throwing caution to the winds, Brünnhilde's ominous words quite belie the triumphal music with which Wagner brings *Siegfried* to a deceptively rapturous close. Beneath the surface, Wotan's revolutionary project, pursued according to a stepwise logic that promised so bright, so forward-thrusting a future, circles back instead toward night and chaos.

Chapter V

Götterdämmerung: Splitting

The Ring ends, as it began, at the Rhine. As the action of *Rheingold* was immersed in the river, the river inundates *Götterdämmerung*'s final scene, reclaiming its ring and its bodies. Return is nature's law.

This opera's most prominent theme is betrayal. Precluding further solution, betrayal completes the cycle of provisional Oedipal solutions with the consummation of death. Even betrayal itself is transcended in the *love-death* of mutual oblivion. Siegfried's fling with Gutrune, as impetuously as he embraces it, is no casual lapse. Vacuous though the relationship may be, it has been spun by Norns into the strands of destiny. Necessity dictates, not so much that Siegfried find bliss in lackluster Gutrune's arms, as that in one way or another, before the strands of time run out, he betray Brünnhilde. Betrayal in *Götterdämmerung* expresses the ultimate insolubility of the Oedipal dilemma: the son may neither possess his mother free of guilt, nor abandon without betraying her.

The prelude opens with a repetition of that cadence-like progression of two chords that accompanied Brünnhilde's awakening in *Siegfried*. The Norns are as startled as she had been. "What light shines there?" the first Norn asks, accustomed to spinning in darkness. "Is dawn breaking already?" (*"Dämmert der Tag schon auf?"*) the second interweaves, using the word *dämmern*, which here (with irony) has the opposite meaning from that in the opera's title. The third Norn: no, it is only Loge's flames glowing around Brünnhilde's rock. "It still is night. Why do we not spin and sing?" The theme here is vision. But whereas Brünnhilde's sight was restored with daylight, the Norns have night vision. They see by *dreaming*. The Norns, perhaps, *are* dreams, as Erda hinted in *Rheingold*. Light is deceptive. "Does the day dawn?" (*"Dämmert der Tag?"* Wagner coyly repeats this irony.) "Or the flame glow? Clouded, my eyes deceive me," says the first Norn. But in sleep comes revelation.[175]

The Norns' colloquy constitutes the recitation of a dream, then, and the dream is *The Ring* itself. For the Norns recount the saga much as Wotan did in his *Walküre* monologue. The dream begins emblematically. "At the World-Ash once I spun, where large and strong a forest of consecrated boughs sprouted green from its trunk. In its cool shade purled a spring, its ripples whispering wisdom; there I chanted holy

---

[175] In *Die Meistersinger*, Act III, scene 2, Sachs tells Walther, " My friend, it is precisely the poet's task/to interpret and record his dreamings./Believe me, man's truest illusion/is revealed to him in dreams:/all poetry and versification/is nothing but interpretation of true dreams ." *"Mein Freund! Das grad' ist Dichters Werk,/dass er sein Träumen deut' und merk'./Glaubt mir, des Menschen wahrster Wahn/wird ihm im Traume aufgetan:/all' Dichtkunst und Poeterei/ist nichts als Wahrtraumdeuterei."*

things." The tree and spring constitute an emblem of parental genitalia: the ash tree, the phallus; the spring, redolent of motherly wisdom, the vagina.[176] "A bold god," the Norn continues "stepped to drink at the spring; one of his eyes he paid as eternal price." The vaginal symbolism of the spring is—by deduction at least—unmistakable, for in *Rheingold* Wotan reminded Fricka that winning her cost him his eye. Wotan's "drink at the spring" is the Norn's euphemism for intercourse.

"From the World-Ash then Wotan broke a branch; a spear's shaft the strong one cut from the trunk." As son, Wotan derives his sexuality from the potency of the father, an acquisition perceived to entail the father's castration. "Over the long course of time the wound sapped the forest; serely fell the leaves; dry, the tree starved; sadly the spring's draught dried: melancholy my song became. Today, though, I weave no more at the World-Ash; the fir must do to fasten the strands to." This emblem of degeneracy suggests the disillusionment with parents that leads to the child's construction of the family romance, as well as the melancholy that attends renunciation of Oedipal ambitions.

---

[176] The symbolic shift is not inconsistent. Hunding's tree in *Walküre* was said to represent the maternal. But that the mother incorporates both male and female parental roles has been repeatedly observed. The pre-oedipal mother is experienced as phallic. Moreover, Wagner's mother, twice widowed, served, like Mime, as "both father and mother" to her children. Symbol derive meaning not only from their shapes, but from their functions as well. In *Walküre*, the tree plays the essentially feminine role of being penetrated by Wotan's sword. The "World-Ash," on the other hand, is phallic; it grows, sprouts branches, then fades, and is cut and left in a heap—cycle of tumescence and detumescence.

The cycle of potency and castration is given another revolution in the vision of the second Norn, who sees Wotan the castrating son in his turn become the castrated father. "Wotan cut runes of truly deliberated covenants in the shaft of the spear; he held it in warrant of the world. A bold hero shattered the spear in battle; to splinters flew the holy warrant of covenants. Then Wotan commanded Walhall's heroes to fell in pieces the World-Ash, trunk and withered branches: the ash fell; the spring dried up forever!"

The Norns' emblem displays the systemic interrelation among the persons of the classic triad. The son, drinking from the maternal spring, breaks a branch from the paternal ash. But the withering tree entails the son's own castration, and with it, the drying up of the spring's longed for waters. A vicious circle. The son cannot realize his wishes without suffering guilt, which in turn, renders fulfillment impossible. He must disarm his rival father, yet be himself unmanned by guilt. No sooner does the wish for a sexual relation with the mother begin to be actualized than guilt intervenes to frustrate consummation. Though each solution to the Oedipal dilemma attempts to side-step this paralyzing guilt through displacement and symbolism, the identical mechanism again comes into play—an eternal round, a circle. Wagner tries to satisfy Oedipal longing in marrying motherly Minna, but once wed, the sexual spring dries up. Minna is frigid, just as mother was depriving and rejecting. Frigidity was the punishment required for investing Minna with the maternal valence. This punishment, in turn, justified the quest for gratification in extramarital affairs. But these adventures merely perpetuated a cycle of infantile response to deprivation experienced as having been deserved.

The third Norn predicts the immolation of Walhall, another disguised castration. Loge (libido) sets it alight. Wotan will pierce the fire god's breast with splinters of his shattered spear, and with them ignite the hall of heroes. Sexuality, that is, exhausts itself in actualization. The Norn's agitation rises musically as she recounts Alberich's theft of the gold. The dwarf's curse gnaws at the frayed strands of fate. The cord breaks. "Ended, eternal knowing! The wise tell the world nothing more. Down to the mother, down!" sing the Norns finally. "The mother" is Erda, spring of wisdom, archetype of the "fountain" at which Wotan is accustomed to "drink."

In Wagner's original conception for *Siegfried's Death*, the Norns' scene functioned as *exposition* of events subsequently *dramatized* in the other operas of *The Ring*. This expository function, accordingly, is replaced in the tetralogy by a strictly thematic one. The audience need not be told what they have already witnessed; this scene, which Wagner regarded as a prologue to Act I proper, prepares the ground thematically for what follows. The Norns' theme of castration achieves its climax in the tearing of the strands of fate, "*Es riss! . . . Es riss ! . . . Es riss!*" Tearing, severing, is castration. But the severed strands also lead thematically to the "prologue's" second scene: Siegfried's departure. In contrast to the Norns, who regress by sinking to mother's protective womb, Siegfried cuts the umbilical cord that ties him to Brünnhilde and departs.

The maudlin tenor of the leave-taking scene throws a veil of denial over the truly traumatic nature of the break. Brünnhilde pretends to relinquish possession of Siegfried. "How could I love you, precious hero, and not release you to fresh deeds?" she asks rhetorically. Yet discernible in this scene of seemingly gracious (indeed selfless) renunciation is the formula that underlies necrophilia: in nourishing her son, mother is sucked dry. To live himself, he must sap her of life. "Just one concern gives me pause," Brünnhilde goes on, "that my merit has brought you too little! What the gods taught me, I gave you, a rich hoard of holy runes; yet the hero, to whom now I bow, has taken from me the virginal strength of my tribe. Bereft of wisdom, yet filled with desire; rich in love, yet emptied of strength—may you not despise the poor one, who can only grant, not give you more."

Siegfried's gratitude is expressed in terms of extravagance. He belittles his own accomplishments: no less than forging his own sword, slaying a dragon, and passing through a ring of magic fire to reawaken a goddess. "You gave more, Wondrous Woman, than I know how to embrace" ("*wahren*"). Life, bestowed by mother, is the gift uniquely beyond measure. Though the awakening of Brünnhilde constitutes the rescue fantasy whereby the son attempts to repay his mother, Brünnhilde's vain effort to remind Siegfried of his deeds indicates how profoundly dependent the hero remains. Only in the compromise of identity can Siegfried resolve this lover's duel over which is the more profoundly indebted.

Brünnhilde bids him, "Bethink the oaths that unite us; bethink the troth we hold to; bethink the love we live: Brünnhilde burns holy then forever in your breast!" They exchange love pledges: his ring for her horse. Here too, Siegfried is self-effacing. "Shall I yet accomplish deeds through your virtue only?" he asks. "You choose my battles, my victories redound to you: on your horse's back, in the shelter of your shield—I think I am Siegfried no longer: I am just Brünnhilde's arm!"

Though the over-arching theme of Siegfried's metaphor is the conventionally romantic merging of lovers, it takes in this instance a very particular turn. Siegfried as Brünnhilde's "arm" represents Siegfried as Brünnhilde's penis. The idea derives from the fantasy that a woman's baby is her penis, an emotional equation that constitutes, in the Freudian view, the normal female resolution of the castration complex. Observation of her mother's lack of a penis convinces the little girl of the irrevocability of her own imagined "castration." She settles for her ability to have a baby as the chance to acquire a substitute penis.[177]

The image of arm as penis recurs near the end of the opera when Hagen tries to seize the ring from Siegfried's corpse. The hero's arm rises magically, threateningly like an erection. Hagen recoils as Brünnhilde strides onto the scene to reclaim her lover, lifeless save for that erectile arm bearing the ring.

Siegfried's farewell suggests the predicament of mother facing an empty nest. Time has turned the tables. At the child's birth, mother was the omnipotent *creatrix*. Out of nothing she made this child born in helpless dependency. Now, it has grown magically more powerful than she. Into the child she has poured (not to say emptied) her whole self — her strength, her knowledge, her affection — and her recompense is to be abandoned by the child who must make his own way in the world. If the child, moreover, is mother's "arm" — as Siegfried

---

[177] See Sigmund Freud, "On the Transformation of Instinct as Exemplified in Anal Erotism," *Standard Edition*, vol. XVII, pp. 127-133; "The Dissolution of the Oedipus Complex," vol. XIX, pp. 173-179; "Some Psychical Consequences of the Anatomical Distinction between the Sexes," vol. XIX, pp. 248-258; Ruth Mack Brunswick, "The Pre-oedipal Phase of the Libido Development," *Psychoanalytic Quarterly* (1940), pp. 303, 309-311.

declares himself to be — his abandonment constitutes a symbolic dismemberment. Likewise, if baby is mother's penis, its loss is a castration, a re-castration (to add insult to injury), undoing what turns out to have been the temporary solution to her impoverished, "castrated" condition. This accounts for Brünnhilde's murderous bitterness, for Siegfried's betrayal is no mere infidelity.[178]

The idea that Siegfried is part of her — that as lovers they share an identity — appeals to Brünnhilde. "If only Brünnhilde were your soul," she says longingly.

"Through her, my courage is inflamed," Siegfried answers.

"So you are Siegfried *and* Brünnhilde?" she asks.

"Wherever I am," Siegfried replies, "both of us sequester." Brünnhilde answers this riddle naively, literally. "Must my rock then be deserted?" she asks. "United, it holds us both!" says Siegfried, completing the paradox.

"Oh holy gods!" croons the Valkyrie, "noble races! Let your eyes graze on this most consecrated couple! Apart — who can separate them?" she muses, proposing a paradox of her own. "Separate — never are they parted!"

The search for psychic origins of the romantic conceit that lovers constitute a single, indivisible person, discussed above

---

[178] The contemporary dispute over sexism inherent in Freud's psychology of the female castration complex and of female sexuality generally is not especially relevant to the present discussion, since the fantasy in question is a man's, not a woman's. In short, we are not for the moment concerned with the truth about female psychology, but with Wagner's conscious and unconscious projection of it. Wagner's view itself might plausibly be characterized as "sexist," to be sure, but that is a separate topic.

in connection with Brünnhilde's sleep, can now be taken a step further back, to the point from which the necrophiliac idea itself springs. Its basis is the primary identification with mother—literally, physically true before birth—that yields in the infant mind only gradually to the reality of separation. As Fairbairn puts it, "Dependence is exhibited in its most extreme form in the intra-uterine state; and we may legitimately infer that, on its psychological side, this state is characterized by an absolute degree of identification and absence of differentiation. Identification may thus be regarded as representing persistence into extra-uterine life of a relationship existing before birth. Insofar as identification persists after birth, the individual's object constitutes not only his world, but also himself."[179]

Freud characterizes exaggerated romantic love as regression. " . . . *Identification has appeared instead of object-choice, and that object-choice has regressed to identification.* We have heard that identification is the earliest and original form of emotional tie; it often happens that . . . object-choice is turned back into identification—the ego assumes the characteristics of the object."[180] Love characterized by identification is immature and backward-looking. Freud sees in it a decidedly destructive element. "Identification, in fact, is ambivalent from the very first; it can turn into an expression of tenderness as easily as into a wish for someone's removal. It behaves like a derivative of the first, oral phase of the organization of the

---

[179] W. R. D. Fairbairn, *Object Relations Theory*, p. 47. Cf., Freud's assessment of Romain Rolland's "oceanic feeling" in the opening pages of *Civilization and its Discontents* as the "primitive ego-feeling" preserved from infancy.
[180] Sigmund Freud, "Group Psychology," *Standard Edition*, vol. XVIII, pp. 106, 107 (emphasis, Freud's).

libido, in which the object that we long for and prize is assimilated by eating and is in that way annihilated as such. The cannibal, as we know, has remained at this standpoint; he has a devouring affection for his enemies and only devours people of whom he is fond."[181] Thus, in the type of love exemplified by Siegfried and Brünnhilde, "the ego has enriched itself with the properties of the object; it has 'introjected' the object into itself . . . "[182]

Fairbairn simplifies the Freudian developmental scheme, which is divided into phases of dominance of different erotogenic zones. He separates personality development into stages of "infantile dependence" and "mature dependence," with a transitional stage of "quasi-independence" mediating between them. "Infantile dependence" is characterized by the primary identification appropriate to the newborn. "Mature dependence," based on recognition of the separateness of ego from object, is the love relation to which adulthood aspires.

Fairbairn concedes, however, that, "The relationship involved in mature dependence is, of course, only theoretically possible. Nevertheless, it remains true that *the more mature a relationship is, the less it is characterized by primary identification*; for what such identification essentially represents is failure to differentiate the object."[183] The implication is that, however appealing and "poetic," the romantic identification of lovers constitutes a fundamentally infantile attitude. The ambivalence of Siegfried's leave-taking—in fact a departure, a splitting apart, the declaration of inseparability

---

[181] *Ibid.*, p. 105.
[182] *Ibid.*, p. 107.
[183] Fairbairn, *op. cit.*, p. 42 (emphasis, Fairbairn's).

notwithstanding—corresponds to the characteristic ambivalence of Fairbairn's transitional stage between infantile and mature dependence. "During this period, accordingly, the behaviour of the individual is characterized both by desperate endeavours on his part to separate himself from the object and desperate endeavours to achieve reunion with the object—desperate attempts 'to escape from prison' and desperate attempts 'to return home.'"[184]

The "prison" from which Siegfried struggles now to escape is the encircling fire of his passionate cathexis to Brünnhilde. The hero's hasty return disguised as Gunther can be regarded as emblematic of his ambivalence over abandoning the maternal figure. For his new attachment to Gutrune is unconvincing from the start. *The abandonment of infantile dependence involves an abandonment of relationships based upon primary identification in favour of relationships with differentiated objects.*[185] But though, under the influence of Hagen's potion, he forgets Brünnhilde, Siegfried never ceases to be bound to her. He rides her horse; he is still her arm. She bears his ring.

Siegfried's escape route up the Rhine is reminiscent of Fairbairn's observation that, "In dreams the process of differentiation is frequently reflected in the theme of trying to cross a gulf or chasm, albeit the crossing which is attempted may also occur in a regressive direction. The process itself is commonly attended by considerable anxiety; and this anxiety finds characteristic expression in dreams of falling, as also in such symptoms as acrophobia and agoraphobia. On the other hand, anxiety over failure of the process is reflected in

[184] *Ibid.*, p. 43.
[185] *Ibid.*, p. 42 (emphasis, Fairbairn's).

nightmares about being imprisoned or confined under-ground or immersed in the sea, as well as in the symptom of claustrophobia."[186]

The romantic ideal of fusion with the "object" is generated from the tension between the fantasy of eternal union with mother and the reality of separation from her. Since the fantasy is regressive, and points (albeit unconsciously) towards the intra-uterine existence of the fetus, its tendency is away from life, towards non-life. The lovers' identity thus reaches its ultimate form in the *Liebestod*, the *love-death*. At the abortive conclusion to their night of love, Tristan invites Isolde to follow him into the country of death: "It is the dark, nocturnal land, from which my mother sent me when I whom she bore in dying, left her in death to reach the light. What when she bore me was her love-refuge, the wondrous realm of night, from which I once awoke: that Tristan offers you, and goes there in advance."

Siegfried cannot lose a battle; he cannot fall to an adversary. He is destroyed only through his betrayal of Brünnhilde, which is fated, and implies that the ultimate insolubility of Oedipal conflict lies in pre-oedipal issues. Not in the triadic struggle with parents does the son succumb, but in the diadic struggle with mother over independence. Separation anxiety is the son's stumbling block, not the threat of the father or the superego. For Siegfried survives the threats of the superego figures, Wotan and Mime. He survives the devouring "terrible mother" in the shape of Fafner. That infantile fear, though commonplace and potent, is never enacted in reality;

---

[186] *Ibid.*, p. 42.

mothers do not eat their young. The insuperable threat is separation from Brünnhilde, which both regard as betrayal. As the fetus perforce departs a mother's encircling body, the adolescent is fated to abandon the narrow scope of her world.

The *love-death* fantasy is further clarified by Freud's observation (alluded to above) of the destructive element in identification: the beloved is cannibalistically "eaten up," and thus annihilated. Exaggerated romantic love is actually narcissistic, argues Freud, an interpretation consistent with the view that the lovers in *The Ring* are projected images of internalized objects. " . . . The object is being treated in the same way as our own ego, so that when we are in love a considerable amount of narcissistic libido overflows on to the object. It is even obvious, in many forms of love-choice, that the object serves as a substitute for some unattained ego ideal of our own."[187]

Identification is mutual cannibalism. The ego eats up and is eaten by the object. In idealizing the beloved (as Siegfried and Brünnhilde obviously do), ". . . The ego becomes more and more unassuming and modest, and the object more and more sublime and precious, until at last it gets possession of the entire self-love of the ego, whose self-sacrifice thus follows as a natural consequence. The object has, so to speak, consumed the ego."[188]

---

[187] Sigmund Freud, "Group Psychology," p. 112.
[188] *Ibid.*, p. 113. In his paper "On Narcissism" (vol. XIV), Freud distinguishes between the "ego-libido" (love of self, stemming from the infant's earliest gratification from bodily processes and sensations), and a secondary "object-libido" (love of others stemming from dependence on mother). Freud observed a reciprocity between them; dominance of one

This destructive quality of narcissistic attachment helps explain the sadistic and necrophiliac components of the final *love-death* of Siegfried and Brünnhilde at the end of the opera. Gored by Hagen's spear, dying, Siegfried cries deliriously, "Brünnhilde! Holy bride! Awake! Open your eyes! Who has locked you again in sleep? Who has bound you in such fearful slumber? The awakener came; he kisses you awake and once more breaks the bride's bonds." In his delirium, Siegfried relives the final scene of the previous opera. The particular language of the delirium, however, refers to the necrophiliac formula: you or I. Only in dying himself can Siegfried Brünnhilde with life; conversely, Brünnhilde must die for Siegfried. The dilemma of union is resolved only by death, in which the lovers romantically, magically "awaken forever" to love. "Now laughs Brünnhilde's joy for him!" sings Siegfried with his dying breath. "Ah, these eyes, open now forever! Ah this breathing's blissful breeze! Sweet dying—blessed dread—Brünnhilde—greets me!"

---

tends to absorb and impoverish the other. He draws an analogy between the relationship of "object-libido" to "ego-libido" and the pseudopodia of cells. When another person is loved (the pseudopodium is extended), libido is drained from its primary object, the self. Conversely, to the extent that self-love is dominant in the personality, libido is withdrawn from external objects. "The highest phase of development of which object-libido is capable is seen in the state of being in love, when the subject seems to give up his own personality in favor of an object-cathexis; while we have the opposite condition in the paranoiac's phantasy (or self-perception) of the 'end of the world.'" (p. 76). *The Ring*'s fantasy of ultimate holocaust, then, is the natural complement of Siegfried's excessively romantic love, in which the object is worshipped at the expense of the self. In narcissism, the self is loved at the expense of the world, to the extent—in its extremest form—of world annihilation.

Siegfried's final version of the *Liebestod* offers up his own life for his beloved's. Yet its logic requires a similar sacrifice of Brünnhilde, one she is not long in carrying out. Of course a murder-suicide pact like this is a son's fantasy (Wagner's fantasy), and not actuality. The son transforms deprivation into martyrdom, and wishes mother (in reprisal) to join him in the flames. Brünnhilde's immolation thus conceals a fantasy of matricide, glossed over by the ardent hyperboles of the Valkyrie's final aria and the musical glories of Wagner's score.

In *Parsifal* it is the mother, not the foolish hero, who dies as a result of his abandonment. But this reversal is merely a variation on the theme. One lives at the expense of the other. Brünnhilde empties herself into Siegfried; Siegfried loses his identity in the gifts of Brünnhilde. One is no more than the other. Betrayal means not just loss of the object, but loss of self, death.

Though death comes by Hagen's hand, it is in effect self-determined, for Hagen is Siegfried's double. Just as Siegfried first appeared as active hero, forging swords, slaying dragons, and so on, but now is "only Brünnhilde's arm," so Hagen, though introduced as scheming antagonist, emerges by the end of Act II as merely the agent of Brünnhilde's revenge. Hagen, with his deadly spear, becomes Brünnhilde's avenging phallus. The parallel lineage of hero Siegfried and anti-hero Hagen also reveals their equivalence. Hagen is son of Black Wotan; Siegfried, son (technically, grand-son) of Light Alberich. Each is charged with carrying out his father's project. Conceived in seduction out of wedlock, both are alien wherever they go. Siegfried remains as out of place in the Hall of the Gibichungs as he was in Mime's cave. Though he swears blood brotherhood with Gunther, it is only to be betrayed, for like Hagen, he is never more than a half-brother.

For that very reason, Hagen refuses to take part in the oath. "My blood would spoil the drink for you," he declares. "Mine does not flow true and noble like yours; stubborn and cold, it stagnates in me; it won't ruddy my cheeks. Therefore I stay away from the fiery bond." Hagen's reference to his sluggish, mongrel blood anticipates somewhat the morbid blood symbolism of *Parsifal*, and the project of the Grail Brotherhood to preserve its threatened racial purity.[189]

Underlying Wagner's concern with brotherhood and blood was the anxiety that he was the "mongrel," fathered not by the legitimate head of family whose blood flowed in his siblings' veins, but by his mother's paramour, who he feared was a Jew. If Siegfried is Wagner's ego-ideal, Hagen is the projection of this fear. Either projection, interestingly, is alien to the "brotherhood" sworn to, because the one is higher, the other lower born than they. Hagen is son to a dwarf, while Siegfried is the son of a god.

Legitimacy and brotherhood are the issue of the first scene between Gunther and Hagen. Gunther asks his half-brother whether his own reputation befits his father's fame, a stinging question, since though born of the same mother, Hagen was not sired a Gibichung. "I think to envy you," he replies, "legitimately titled. Dame Griemhild who bore both us brothers gave me to understand that."

---

[189] See Robert Gutman, *Richard Wagner*, pp. 594-601.

"I envy you," Gunther objects; "do not you envy me! If my legacy was primogeniture, wisdom was yours alone: half-brother strife (*Halbbrüderzwist*) was never better mastered; only to praise your counsel do I inquire about my fame."

A moment later, though, Gunther rebukes Hagen for stirring up *Halbbrüderzwist* by whetting his appetite for the unattainable. For Hagen has counseled the king to win Brünnhilde for his queen. "Why do you waken doubt and strife? (*"Was weckst du Zweifel und Zwist?"*) You stir desire in me for that which I cannot command!" Hagen is the true brother after all. Love, peace, unity are but a mask for rivalry. "Brotherhood is always a quarrel over the paternal inheritance."[190] Hagen is excluded from Gibich's legacy of power; Gunther reigns unchallenged. But the legacy of Hagen's own father (is it Alberich or Wotan?) is the ring, whose omnipotence could displace the paltry power of the Gibichung. Hagen has a plan. Could Gutrune capture Siegfried's heart with the aid of a potion of forgetfulness, then Siegfried might win for Gunther the otherwise unattainable bride of fire. "Now speak," Hagen gloats, "What do you think of Hagen's counsel?"

Gunther is all adulation. "Praised be Griemhild who gave us this brother!" he exclaims. Yet behind Hagen's apparent collusion with Gunther and Gutrune lurks his own ambition to acquire the ring, "the paternal inheritance." When Siegfried happens by in his skiff, it is precisely the parental inheritance that Gunther rhetorically offers him, in token of friendship, or, as it turns out, brotherhood. "Greet joyfully,

---

[190] Norman O. Brown, *Love's Body* (New York, 1966), p. 17.

Oh hero, the hall of my father; wherever you walk, whatsoever you see, consider now your own: yours is my legacy, land and folk."

This gift seems calculated to stir brother Hagen's jealousy, who must never aspire to such a prize. But Hagen has set his heart on the ring anyway. Though the "brotherhood" trope conventionally epitomizes love and unity, the *archetypal* brothers are, as Norman O. Brown observes, "Romulus and Remus, Cain and Abel, Osiris and Set; and one of them murders the other. Or rather they both accuse each other of fratricide and put each other to death for the crime. . . The mutual relations of the brothers reenact the primal scene, the cannibalistic intercourse, and the primal crime, the dismemberment. The brothers are brothers to dragons, dragon seed sown (*Spartoi*), that comes up as young men armed for a Pyrrhic dance in which they mow each other down. All fraternity is fratricidal."[191] Platitudes about "brotherhood," then, are civilization's denial that the most intense rivalries are among siblings.

Hagen quickly takes over the interview with Siegfried from Gunther. Even the ingenuous Siegfried observes that Hagen knows him better than circumstances account for. "You called me Siegfried: have you seen me before?"

"I recognized you," Hagen replies evasively, "by your strength alone." Hagen's mysterious knowledge of Siegfried derives from his role as double, or shadow. He knows Siegfried as he knows himself. Hagen is consciousness, guilt, evil, death. Siegfried, who is unconsciousness, instinct, virtue,

---

[191] *Ibid.*, p. 26.

life, is as ignorant of Hagen as he is of the gold hoard he has acquired. "I nearly forgot about the treasure," he tells Hagen; "that's how much I value its idle worth! I left it lying in a hole where once a dragon guarded it."

But Hagen knows the value of the treasure and the virtues of the Tarnhelm, and recites them for the naive hero. "Did you take nothing else from the hoard?" he asks, aware that Siegfried has taken the ring, whose virtues he understands, but conceals. "You guard it well?"

"A noble woman keeps it, "Siegfried replies.

"Brünnhilde!" murmurs Hagen knowingly.

Cunning Hagen now gives Gutrune the draught of forgetfulness with which he lures Siegfried into adultery. Siegfried's toast is freighted with obvious irony; the opera's audience knows he will violate his pledge to the Valkyrie. "Were I to forget all you have given me," he begins, "yet one lesson would I never let go: to true love, Brünnhilde, I offer you this first drink!"

The irony here bears closer scrutiny, though. For Siegfried's words have also a straightforward meaning. After all, Siegfried is guileless, and immune to the charge of hypocrisy. Wagner's ideal of liberation was a sexuality unfettered by social convention — unconscious, instinctual. In a concrete sense, true love, liberated love is the love of impulse, of forgetfulness, of unconsciousness. For the revolutionary Wagner, this is a lesson more important than mere bourgeois fidelity. The character of Gutrune is beside the point. What matters is the liberation of instinct, which is the equivalent of creation of the hero, the man of the future.

Siegfried drinks the draught of forgetfulness unhesitatingly, unashamed. Gutrune, who knows its nature, "casts down her eyes from him, ashamed and confused," for shame accompanies consciousness. But Siegfried woos Gutrune as impulsively as, in the foregoing opera, he splintered swords, smashed bowls, and cleaved anvils in twain. Passion burns in him; he is unencumbered by rationality. "Gunther — what is your sister called?" he asks, and in the next few breathless moments in the action proposes marriage, swears blood brotherhood, and vows to win Brünnhilde in Gunther's place.

"How will you deceive her?" Gunther asks, reasonably enough.

"Through the Tarnhelm's deceit I'll trade my form for yours." Siegfried is impatient and unreflecting — heroic. Yet the strands of fate have been spun and severed. Brotherhood is betrayal; doom, ineluctable.

Hagen knows the force of instinct. "See how he is driven to win you to wife!" he says to Gutrune, as Siegfried rushes off to deceive Brünnhilde. Left alone, he gloats over the success of his machinations. "Here I sit on guard, protect the court, defend the hall from the enemy. The wind blows for Gibich's son; he sails off a-wooing. He is led by a powerful hero at the helm, who will weather danger for him: his own bride he'll bring him here to the Rhine; to me, though, he brings the ring! You free-born, happy companions, just sail merrily on! Though he seems lowly to you, you serve him nonetheless — the Nibelung's son!" ("*Dünkt er euch niedrig, ihr dient ihm doch — des Niblungen Sohn!"*) Although *niedrig* is here used in the sense of class, "lowly," it is also connotative of Hagen's dwarvish lineage. His bitter fantasy of revenge is another reflection of Wagner's anguish over his diminutive stature and feared Jewishness. Hagen's vengeful megalomania functions as Wagner's retaliation in fantasy against a world that neglected and despised him, more importantly against a mother whose deprivation had left his ego stunted[192] and "impoverished."

Niebelung megalomania is the topic of the dream colloquy between Hagen and his father with which Act II begins. Hagen becomes another of *The Ring*'s fateful "sleepers," but his is the troubled sleep of the insomniac. "Do you sleep, Hagen, my son?" asks Alberich. "You sleep, and do not hear me, whom rest and sleep betrayed?"

"I hear you, terrible imp," Hagen reassures him: "what have you to tell my sleep?" Alberich incites him to remember the strength he might put to use, were he still as courageous as the day his mother bore him. "Though my mother gave me courage," Hagen counters, "yet I cannot thank her for yielding to your guile: old too soon, wan, and pale, I hate the happy, am happy never!"

The dwarf is satisfied with this dark assertion. "Hagen, my son, hate the happy! Thus you love your joyless, pain-burdened father as you should!" Alberich no longer fears Wotan, he tells his son, for Wotan's own offspring has given

---

[192] That is to say, his true, *inner* ego, as opposed to the grandiosity he habitually displayed to the outside world.

him comeuppance. Now he must fall with the rest of the gods.

"The everlasting Power," asks Hagen—"who inherited it?"

"I—" answers Alberich, "and you: we shall inherit the world, if I have not mistaken your fidelity, and you share my affliction and rage." Siegfried now has the ring, he tells him, but, ignorant of its virtue, the childish hero puts it to no use whatever. "Laughing in flames of love he burns his life away. To bring him to ruin is now our only task . . . Do you sleep, Hagen, my son?"

The dream form shows that Hagen and Alberich share their identity as Wotan and Siegfried do. When Alberich urges his son to swear to retrieve the ring, Hagen answers (much as Wotan reasoned in *Walküre* that talking to Brünnhilde was in essence talking to himself), "I swear it to myself: cease your worry!" Each, moreover, appears as the creation of the other's fantasy, a projection of the self. For while Alberich appears because Hagen dreams him, Hagen exists because Alberich has physically conceived him to carry out his project of recapturing the ring.

"After all, I begot you, unflinching one, that you would stand firm for me (*dass . . . hart du mir hieltest*) against heroes. Though not strong enough to stand up to the dragon—which was destined only for the Volsung—yet I raised Hagen up to tough hate; he now shall avenge me, win the ring, to the mockery of the Volsung and Wotan!" The verbal formulation suggests that here once more the unconscious equates the son with the penis. Alberich's tragedy stems from the Rhinemaidens' blow to his virility. Well then, his son, not a dwarf, but a stalwart warrior will defy those of heroic proportions, "laughing in flames of love," and annihilate them.

Of course the pathetic megalomania of the Nibelungs is the grandiose megalomania of Wotan and Siegfried turned on its head. Freud described the process of repression as a "detachment of the libido from people — and things — that were previously loved,"[193] a phrase felicitously appropriate to *Rheingold*, which engenders the final holocaust. Alberich's response to the sexual rebuff of the Rhinemaidens is to detach libido from the women he has lusted for. As noted in that context, however, the human being cannot actually desexualize himself — he can only seem to. The libido detached from an object formerly loved is sooner or later reattached to some substitute — in Alberich's case, the ring. Megalomania, writes Freud, "we may regard as a *sexual overvaluation of the ego* . . . "[194] In transferring his single-minded interest from the Rhinemaidens onto the ring, Alberich was symbolically renouncing an external love-object for the narcissistic gratification of anal-erotism. "What use is made of the libido after it has been set free by the process of detachment? A normal person will at once begin looking about for a substitute for the lost attachment . . . But in paranoia the clinical evidence goes to show that the libido, after it has been withdrawn from the object, is put to a special use. It will be remembered that the majority of cases of paranoia exhibit traces of megalomania, and that megalomania can by itself constitute a paranoia. From this it

---

[193] Sigmund Freud, "Notes on a Case of Paranoia," *Standard Edition*, vol. XII, p. 71.
[194] *Ibid.*, p. 65 (emphasis, Freud's).

may be concluded that in paranoia the liberated libido becomes attached to the ego, and is used for the aggrandizement of the ego. A return is thus made to the stage of narcissism . . . in which a person's only sexual object is his own ego."[195]

Overvaluation of the cathected object — the fantasy in this case that omnipotence resides in the anal sphincter — is the psychic defense against the sense of dwarvishness and un-worth. Overvaluation of the self is one side of the coin; destruction of everything other than the self is the obverse. The ego that feels itself small in relation to the world becomes big by reducing the world to a heap of cinders. The vision of *Götterdämmerung*, of universal annihilation, is both a projection of the sense of devastation already residing within the ego, and an active strategy for counteracting it. If the dwarf can bring about the destruction of the gods, who tower above him, he transforms himself into a giant. Hagen and Alberich's dream of world domination expressed in terms of inheritance shows to what extent the megalomaniacal fantasy is directed specifically against the constellation of siblings who compete for the patrimony, mother's love.

Mother's love, mother's body are, finally, that possession of the father the sons most desperately covet — the legacy, the inheritance. The external world (*die Welt Erbe*) which the Nibelungs long to rule is merely a substitutive symbol. The final scene of Act I, in which Siegfried, disguised as Gunther, weds Brünnhilde for the second time is a fantasy in which this primal wish is acted out. For Siegfried and Gunther are now

---

[195] *Ibid.*, p. 72.

brothers, doubly so since they have both sworn blood-brotherhood, and promised to become brothers-in-law. In the rape of Brünnhilde, the brothers ritually share their woman. For Siegfried, through the magic of the Tarnhelm, is also Gunther. Moreover, the purpose of the deception is for Siegfried to transfer his bride to his new brother. It is an ingenious fantasy, however, because although in the person of Siegfried, the brothers communally rape the maternal stand-in, simultaneously Siegfried clearly triumphs over his brother, who is too weak to accomplish the unique deed except vicariously, voyeuristically.[196] Siegfried's sword between his

---

[196] Margaret Mahler-Schoenberger, "Pseudoimbecility: A Magic Cap of Invisibility," *Psychoanalytic Quarterly*, vol. XI, no. 2, (New York, 1942), pp. 149-164, interprets the mythological device of the *Tarnkappe*, the cloak of invisibility, as a symbolic form of "pseudoimbecility," the pose of ignorance or stupidity that ". . . enables children as well as infantile adults to participate in the sexual life of parents and other adults to an amazingly unlimited extent which, overtly expressed, would be strictly and definitely forbidden." p. 149. She elaborates, "The small child's keen powers of observation, its bold intuition, become unwelcome. This applies especially to perceptions in the sphere of sexual exploration whose failure to reveal the secret of the sexual relationship between the parents marks the beginning of the latency period which is characterized by repression of overt sexual interests and a slowing down of development of the child's so far brilliant exploratory intellect." pp. 151, 52. Even more pertinent to the Siegfried/Gunther/Brünnhilde triangle is Mahler-Schoenberger's observation of "still another essential function of stupidity: to restore or maintain a secret libidinous rapport within the family." p. 154.
The concept of pseudoimbecility invites consideration — beyond the scope of the present study — of this essential element in the character of *Parsifal*, "der Reine Tor."
See also footnote 109, p. 107, above.

body and Brünnhilde's is an unconvincing hedge against infidelity.

The text indicates unmistakably that in wresting the ring from Brünnhilde, Siegfried accomplishes a rape. "A monster leapt onto this rock!" Brünnhilde cries when she sees him. "An eagle came flying to tear my flesh to pieces!" (*"Ein Aar kam geflogen mich zu zerfleischen!"*) This image presents another apparent distortion of the vulture Geyer. Taking possession of his inheritance, the son usurps his father's place, becomes his father. The stage directions specify further: "He forces himself upon her; they struggle. Brünnhilde wrenches herself free and flees, turning as if to defend herself. Siegfried seizes her again. She flees; he overtakes her. The two struggle with each other. He grabs her by the hand, and draws the ring from her finger. She shrieks loudly. As she sinks into his arms as though defeated, her unconscious glance grazes Siegfried's eyes. [He] lets the powerless [Brünnhilde] slide down onto the stone bench in front of the rocky chamber."

"Now you are mine!" Siegfried cries exultantly. "Brünnhilde, Gunther's bride — grant me now your chamber."

"What defense did you have, wretched woman?" Brünnhilde reproaches herself, as "Siegfried drives her on with an imperious gesture: trembling and with faltering step she goes into the chamber."

"Now, Notung give witness, that I have wooed chastely," Siegfried declares. "Preserving my fidelity to my brother, separate me from his bride." But after this manifestly erotic struggle over the ring, and Brünnhilde's orgasmic exhaustion and defeat, Siegfried's gesture of separating himself from his wife with the sword freighted throughout *The Ring* with phallic symbolism seems perfunctory, not to say disingenuous.

Act II is a tragedy of errors. At its emotional center is Brünnhilde's confrontation with Siegfried in the hall of the Gibichungs. The dramatic impact of the scene is generated by marital confusion over whose spouse belongs with whom, confusion in which one might see reflected Wagner's uncertain paternity, or his relation to Hans von Bülow and his wife Cosima.

Brünnhilde arrives as Gunther's wife, but recognizing Siegfried (who appears betrothed to Gutrune) she swoons. "Gunther," says the naive hero, "your wife isn't well!" He paraphrases the words with which he tried to awaken her to love in Siegfried: "Awake, woman! Here stands your spouse!" (*"Erwache, Frau! Hier steht dein Gatte."*) Since *Frau* means both "woman" and "wife," Siegfried could just as well be addressing her as his own wife (as indeed she is), an ambiguity that adds to the mounting confusion.

Focus shifts now to the ring. It flashes on Siegfried's hand. Yet Gunther (or so Brünnhilde thinks) took the ring from her. How did Siegfried come by it? Not from Gunther, but from a dragon Siegfried got it, he avers. Hagen meanwhile sows suspicion and urges revenge against Siegfried. Brünnhilde turns to Gunther: "Where do you hide the ring you seized from me?" As Gunther continues nonplussed and speechless, she concludes correctly (though still confused), "Ha! He is the one who tore the ring from me: Siegfried, the treacherous thief!" Railing against his betrayal, she calls on the gods to avenge the outrage. By the time Gunther, ill at ease over this turn of events, asks Brünnhilde (whom he thinks his wife) to compose herself, she has decided. "Stay away, traitor! yourself betrayed! Know then all of you: not to him, but to that man over there am I wed," meaning, of course, Siegfried.

Brünnhilde's certainty is the complement of her earlier confusion. The Latin tag cited by Freud in "Family Romances" to the effect that *pater semper incertus est*, while *mater* is *certissima* applies here. If the motif of marital confusion reflects Wagner's paternity, Brünnhilde's sudden certainty is a declaration of the un-severable maternal tie. Un-severability and betrayal are (as we have seen) the antithetical sides of the filial relation to mother, paralleling her opposing good and terrible faces, as well as the contradictory urges of clinging and weaning.

It is true that her first accusations pertain to Siegfried as lover. "He wrested pleasure and love from me," she charges. And when Siegfried protests that his sword between them has preserved chastity and blood-brotherhood, Brünnhilde chides, "Cunning hero, see how you lie! how falsely you invoke your sword! Well I know its keenness; yet I know too its sheath, in which it happily rested on the wall, Notung, true friend, while his master wooed his beloved." The phallic nature of the sword (indeed, the transparent emblem of intercourse represented by the sheathed sword) is barely concealed by the logistical nicety of Brünnhilde's accusation. Symbolism aside, however, we know the sexual encounter was consummated.

Later, complaining that Siegfried holds her in bondage through sorcery, she asks, "Who now offers me the sword with which to sever these bonds?" (*"Wer bietet mir nun das Schwert, mit dem ich die Bande zerschnitt?"*) *"Bande"* is ambiguous here. In this metaphorical context, it means the bonds with which prey is held captive. But *"Bande"* also signifies bonds of family. "Oh, thankless; most shameful reward! Not one art known to me that did not work to the good of his body! Unaware, he is wound about by my magic spells that protect him from wounds." A mother might be speaking here of a child she has nurtured and worried over. And to be sure, Siegfried is the child of her creation. This accords with Wagner's conscious allegory: Brünnhilde is Wotan's innermost thought, the "womb" in which the hero has been conceived.

As Act II reaches its chilling culmination, Brünnhilde — wronged not just by her lover, but by all men — tells Gunther, "He betrayed you, and all of you have betrayed me! Should I be avenged, all the blood in the world would not atone for your guilt! Yet the death of the one serves me for all: let Siegfried fall — as atonement for himself and for you!"

This idea resonates with Christian meaning. And in the Christian context, the *one* who atones for *all* is, of course, the *son*. Brünnhilde's sense of having been wronged by all men expresses resentment against that entire half of humanity in possession of a penis. Yet of all men, only the son has committed the unforgivable crime, requiring the punishment of death; the son alone had power to restore the penis her sexual destiny denied her. Instead he castrates anew by abandoning her.

This insight warrants restating the observation that pre-oedipal issues persist to block resolution of the Oedipus Complex. While the paternal threat of castration urges renunciation of Oedipal wishes, guilt over complicity in mother's castration prohibits renouncing them. Renunciation means abandoning mother. The son's penis is not excised; he himself is the penis (as it were) cut from his mother's body. Separation anxiety is translated into castration anxiety. The trauma of birth is the prototype (as Freud observed) of both separation anxiety and castration anxiety.

The equation can be stated from another perspective. If the father, threatening castration, demands renunciation of mother as love object, that resolution is just as strenuously opposed by mother in order to save herself from the castration of relinquishing her son's dependence. The son faces an insoluble dilemma: the commands of the superego are countermanded by the introjected mother, though she herself shares in the identity of the superego. It is difficult to distinguish the son's guilt over mother's castration (on the one hand) from anxiety over his own (on the other) since the introjected mother is in fact part of himself. Loving mother means (as the fantasy of romantic fusion with the beloved indicates) becoming like mother — viz., castrated.

As the curtain rises on Act III, *The Ring* has come full circle to the finny Rhinemaidens warbling over their pilfered gold. It is as much Hagen as Siegfried the nixes long for when they sing, "Dame Sun, send us the hero who would give us back the gold!" Though one assumes they mean Siegfried (who enters once more pursuing a bear — one he is hunting, this time, not just toying with), in fact they cannot coax the ring from him. They charge him with the conventional Jewish vice: "Are you so stingy? . . . So tightfisted in trade? . . .You should be generous with ladies . . . so handsome! . . . So strong! . . . So desirable! . . . A pity he's so stingy!"

This accusation hits home, and calls forth protestation reminiscent of the prodigious denials of Mime's paternity in *Siegfried*. "Why should I suffer this meager praise? Should I let myself be so slandered? Were they to come again to the water's edge they could have the ring. Hey, hey! You lively water-lovelies! Come quick: I'll make you a present of the ring!"

But the Rhinemaidens now are coy. "Hold on to it, hero, and guard it well, till you discover the evil you harbor in the ring. You would be happy then, should we free you from the curse."

Their threat makes Siegfried perversely retract his offer. "You cunning ladies, leave off! If I hardly trusted your wheedling, your threats frighten me even less! . . . For love's favor, I'd gladly give up [the ring]. I'll give it to you should you offer me pleasure. But if you threaten my life and body, though it be not worth a finger, you'll not wrest the ring from me!"

Now Siegfried performs a remarkable gesture. "For life and body—look you—thus I toss away!" He picks up a clod of earth and throws it "over his head behind him," as the stage directions specify: a symbolic defecation, the psyche's instinctive repudiation of the charge of stinginess. Yet cunningly, he retains the ring itself, thus fulfilling the necessities of destiny and plot. The compromise gesture neatly embodies Wagner's ambivalence, himself both spend-thrift and hoarder.

This gesture bears a relation also to the issue of independence. " . . . The task of differentiating the object tends to resolve itself into a problem of expelling an incorporated object, i.e., to become a problem of expelling contents," writes Fairbairn. Siegfried throws the conveniently symbolic clod, but actually retains the ring. "Owing to the intimate connection between primary identification and oral incorporation, and consequently between separation and excretory expulsion, the conflict of the transition period also presents itself as a conflict between an urge to expel and an urge to retain contents. Just as between separation and reunion, so here there tends to be a constant oscillation between expulsion and retention, although either of these attitudes may become dominant. Both attitudes are attended by anxiety — the attitude of expulsion being attended by a fear of being emptied or drained, and the attitude of retention by a fear of bursting."[197]

Though separate, and displaying opposite natures, Siegfried and Hagen represent two sides of a single psychic entity. Siegfried appears to toss his life away as easily as a clod, that is, to spend freely. Hagen, on the other hand, is cast in the mold of the covetous Jew. Yet it is from Hagen, finally, not Siegfried, that the Rhinemaidens have their ring back. Hagen seizes it from the ashes of the hero's funeral pyre, whereupon the Rhinemaidens, throwing their arms like garlands round his neck, draw him and the ring into their deeps, fulfilling Alberich's original, amorous wish in *Rheingold*.

---

[197] Fairbairn, *op. cit.*, pp. 43, 44.

Hagen is the despised, rejected and denied self; Siegfried is the idealized self. "The most prominent symptom of the forms which the double takes is a powerful consciousness of guilt which forces the hero no longer to accept the responsibility for certain actions of his ego, but to place it upon another ego, a double, who is either personified by the devil himself or is created by making a diabolical pact," writes Otto Rank. This double is in essence a "detached personification of instincts and desires which were once felt to be unacceptable, but which can be satisfied without responsibility in this indirect way . . . "[198]

Though Hagen is the despised villain, he expresses Wagner's wish—allowed to rise to consciousness disguised beneath the cloak of denial in the context of a mythological fiction. If Hagen can take possession of the ring, if the dark, Jewish, Geyerish side can be ascendant, Wagner could revel in narcissistic omnipotence. Hagen is the repressed. Siegfried's naïve pleasures are impossible. Siegfried himself is impossible. Hagen must murder Siegfried not only because the self punishes its own guilt, but because Hagen, openly, shamelessly evil, is also the self's last chance, the final return of the repressed. Hagen's hand is the last to clutch at the ring, and his words conclude the tetralogy: "Away from the ring!" He reenacts Alberich's theft, Alberich's retreat from object love into narcissism—no less a dead end for Hagen than for his father.

Partly, the struggle between Hagen and Siegfried is the struggle between consciousness and unconsciousness.

---

[198] Otto Rank (1914). *The double: A psychoanalytic study*, (Chapel Hill: University of North Carolina, 1971), p. 76.

Siegfried's strength lies in his lack of fear, his lack of consciousness, his spontaneity. Hagen's strategy, accordingly, hinges on restoring Siegfried's memory, driving into consciousness the forgotten sexual relation with Brünnhilde, and luring him into acknowledging what must appear as treachery against Gunther. Siegfried represents that heroic stage during which the infant's ignorance of taboo and the realities of power makes all desires possible. Siegfried walks unscathed through the magic fire simply because he does not fear it; the infant enjoys imaginary monopoly over its mother unaware of its rival's power. When Hagen makes Siegfried conscious, Siegfried must die; consciousness means death. The infant dies into the adult. Innocence dies into guilt.

The form of Siegfried's murder reveals his self-reflexive relation to Hagen. Resting from the hunt, Hagen elicits the hero's life story, the last of *The Ring*'s notorious rehearsals of past events. As Siegfried admits to his sexual relation with Brünnhilde, Wotan's two ravens start ominously from a bush. Siegfried turns to see them fly off, and Hagen thrusts his spear into the hero's back. The ravens function doubtless as another manifestation of the disguised vulture, especially as they are associated with father Wotan. They are his double; they are Alberich, "Black Wotan." Their role in Siegfried's murder reflects the participation of the superego in the revenge plot, since Oedipal guilt is mixed with pre-oedipal clinging. Still, Hagen's hand commits the act suggestive of anal rape—the phallic spear thrust into Siegfried's body from behind.

The murder could serve almost as a pictorialization of a process ascribed by Freud to certain forms of melancholia, in which the "lost object" is incorporated into the ego as a strategy for retaining it. He describes " . . . the ego divided, fallen apart into two pieces, one of which rages against the second. This second piece is the one which has been altered by the introjection and which contains the lost object. But the piece which behaves so cruelly is not unknown to us either. It comprises the conscience, a critical agency within the ego, which even in normal times takes up a critical attitude towards the ego, though never so relentlessly and so unjustifiably [as in melancholia]."[199] Brünnhilde mourns the lost object (that part of the self embodied in Siegfried), and rages against it through the agency of Hagen. The affect of mother mourning her son, and of son mourning his renounced mother are here treated as interchangeable.

The thinly veiled fantasy of anal rape suggests a homosexual component in *The Ring*'s meaning. In fact, an erotic undercurrent often characterized Wagner's closest relationships with men.[200] But homosexuality is not at issue in *The Ring*. No overtly homosexual behavior occurs. If a latent tendency or a sub-rosa theme is discernible, its importance lies in its symptomatic relation to more primitive developmental stages, pre-oedipal attachment and narcissism. Though also homosexual, the fantasy of anal rape by the double is fundamentally *autoerotic*, and links Siegfried's death thematically with the anal-erotism of *Rheingold*.

---

[199] Sigmund Freud, "Group Psychology," p. 109.
[200] Cf., Hanns Fuchs, *Richard Wagner und die Homosexualität* (Berlin: Bersdorf, 1903), who concludes somewhat naively, however, that Wagner was neither actively nor truly latently homosexual—that rather his homophilic relationships were on a strictly Platonic and ethereal plane. The book is a work of apologetics that affirms the evidence of homosexual tendencies on Wagner's part only in order to deny the conclusion it seems to be pointing to.

To the tetralogy as a whole, Wagner gave the over-arching (and on reflection quite surprising) title *Der Ring Des Nibelungen*. The ring that is the token at the center of the whole epic sweep of the action is neither Wotan's, nor Siegfried's, nor Brünnhilde's, nor even the Rhinemaidens'. It belongs to Alberich — the dwarf who has renounced love, and whose realm is below ground, in the bowels of the earth. *The ring of the Nibelung is the token not of the lofty and heroic, but of the shameful and the repressed.*

Below the narrative level of the operatic saga, the ring is redolent of the symbolism of the anal sphincter, earliest source of independent erotic gratification, solution to the frustrations of object love; enjoying it, the infant is self-contained, self-fulfilling, complete, albeit alienated. This autoerotic equivalence between Alberich's theft of the gold and Siegfried's murder, gives *The Ring* a circular structure in a deeper sense than the return of the action to the river. In anal-erotism the male infant becomes androgynous, possessing both a penis and a vagina. Hagen and Siegfried. Siegfried is in possession of the ring; Hagen, of the spear. The murder unites hero and anti-hero like lovers. It is the *love-death*. Dying into one another, they cease to be doubles. Hagen becomes Siegfried, fulfilling his aborted gesture of restoring the gold to the Rhine. In its waters their two bodies dissolve and mix.

If this is redemption, however, it is only the dubious redemption of oblivion. The ecstatic music proclaims hope, of course. But Wagner's music has beguiled us before. The edifice of culture, the sensible, the *conscious*, functions to deny, not confirm the unconscious reality buried under it.

Brünnhilde's ashes mix with Siegfried's, along with those of Grane and all the divinities and warriors from Walhall. But the common interpretation that the music of immolation expresses "redemption through love" is born out neither by the drift of *The Ring* as a whole, nor by Wagner's stated intentions.

It is true that in his original draft of *Siegfried's Death* Brünnhilde's immolation speech expressed this idea. But Wagner was uneasy about so optimistic a conclusion from the start, and tinkered with the speech until, by *The Ring*'s publication in 1872, all trace of what he considered "tendentious" moralizing about love had finally been excised, and replaced with "heroic negation."[201] He had at one point during a phase of enthusiasm for Buddhism given the Valkyrie's immolation a distinctly Eastern tone. Drawing on the doctrine of reincarnation, Wagner had Brünnhilde proclaim her round of birth and death at an end. "I depart the home of desire, I flee the home of illusion forever; behind me I close the open door of eternal becoming: the illuminated one now journeys forth, freed from re-birth, towards the goal of world-wandering, holiest, chosen land of neither desire nor illusion." Though he deleted these words too, Wagner nevertheless thought them near enough the idea he was after to append them as a footnote to the immolation scene in the 1872 publication of *The Ring*.[202] Life is as much a curse for Brünnhilde as for the Flying Dutchman. Contrary to the popular misconception that the final immolation with its

---

[201] Robert Donington, *Wagner's 'Ring' and its Symbols* (New York, 1974), pp. 270, 71.

[202] One can follow the course of Wagner's gradual revisions in Newman's chapter, "Difficulties in the Rounding of the 'Ring,'" vol. II, pp. 347-361.

gorgeous music, opens the prospect of redemptive rebirth, Brünnhilde clearly says she shuts the door of rebirth, which leads not to "redemption through love," but to the same eternal round of desire and illusion—of suffering. In the Buddhist conception, only the individual who has lived without inflicting suffering on any other creature has merited the nirvana of annihilation. So much cannot, of course, be said for Brünnhilde, who has contracted with Hagen for Siegfried's murder. It is clear, nonetheless, that oblivion, not rebirth, is the longed for consummation.

Wagner set forth his pessimistic rationale in a letter to Liszt (June 7th, 1855). " . . . The true men of genius and the true saints of all times have . . . seen nothing but suffering and felt nothing but compassion. For they recognized the normal state of all living things and the terrible, ever self-contradictory, ever self-mutilating and blindly egoistic nature of the 'will to life,' common to all living things. The terrible cruelty of this will, which first in sexual love aims only at its own reproduction, appeared for the first time reflected in the organ of perception, which in its normal state had felt its subjection to the Will to which it owed its own existence. In this manner the organ of perception was placed in an abnormal sympathetic condition. It sought to free itself continuously and finally from that disgraceful thralldom, and this it at last achieved in the perfect negation of the will to life. This act of the negation of will is the actual mission of the saint: that he finds ultimate fulfillment only in the absolute termination of personal consciousness . . ."

Next he expounds the Buddhist doctrine of reincarnation, and avers that Christianity no longer reflects the same true longing for annihilation, "because we know it only in its mixture with, and distortion by, narrow-hearted Judaism . . . In early Christianity however we still see distinct traces of the perfect negation of the will of life, of the longing for the destruction of the world, i.e., the cessation of existence."

Universal conflagration is an extension of the fantasy of the womb. Womb and intra-uterine self *are* the universe. Siegfried and Brünnhilde are blended in the flames and ashes, but so are the gods. And then the Rhine overflows its banks and washes the ashes into itself, drawing Hagen into the stew as well. Annihilation is unification, resolution of the Oedipus Complex, end to the anxiety of separation. The very unreality of the mythological Nordic Ragnarok, however, raises the question what Wagner's apocalyptic fantasy refers to in actual life. *Götterdämmerung* is a grand idea, but like the other elements of *The Ring*'s narrative, it represents a mythical inflation of a more mundane reality. Identity with mother, namely, is a fantasy. The dream of slipping bodily into the womb cannot be realized. In this more practical light, to what does the conclusion of *The Ring* refer? Recalling of Wagner's memory of dozing in that hotel in Spezia, imagination fecund as a jungle, dreaming the watery prelude to *Rheingold*, we might regard the culmination of *Götterdämmerung* also as a dream—a dream of conflagration and inundation. If fire is libido, then this dream might constitute the equivalent of a grandiose nocturnal emission—smoldering passion climaxing in ejaculation.

The "wet-dream," in turn, rests on the infantile basis of eroticized enuresis. "As far as can be seen," writes Melanie Klein of the common fantasies of flooding the world with urine, "the sadistic tendency most closely allied to oral sadism is urethral sadism. Observations have confirmed that children's phantasies of flooding and destroying by means of enormous quantities of urine in terms of soaking, drowning, burning and poisoning are a sadistic reaction to their having been deprived of fluid by their mother and are ultimately directed against her breast."[203]

We circle back, then, to deprivation. To be deprived of the first basis of life, the contents of mother's breast, and her love, elicits the most grandiose fantasy of revenge. No trauma is so devastating as this loss; only global devastation can represent its magnitude. The wet-dream repeats the autoerotic solution to deprivation, of course. But autoerotism only increases the impotent rage of a dwarfed ego, calling forth ever more terrible, ever grander and more universal retribution. Yet the revenge fantasy is barren too, and returns inevitably to the deprivation that spawned it. Hence, Wagnerian pessimism, and the ideal of oblivion. Only death—not of the body merely, but of consciousness—redeems the guilt and pain of having lived.

But the ending of *Götterdämmerung* is ambiguous. Though the Hall of the Gibichungs tumbles and Walhall burns, the world does not end—the Rhinemaidens go on swimming in the Rhine, and human beings remain on earth to carry out Wagner's final stage direction: "From the rubble of the demolished hall, the men and women, struck with amazement, watch the growing firelight in the sky. As this finally glows at its intensest brightness, one glimpses the hall

---

[203] Melanie Klein, *The Psychoanalysis of Children*, pp. 128, 29.

of Walhall, in which the gods and heroes sit gathered . . .
Bright flames appear to start up in the hall of the gods. When
the gods are entirely engulfed in the flames, the curtain falls."

Although *The Ring* proclaims the ideal of annihilation, in
reality the fate it adumbrates is not so grand. The world is
doomed, as it were, to grim continuation. *"Götterdämmerung,"*
"Twilight of the Gods," is a denouement pointedly distinct
from the Buddhistic void of annihilation, on the one hand, and
the Christian glory of resurrection on the other. "Twilight"
conveys just the ambiguity of Wagner's peculiar pessimism.
Alberich's ring has returned to the depths of the Rhine, but
only — we foresee — to be repossessed by some future avatar.
The cycle of birth and death will have to be repeated; return to
the womb repeats the necessity of being born. Birth is trauma,
separation, loss, death. If *Götterdämmerung's* ending implies
rebirth, it is not to a loftier plane. Rebirth is subsumed under
mere continuation because that cycle is the form life happens
in reality to take.

Appendix

a Note on Fairbairn's "Internal Saboteur"

Fairbairn's departure[204] from Freud's premise that libidinal impulses are repressed offers a further rationale for Wotan's punishment of Brünnhilde. In Fairbairn's view, not impulses *per se* but the *objects* of those impulses are repressed. Thus one could avoid the somewhat awkward formulation that the sleeping Brünnhilde embodies the repressed Oedipal wish by regarding her simply as the loved object, the introjected maternal figure. The mechanism is somewhat as follows. The infant's first love object is its mother, with whom it is wholly identified. Only as the infant becomes aware that sometimes its desires for mother and her breast are ignored or denied is some measure of differentiation forced upon it. In response to this frustration and deprivation, the infant splits its maternal image into a good, satisfying mother and a bad, denying mother. The good mother, who gratifies the infant's desires in reality, is enabled to pursue a differentiated, external existence. The bad mother, however, is internalized in an effort to control the painful experience of her rejections.

In the process of this introjection, the bad mother is split once more. For she is bad only in the sense that she denies herself to the infant, not that she is undesirable. On the contrary, she

---

[204] W. R. D. Fairbairn, *An Object Relations Theory of the Personality* (New York, 1954).

is all the more desirable and provocative an object for being unattainable. The aspect that is desirable, which Fairbairn names the "exciting object," is split off from that aspect that denies gratification, which he calls the "rejecting object." Attached to these images of the bad mother are those portions of the ego identified with them through libidinal cathexis. Differentiating these split off portions from the central ego, Fairbairn names them respectively the "libidinal ego" and the "internal saboteur." Fairbairn's "internal saboteur" incorporates many of the functions of Freud's superego, but predates it developmentally, and is formed upon a maternal, not a paternal image. The Freudian superego is seen as a later and relatively weaker superimposition over the internal saboteur. Thus, the superego's moral basis is outweighed by the more primitive internal saboteur's sadism.

The infant's control over the bad mother is now manifested in repressing both these aspects, driving them into unconsciousness by means of the aggression that mother's frustrations have awakened in him. Fairbairn surmises that neither aggression nor ambivalence would ever arise in the absence of frustration. Repression of these two aspects of the bad mother have not solved the dilemma of frustration, however, for the infant continues to face frustration in reality.

Yet to express his anger against the externally denying mother openly risks provoking her anger, making her even more depriving, and thus increasing her "badness." Simultaneously, to the extent that the deprivation dominates the maternal picture in external reality, it is equally dangerous to express positive libidinal desire, for the bad mother is the rejecting mother, and for the infant to have its love rejected means further loss of the loved object (which in turn through the primary identification is tantamount to a loss of self, a diminution of the ego).

The dilemma is resolved by turning both anger and desire inwards. As Fairbairn explains, "The child seeks to circumvent the dangers of expressing both libidinal and aggressive affect towards his object by *using a maximum of his aggression to subdue a maximum of his libidinal need*. In this way he reduces the volume of affect, both libidinal and aggressive, demanding outward expression" (emphasis, Fairbairn's). These abstract forces, Fairbairn associates with concrete psychic structures. He goes on accordingly to attribute aggression to the internal saboteur, and libido to the libidinal ego. "The child's technique of using aggression to subdue libidinal need thus resolves itself into an attack by the internal saboteur upon the libidinal ego. The libidinal ego in its turn directs the excess of libido with which it becomes charged towards its associated object, the exciting object. On the other hand, the attack of the internal saboteur upon this object represents a persistence of the child's original resentment towards his mother as a temptress inciting the very need which she fails to satisfy and thus reducing him to bondage — just as, indeed, the attack of the internal saboteur upon the libidinal ego represents a persistence of the hatred which the child comes to feel towards himself, for the dependence dictated by his need." (pp. 114, 115.) This last is a crucial point: the attack of the internal saboteur is simultaneously against the mother and against the self, insofar as the mother figure is incorporated as part of the self.

This scheme may be offered to shed light on the relations of Wotan with Fricka and Brünnhilde. The women can be seen as corresponding to the two aspects of the bad, or frustrating, mother. Brünnhilde is the exciting object, the temptress, who lures Siegmund into battle by promising to protect him from the consequences of his incestuous relations, although she fails to deliver on her promise. She is equally frustrating to Wotan, though he loves her above all women. Fricka, by contrast, though also a maternal figure, is the depriving, rejecting object, and incorporates the internal saboteur. This scheme has the virtue of making sense of Wotan's (superego's) pathetic weakness in relation to her. Fricka's unrelenting hatred of Brünnhilde forces Wotan to act against his own wishes. The superego that emerges from introjection of father is, in Fairbairn's hypothesis, weakly superimposed on the internal saboteur. Thus Wotan goes to the wall as easily as his own moral precepts. It is Fricka whose will is fulfilled, first in the destruction of Siegmund, then in imprisoning Brünnhilde in sleep, the repression, that is, of the "exciting object."

Though she offers moral principles as her rationale, it would appear in this light (as indeed it appears in the text from her icy rage) that moralism also in her case overlays more powerful sadistic aggression. "The attack of the internal saboteur upon the libidinal ego must obviously function as an extremely powerful factor in furthering the aims of repression; and it would appear to be on this phenomenon that Freud's concept of the superego and its repressive function is largely based." (p. 173.)

The concept of the internal saboteur may also illuminate Siegfried's murder. In Fairbairn's view, the internal saboteur (or any of the endopsychic structures, for that matter) is protean, represented now by one person, now by another. In *Götterdämmerung* Hagen might be regarded as taking over from Fricka the role of "internal saboteur." Though this agency is originally an aspect of the mother, i.e., female, Hagen's masculinity may represent the phallic attribute of the "bad mother." Moreover, as part of the masculine ego-structure, the introjected mother is equally male and female.

If Hagen assumes the role of internal saboteur, however, what of Brünnhilde, who played "exciting object" in *Walküre*, but who now connives in Siegfried's murder? Even here she may be regarded as "exciting object," an aspect, after all, of the "bad mother."

"The trouble about such an internal object," explains Fairbairn, "is that, after internalization, it continues not only to be unsatisfying, but also to be desired (cathected). It thus presents a duality of aspects which constitutes as great a difficulty in the inner world as that formerly constituted by the ambivalence of objects in the outer world. This duality of aspects has already been referred to as providing the basis for a split of the internalized bad object into (a) an exciting object, and (b) a rejecting object—a split which is now seen to be effected by the original ego in an attempt to deal with the difficulties ensuing upon the internalization of bad objects." (p. 172.)

But Hagen's attack is carried out against Siegfried, not Brünnhilde. Fairbairn's scheme calls for the internal saboteur to attack the libidinal ego and its attached exciting object. Siegfried, however, *is* Brünnhilde, as Wagner has made clear through his unceasing emphasis on the romantic hyperbole. In attacking Siegfried, Hagen is murdering Brünnhilde too. Indeed, Brünnhilde follows Siegfried onto the funeral pyre in short order. Moreover, Siegfried adopts the feminine (that is to say, the passive, masochistic) attitude in the murder, relinquishing his role as masculine hero, assuming instead the identity *proper* to Brünnhilde — the woman raped with the phallic weapon. To be raped has been Brünnhilde's destiny, imposed by Wotan and enacted by Siegfried, who submits, in turn, to an equivalent destiny.

ABOUT THE AUTHOR

Tom Artin was educated at Princeton University. His previous books are *The Allegory of Adventure*, a study of Arthurian Romances by Chrétien de Troyes, poet at the 12th century court of Champagne, and *Earth Talk: Independent Voices on the Environment*. He lives with his wife, Cynthia, in Sparkill, NY.

Made in the USA
Middletown, DE
24 July 2015